The Downsizing of Asia

The recent Asian financial disaster has prompted many questions. How did it happen? Was it due to poor public policies and a lack of market regulation? Is it part of a systemic and global disorder? Has the Asian model come to an end?

This book charts the economic fortunes of Asia from the early 1990s to the collapse in confidence in 1997 to 1998. It examines the reasons behind the economic crisis and surveys the likely social and political impact on Asia – the questioning of Asian values and the reappearance of ethnic and religious divides.

François Godement argues that the Asian economies have reached a crisis of maturity. The main components of healthy commercial growth remain in place, the damage has been caused by a lack of financial regulation, organization and discipline, and now there is a profound sense of pessimism. Cooperation between states in the region is now essential if they are to regain their economic momentum.

François Godement is a Senior Research Associate at the Institut Français des Relations Internationales, Paris. He is also the author of *The New Asian Renaissance*.

The Downsizing of Asia

François Godement

London and New York

First published 1999 by Routledge
11 New Fetter Lane, London EC4P 4EE

Simultaneously published in the USA and Canada
by Routledge
29 West 35th Street, New York, NY 10001

© 1999 François Godement

Typeset in Baskerville by The Florence Group, Stoodleigh, Devon
Printed and bound in Great Britain by TJ International, Padstow,
Cornwall

British Library Cataloguing in Publication Data
A catalogue record for this book is available from the British Library

Library of Congress Cataloging in Publication Data
A catalog record for this book has been requested

ISBN 0–415–19833–X (hbk)
ISBN 0–415–19834–8 (pbk)

Contents

Acknowledgements

This book has been written in trying times, as the Asian crisis unfolded and spread its consequences. I would never have finished the project without the encouragement and assistance at various stages of Régine Serra, Arnaud d'Andurain and R. Bin Wong. Ning, Noémie and Olivier have had to endure the permanent urgency that came with the topic. I wish to thank them all for their patience.

1 Introduction

A crash course in history

Great financial crises, like major political revolutions, lend themselves to two major undertakings: scapegoating, and looking for the root of the trouble. The first pursuit is an understandable reaction in the face of such change: somebody must be responsible. The search for culprits – speculators, the West, the Asian model or Asian debtors themselves – is only too tempting. The second pursuit is akin to asking whether the French Revolution started on 14 July 1789 because the price of bread reached a high on that day, or whether it happened because the French monarchy could not cope with the crisis in fiscal revenue or with the Enlightenment. Like revolution, financial mayhem is a major historical event. In the post-Cold War era, and particularly in East Asia, where geoeconomy has largely displaced geopolitics as the major agent of change, a financial collapse *is* history in the making.

A crisis of transition

The closest that one can get to the cause of the 1997 to 1998 Asian economic crisis ('the Crash') is that Asian economic models met their fate when they embarked upon a course of international trade and financial liberalization that followed the Western model. Most Asian countries (with the important exceptions of Hong Kong and Singapore, which are very special enclaves) failed to set up adequate regulation and supervision that would have allowed capital markets to develop without dangerous imbalances. Overwhelmed by capital inflows from the world's industrialized economies (and first and foremost from Japan), they overborrowed, overinvested and overreached themselves, until confidence snapped like a taut wire. What happened next is now well known. Net private capital inflows to Malaysia, the Philippines, South Korea and Thailand reached 93 billion dollars in 1996. But by 1997, the movement had reversed, with an outflow of 12 billion dollars.

The Crash was a crisis of transition, heightened by a lack of regional government cooperation at a time when economies and markets had become interlocked. The event points to the late adjustment of Asian governments and institutions to the kind of momentous changes that were happening in the economic field, changes that governments themselves had usually encouraged.

A paucity of predictions

On the surface, the Asian events of 1997 appear at first to be a financial tragi-comedy, devoid of much historical and cultural depth. The cast includes, besides many pinstriped international bankers, the Indonesian president of a taxi company ironically called Steadysafe, which failed miserably, as well as innumerable owners of 'bubble' properties and short-term debts. Japanese high officials committed suicide to atone for the local equivalent of three-martini lunches with the firms they regulated. Korean auto firms that had been legally declared bankrupt went on acquiring dealerships in America and, in one instance, a lorry company in the United Kingdom. Asia-Pacific pundits kept chanting the mantra of sound fundamentals, although this did not sway the markets.

Much of the real debate on the crisis, its roots and its cures happened in fact outside the region. Asia became a proxy for debates between IMF and World Bank factions, used to propping up much smaller economies. Reform agendas for Asia were often discussed with no consideration at all of Asian realities. The problems of such complex societies cannot be cured by a few neo-liberal or monetary prescriptions, or by a blanket denunciation of Asian sins.

What caused the Crash? Was it the mere flutter of a butterfly's wings – the failure of a Thai finance company for instance – which threw the entire regional system into a spin? Unlike the econometric models of quantitative economists, real financial systems share the weaknesses of all other human constructions. Panic, psychological contagion and herd-like behaviour can spread a disaster far beyond the boundaries and linkages that macroeconomic models can predict. Several economists, and a few international institutions, issued words of warning about some Asian economies after the Mexican crisis of 1994.[1] But precious few translated these warnings into a general argument. Even Paul Krugman of the MIT – considered by some of his peers as a popularizer – who came closest to a prediction, was not completely on cue. He later reformulated general arguments on the pattern of Asian growth (including the celebrated 'sausage factory' argument regarding productivity stagnation in Southeast Asia) to fit the actual events:[2] the Crisis of 1997 was not born in the physical economy of Asia but in the financial arena where regulations were not in place. Confidence snapped. To its credit, the grand old lady of all international economic institutions, the Bank of International Settlements (BIS) in Basle, foresaw the impending disaster with clarity, and issued a warning in the most blunt language that could be used by bankers.[3] But the BIS is entrusted with advising, rather than deciding. And its advice is aimed at saving lenders from themselves, not at rescuing hapless debtors. The lonely journalist, Bill Emmott, had single-handedly predicted the stagnation of Japan's economy much earlier.[4] His prediction was received as eccentric. In fact, he managed to anger both Japan's friends (who saw the country acquiring a quasi number-one status internationally) and its enemies (who needed to depict Japan as a threat, and not as an invalid). Finally, there had been no dearth of dire warnings regarding the Chinese economy in previous years: overheated, overextended and riddled with confusion between market and bureaucratic forces, China's economy had been the leading candidate in Asia for a so-called 'hard landing'.

No one, however, had foreseen the chain of events that unravelled after 2 July 1997, the day when Thailand's government gave up the struggle to defend the parity of the baht with the US dollar. Not even the staunchest critics of Asia's economic policies, who berated either its growing social inequality or the lack of investment into education and technology, had foreseen the sudden wave of monetary and financial destruction that caught the region unaware. Only five months later, Alan Greenspan, the chairman of the Federal Reserve, would put this destruction of capital at 700 billion dollars, and the losses are still mounting. The region's economy, in which international trust had become the modern-day complement to the celebrated Asian personal relationships as the basis for successful business, has ground to a halt.

The West has grown accustomed to a rose-tinted view of Asia, where one continuous and miraculous growth pattern apparently spread from one corner of the region to the other. As a matter of fact, Asian economies have gone through boom and bust cycles in the past. In 1980, for example, Korea underwent an 8 per cent recession of its GDP, and was bailed out by Japanese loans in 1983. In 1985, China's reform programmes skidded off the rails, with Chinese foreign currency reserves very nearly disappearing. Southeast Asian economies also went through a rough patch in the mid-1980s. In the wake of the 1989 Tiananmen repression, Hong Kong's stock market and real estate fell through the floor. Hong Kong's market, deriving its collective psychology from traditional Chinese money markets, has gyrated up and down many times throughout its history. Taiwan's growing financial centre, resting on many insider

deals and far too many 'grey' – or technically illegal – security broker-
ages, had also collapsed before: for instance in 1987, when its decline
predated Wall Street's Black Monday on 19 October 1987 by a few weeks.
Even Japan's Kabutocho fell from a high of nearly 39,000 in 1990 to a
low of 14,300 in 1991, and although this can be seen in retrospect as a
turning-point for the Japanese economy, it did not grow at the time into
a full-scale regional crisis. Yet, with two-thirds of Asia's GNP, Japan
appeared as a far more potent actor than the small financial and currency markets of Thailand, Indonesia and even Korea. In short, massive
fluctuations which take their cue from traditional money markets and
from a speculative streak present throughout the emerging world are
bad for small, or poorly connected operators. However, the market never
falls to rock bottom for the main actors of bureaucratized and hierarchical societies, where foreknowledge is the name of the game. It may
not look like it to the small investor losing his life savings, but Asian
markets have historically rebounded almost as quickly as they fell. After
all, the Chinese were the inventors of the wheel of fortune.

For these reasons, many in Asia have chosen to consider the crisis as
a temporary setback, a case of market overreaction or at most a normal
growth crisis, in a region where the fundamentals still point towards
prosperity. These were almost, word for word, the reassuring thoughts
that President Clinton aired at the Asian Pacific Economic Cooperation
(APEC) Vancouver summit on 14–15 November 1997. He reduced the
financial crisis to mere 'glitches', thus missing the sense of panic that
was sweeping the region. But prosperity has failed to show up around
the corner, and the relentless beating taken by these markets gone astray
has now drowned out sound economic fundamentals.

The separation of economics and politics

I will now focus attention on the explanation for the Crash. What matters
here is the separation of economics from politics, and its unexpected
consequences. Investment, capital flows and growth belong to the
economic sphere. But regulation, supervision, transparency and –
perhaps above all – a sense of balance between dynamic growth and
system stability can only be generated in the public and political sphere.
Asia performed well in the first area, and failed miserably in the second.
This verdict includes Japan, the world's second-largest democracy.

A history of the Crash and its aftermath cannot therefore be an exercise in economic theory alone, much less an ideological exercise which
compares the respective virtues of market democracy with the guiding
hand of the state. Economics must certainly be brought in. Yet out there

in the real world it is not only abstract economic laws that drive markets. Human decisions and collective psychology also shape economies, or even bend them out of shape. These elements are beyond the reach of scientific determinism.

The analysis of such a history can carry with it more than a whiff of ideology. A crisis is first of all a mirror for critics who seek the confirmation of their views in events. It is an exercise ground for experts and institutions with pet theories. Globalization has given economists and market analysts, two categories of professionals, often with limited knowledge of Asian history and culture, a license to apply schemes lifted from other contexts. Perhaps this is just retribution for the complacency of many Asianists and Orientalists who have relied too heavily on their belief in the uniqueness of Asian culture and institutions.

What is more, ideological debate about Asia also marks the return of a suppressed yearning. The region has been ahead of all others in witnessing the obsolescence of ideologies. It was once an economic and political battleground, where the Cold War was played out between the two superpowers and where communism made one of its strongest attempts at social revolution. From the twin defeat of the former Soviet bloc and communism, the present world order has been constructed. Both defeats happened in Asia. The age of revolutions ended in Asia. China's reformist transition predated the fall of the Soviet model. Today's world, especially after the demise of communism and the end of the Cold War, has effectively brought an end to the possibility of politically based revolution in the foreseeable future: this is what Francis Fukuyama's 'end of history' is really about. The inspiration for his thesis came from Asia, where Chinese communism converges with state capitalism, and where revolutionaries of yesteryear, such as Pol Pot, end up literally in the trash can.

It is over Asia that the proponents of authoritarian development have locked ideological horns with the advocates of liberal democracies. It is in Asia that political stability has been designated as the pre-condition for economic growth, in spite of some noteworthy evidence to the contrary.[5] Strong states and fast economic growth have reduced the range of dissent and alternative policies. There remains a debate in Europe and America between progressive and conservative worldviews, although on both continents the successful progressives are often enlightened conservatives in disguise. In East Asia, liberalism and democracy are the only currency that effectively counters the established systems, while the advocacy of socialism in any form has simply disappeared from sight.

Given this separation of economics and politics, it is not surprising that Asian history is being reshaped by an economic upheaval. Asian societies have exhibited a marked preference for stability. Many customary social arrangements already existed to foster this stability – in addition to coercive political rule in some places. Upheaval could hardly have come about from self-conscious political forces. These forces often failed, whether they were China's political reformists of the 1980s, Japan's fresh faces in the politics of the 1990s, or Southeast Asia's NGOs.[6] As in the era of failed revolutions in the Europe of the early nineteenth century, conservative priorities and evolutionary tactics gained the upper hand in Asia while ebullient and politically based movements regularly dissolved.

Or at least they did until the Crash. The 'separation of economics from politics' has been a major tenet of Asia's long-term evolution. Extraordinary advances were made in the economic field, with Asia becoming the world's centre of dynamic growth. To the sceptical reader, we should point out that even the present economic recession in Asia will hardly take it back to its starting-point of the early 1960s. For 30 years, East Asia's overall yearly growth rate has exceeded 5 per cent. According to World Bank criteria, the number of people living on or below the poverty line has been reduced from 60 per cent to 20 per cent of East Asia's population. But although democratization advanced in the industrialized economies of Asia (South Korea, Taiwan and Hong Kong), the politics of economic growth remained largely unchanged. In Northeast Asia (except Taiwan, which now possesses a more sophisticated entrepreneur culture) and in Singapore, Japanese-inspired policies of nurturing economic growth are in place and a holy trinity of bureaucrats, large firms and politicians work hand in hand. The less developed parts of Asia have been able to adopt from Japan only its policy of export promotion and import substitution. There, the nexus of the relationship between politics and the economy has more to do with traditional protection, community policies and that long-forgotten idiom: 'squeeze'. In some cases, such as the post-Tiananmen Square Asian communist systems, the separation of politics from economics is an ever-present, if undeclared dogma.

Self-conscious political action, including the active repair and reform of collective institutions and laws, is usually the most visible top strata of human society. Economic change is the underlying bottom strata, whose shifts can go unseen but are none the less powerful. In any liberal society, the top and the bottom strata interact without any predominance. But Asian societies have been different. They have combined guided or even forced development with political authoritarianism or attachment to political tradition, as in the Japanese case. Even in the most obvious cases of political upheaval in recent Asian history, restoration rather than revolution has been the key. For example, Corazon

Aquino and Fidel Ramos re-established Philippino democracy after the Marcos era. Other ASEAN states, Malaysia and Singapore, for example, which have more tolerance for a political opposition, have somewhat relaxed the state security limitations on personal freedom, without going back to the administrative practices and political systems of the immediate post-colonial era. Certainly, there have been strong political and social movements. One need only look at China's turbulent history under Deng Xiaoping or at the simmering political and religious tensions in Indonesia that predated the Crash.

Yet, by and large, the surface of the Asian political sea has mostly been unruffled, with national captains firmly in charge. Economic change, and perhaps the modern information revolution instigated by the Internet, have been the only areas in which horizons could infinitely widen, and where the individual spirit has flowered.

When political rigidity prevents institutions and laws from yielding to powerful shifts in economic and social forces, there are two outcomes: either economic growth and social renewal stop, leading to a closed society, or one day the ground erupts under pressure from deeper tectonic forces. The Crash represents such an eruption.

A revolutionary agenda without revolution

The Crash therefore does not only pose questions about economic policies or political disruption, social suffering and the chaos that may result from them. In fact, we remain convinced that those nostalgic for Asia's revolutionary era, who would like to see a return to messianic revolutionary upheaval, will be heavily disappointed. Notwithstanding the fall of Suharto, along with that of every other Asian government that has come under the International Monetary Fund (IMF)'s helping hand, there is no major challenge arising from within Asia's stricken societies. What is at stake is indeed more serious than nineteenth-century-type political revolutions, complete with the storming of the president's palace, a new flag and perhaps a new national anthem. Left–right politics are dying out in Europe and America; although astute politicians still ride on their coat-tails, yet rely more on market research than on political ideology to win elections. Asians are far too pragmatic to return to this Old World game. In fact, Asians are going to be so nostalgic about the past prosperity of their economies in the near future that one of the main political issues, and a real danger, will lie in attempts to rebuild that past along the same lines. A withdrawal into nationalism, hostility at foreign presence and intervention and confusion over democratic gridlock, will be part of Asia's new political scene.

The difficulty, which we are already seeing in Japan's political system, will be in bringing Asians themselves to look at systemic, yet non-revolutionary changes to the top strata of their societies. These changes include the following priorities: a limit to state intervention in the economy; reform in the structure of capital and large firms; freeing property rights and ending the closed management system for domestic savings; building a welfare net, if not a welfare state, which can replace the protection of customary relationships; and building regional interdependence in the monetary and financial fields. These changes also imply open economic (and therefore, political) information and above all, government accountability for policy mistakes or fraud. It is a tall order. Without these changes, Asia's tigers will become cowering cubs in the open spaces of international finance. These mighty animals prospered because they were always guaranteed a free lunch by the governments that nurtured them. Now that global economic rules forbid this guarantee, they have to earn their lunch on a daily basis, not over the five-to-ten-year stretches of the developmental state model.

The lack of elasticity in Asia's public policies, administrative systems and social organizations is another major topic of this book. The massive disruption caused by the record growth of the past two decades, the devastating effects of foreign capital on time-honoured structures, will receive due attention. Yet we do not view the Crash of 1997 so much as an economic crisis – although indeed it has borrowed many feathers from that particular bird – but rather as a collision, if not a 'clash of civilizations' (Samuel Huntington). It is a clash of systems, between formerly mercantilist Japan and triumphant neo-liberal America. While East Asian economies have been popularly classified as tigers and dragons, they are no match for the market economies. With the advent of sudden and almost full liberalization, the market has become a blunt instrument, while East Asian economies caught in a transitional stage from their former mobilization model are paralysed by this sudden change of rules. It is a clash of cultures, between Asian models of cooperation and hierarchy, and Western individualistic market behaviours. This involves heartbreaking decisions for Asians which are largely misrepresented in the hype about corruption or cronyism. This focuses only on the deviant elements in more fundamental patterns of social relationships. There is also a clash of long-term strategic choices. Industry-based Asia has cornered successively the auto, shipbuilding and semiconductor sectors only to find that these are now glutted and devalued. The West rests more and more on service activities, from the financial sector to the new information 'industry', and the worldwide marketing of brands that become generic products in all languages, from Coca-Cola and Gillette to Mercedes-Benz or Nestlé.

The Crash may well have started as a classic case of liquidity crunch. 'Overloaning' is certainly not a Western nor an Asian twentieth-century invention. Traditionally, when the year drew to an end in the centre of traditional banking of Ningbo (in Zhejiang province, China), merchants and bankers alike followed the time-honoured tradition of paying their debts before the New Year. To do so, of course, they had to call in outstanding loans. Since there were always more paper loans than currency available, the rush to do so inevitably left someone standing with worthless paper in hand on the eve of the Spring Festival, which marks the beginning of a new cycle. Every year in Ningbo, hapless merchants went under as a result of standing last in line to recover short-term debts.

In 1997, the 'change of rules' of several banking systems and capital markets – and most identifiably the adoption by banks of the celebrated 8 per cent Cooke ratio of reserves and assets to outstanding credit – created a massive stampede to reclaim cash from outstanding loans.[7] Any Ningbo merchant at the beginning of the twentieth century would have understood what went on. An insolvency crisis, stemming from excessive short-term credit unexpectedly falling due, is also a standard cause for a financial crisis in an emerging economy. It is therefore not uniquely Asian, especially since Western banks joined the party *en route*. What is uniquely Asian is the reliance on large infusions of capital, whether from domestic savings or foreign sources, to fund rising industries, spawn international firms and garner political and social support. With the capital liberalization movement under way since the mid-1980s, the long-term focus of Asian economies on industry, and their short-term disregard for returns on capital, have become untenable. The changeover to financial bubble economics in the hope of quick profits reflects this problem. The liberal transition to international market rules kills the Asian goose which took its time to lay a golden egg. The jolt from the Asian financial sphere quickly became a revolution, or, literally, an epochal transformation that destroys entrenched customs and institutions, leaving open the possibility of chaos – or of a complete reconstruction.

No measure of modernization, Westernization or globalization has created a political revolution in East Asia since the Second World War. Yet the thunder from the hooves of a thousand Western bulls heading back to the safety of home, and from millions of smaller Asian bears fleeing their markets to join them, create the setting for revolutionary change. It is no use blaming the celebrated herd instinct, which makes almost every mutual fund manager mimic his colleagues, nor challenging the incredibly lightweight judgement of many celebrated gurus. Barton

Biggs is no Voltaire, George Soros is no Rousseau. Several conservative political leaders in Asia have rightly pointed out the bias of market judges who stand to make money from quick variations in pricing. That does not lessen their influence, at least not in the short term, nor the possibility that this short-term influence creates a more lasting spiral.

We are reminded of the famous financial experiment by John Law in France between 1718 and 1720. He created a capital market by selling debt papers for his South Sea venture. The historical inventor of bubble economies saw his debt paper fall in spite of official backing by the Regent. The resulting crisis of confidence would draw many to the revolutionary camp. John Law had invented a fundamental feature of capitalism, but he knew little about the necessary regulation of markets, and even less about the need for transparency in accounting. The financial *apprentis sorciers* of the Asian miracle are his children.

From the first to the second Crash?

The Asian crisis is not merely a systems failure that the political leaders of the Asia-Pacific can solve by putting their heads together, or that the men in white at the IMF's emergency ward may cure by prescription. True, an initial failure of these leaders and institutions has aggravated the crisis of confidence. The restoration of trust is the essential ingredient of any solution, as Jeffrey Sachs remarked quite early on.[8] Leaders like Dr Mahathir, the Prime Minister of Malaysia, who waved their arms wide in an effort to slow down the flow of capital responding to panic and speculation, failed to understand that trust could no longer be decreed, but had to be rebuilt from scratch.

The reason for these leaders' failure to ward off the crisis does not rest only with their flawed understanding of markets. By the early autumn of 1997, the financial collapse of a region that had, in any case, been bound together by very thin glue was leading to a far more momentous event. A social and political breakdown was also on the way, and it challenged the roots and the legitimacy of political systems throughout the region. This was no longer a case of the lonely butterfly over the Gulf of Siam stirring a typhoon hundreds of miles away. It looked more like an elephant that had been thrashing around in the jungle, suddenly charging into a clearing. The political structure that had provided the real glue for the region's economic success suddenly became the fatal flaw that prevented the region from putting itself right. 'Corruption', 'crony capitalism' and 'bureaucracy' were the key words used by observers to describe a general loss of faith in Asian states and their ability to manage capital into open markets.

True, there is much hypocrisy in this sudden flurry of denunciations. In many cases, capital has been drawn to the region precisely because a strong public hand guaranteed large returns. Crony capitalism, heavy-handed bureaucratic intervention and state-induced economic strategies are not new in Asia. They have been around for decades, and were usually seen as facilitators of the high growth rate of Asian economies. Even those who defended a free market approach against government interventionism had come around, seduced by the success of Asia's emerging economies. In 1993, the World Bank had only praise for the Asian governments who 'intervened systematically and through multiple channels to foster development . . . , targeting and subsidizing credit to selected industries . . . establishing and financially supporting government banks'. The World Bank noted without any apparent regret that 'some of these interventions violate[d] the dictum of establishing for the private sector a level playing field'.[9] These very same practices would later be called 'bad loans to good friends', thus becoming the basis for an indictment against several Asian governments in 1997.

Only five years before the Crash, the literature on the economic miracle applauded the long-term perspective of Asian state intervention and corporate planning. This was seen in stark contrast to the Western financial dictatorship of quarterly reports to shareowners, and to the lack of strategy due to an insistence on short-term financial results. In 1997, the dismal science of economics once again reversed itself. 'Short-termism', as critical economists used to call slavish attention to immediate financial results, has become respect for 'shareholder values'. It has fled the West to rule East Asia. Governments and bureaucracies that were praised for creating a favourable long-term investment climate are now requested to demolish the means whereby they steered, and sometimes controlled, their economies. The Asian model is now fair game.

Domestically, Asian public opinion certainly hovers between blaming international capital and indicting local political leaders for incompetence or worse. This crisis within a crisis has been felt with varying degrees of severity around Asia. In South Korea, the incumbent ruling parties have suffered a defeat at the polls by their eternal opponent, Kim Dae-jung. This change at least provides a quick political alternative within a democratic system that moderate politicians and realistic generals had put in place over the previous decade. In Japan, police cars screeching to a halt in front of large corporate headquarters, heads bowed in shame on the top floor and promises to end the insider deals are certainly nothing new. But the arrest of top civil servants at the nation's most prestigious institution, the Ministry of Finance, and the suicides of several of them,[10] are novel indeed. Top civil servants were spared by the anti-corruption drive in previous years. To commit suicide was an act of despair for small businessmen or ordinary crooks, not for connected insiders. It is not enough to note that the Hashimoto government fell to new depths in the polls: this had happened to several previous governments. But never had faith in the system sunk so low, and Japan been so far from playing a positive role in regional affairs as in 1997 to 1998.

In Indonesia, President Suharto and his clan were initially very far from committing political suicide. That would have been the practical requirement that was thrown at them by the IMF and a grim Mr Camdessus, who presided over the signing of a deal with Indonesia in January 1998. The first family, in power since 1965, was at the centre of the storm created by the financial crisis, and was also the symbol of what prevented its resolution. Rather than give up Indonesia, Inc., Suharto, the Javanese king, his children and his courtiers began playing an old game of shadow puppets. They kept open the very firms that were supposed to have been shut down and equivocated on key rescue measures. Even more ominously, they seemed unable or unwilling to check the storm of ethnic hatred and xenophobia that was rising against the Indonesian Chinese minority. Although the police and armed forces contained the worst disturbances up to Suharto's fall in May 1998, there was no mistaking the direction of the wind. Extreme Islamist forces and well-connected businessmen were using the Chinese as scapegoats for the financial crisis.

The Indonesian New Order that held together since 1966 has come unstuck, and the potential for chaos is great. Perhaps this was Suharto's trump card in confronting the international financial community and the United States, as trouble in Indonesia will reflect on its neighbours and create strategic uncertainty throughout Southeast Asia. In retrospect, his departure from power has done nothing to slow down the Indonesian economic crisis, and nor to prevent it from throwing its regional neighbours into recession. By June 1998, the rupiah had lost 78 per cent of its value on the dollar, a precipitous fall which inexorably triggered an economic implosion.

Indonesia's crisis and instability are by far the most severe in the region. Huge forest fires over much of Borneo and Sumatra have been an additional plague. In the autumn of 1997 the fires disrupted the entire Southeast Asian area, weakening revenue from tourism and worsening the plight of rural people. The spell of rural drought that fuelled the fires also created a shortage in edible grain and cooking oil. President Suharto had succeeded in his New Order by feeding the hungry multitudes in Java, and was awarded a medal from the Food and Agricultural

Organization (FAO) for this feat. The fact that largely protectionist and monopolistic recipes had achieved this is an irony which is lost on the International Monetary Fund (IMF). The IMF challenged Indonesia to liberalize and in effect dismantle the agricultural and primary material distribution system at precisely the moment when heavy shortages materialized. The ensuing panic, the Suharto government's well-meaning attempt at restoring food security by a temporary ban on some exports, and food riots and famine in parts of the archipelago, spelt disaster. Millions of factory workers lost their jobs and were heavily 'encouraged' by the armed forces to return to their home villages, in an effort to avoid demonstrations in the urban centres. Suspended for 32 years by the wily general, history is back and knocking on Indonesia's door. The political forces that had been suppressed are now straining at the leash in the first revolution achieved by the Crash of 1997.

Other Asian societies prove much more resilient than Indonesia. Korea, Malaysia, Thailand and the Philippines all saw their currencies decline by about a third against the dollar in the year after July 1997. Thailand was hard hit by a recession that destroyed the middle classes' financial savings and impoverished farmers. Yet popular anger hardly rose beyond a widespread disbelief in the government's ability to solve the problems. Almost a year later, more organized political opposition surfaced ominously, combining legitimate social discontent with some of the worst offenders from the pre-Crash era. Malaysia, which had seemed to be heading for a free fall after Dr Mahathir unwittingly drew the attention of market operators by his sharply anti-liberal polemics against 'speculators', has proved to be much more cohesive. This is due in good part to the strength of existing foreign industrial investment, and to the fact that its foreign debt was largely publicly held. Had it not been for the regional sense of panic, there was nothing that government austerity could not cure. The Philippines, thanks to their comparatively late arrival in the Asian fast lane, have less international debts, less financial bubble and simply less acquired wealth to lose.

At the time of writing, the other Asian shoe has not dropped yet. That shoe belongs to the Chinese world in Asia. Singapore, Hong Kong, Taiwan and China itself are not immune from the region's woes. Singapore let its currency slide downwards as early as July 1997, and Taiwan did so in mid-October. By early June 1998, this devaluation was contained to less than 20 per cent against the dollar. Stock markets were affected, too, and Hong Kong suffered the biggest onslaught, losing more than 50 per cent from its 1997 peak, although the Hong Kong dollar, pegged to the US dollar, held steady. The price to pay for this monetary stability is a steep decline in financial and real estate values, with an economic recession officially announced in late May 1998.

The situation in China remains unique. It is either half-open, or half-closed to the winds of international markets, depending on one's viewpoint. Its currency is partly convertible for commercial, but not financial, transactions. Only a panic from within China, leading to black market currency transactions, can really destabilize the renminbi. But in other respects, China is hard hit. International investment, frightened by regional prospects, began to dry up in 1998, regional exports are down. Furthermore, many observers draw from the regional disaster an analogy with China's own domestic financial bubble. These prospects are disquieting. In the course of a year, the Chinese went from fast growth with inflation to price deflation with much reduced growth. As it does so, the state and public enterprise deficit is bound to build up, while a burst of spending is required to fuel the domestic economy. The social spectre of unemployment looms large on the Chinese horizon.

The Chinese leadership has worked hard, however, to contain the consequences. It has pledged to abstain from a devaluation of the renminbi that would trigger another round of currency depreciation throughout the region. It confirmed, albeit cautiously, the ongoing reforms and talked about restructuring, once more, the giant public banks of China. This show of will, though useful, will not prevent observers from questioning the feasibility of these policies eventually.

The Asian model under siege

Overall, the Crash raises a host of inescapable questions. First and foremost, there is the issue of the so-called Asian economic miracle. Had it all been a mirage? And even more importantly, will it return? Even though few professional economists accept the notion of an integral Asian economic model, fast growth has become something we expect from the region. Yet in 1997 to 1998, the advice most frequently thrown at Japan's leaders was to jumpstart their economy by a mixture of Keynesian measures and economic deregulation. This advice came from Western-style prescriptions against recessions. It neglected the fact that Japan's budget ran a high deficit. That successive Japanese government essentially threw good money after bad, and that no amount of loose public spending can bolster the Japanese consumer and investor's shaken confidence are two facts perhaps conveniently overlooked by Japan's partners. In this sense, they seem to expect a cure that would come from adopting Western financial recipes, after discarding the Asian miracle cook book.

A 'miracle' is shorthand for the mix of policies and institutions that created the successes of Japan, Korea, Singapore and, to a lesser extent Taiwan, and which the rest of Asia sought to emulate with varying degrees of loyalty to the original model. I believe that the Asian miracle or model was no mirage. For a very long time, however, it was denounced or denied by most international economists – the World Bank only came around and recognized it in the twilight of the early 1990s, when it was already passing away at Asia's economic heart, Japan.

The Asian model was stretched thin, over predominantly agrarian societies in Southeast Asia where education and cultural cohesion were less obvious. It was also scuttled in Northeast Asia under the pressure and demands of global trade partners. Being good at playing *go* is not a guarantee you will win a game of chess. While Western observers rail against the lack of objective and clear rules in an Asian economic environment that to them appears to be rigged, Asians, who place personal trust and mutual reliance over rules, are nostalgic for the intuitive and collective economic strategies that made their success. Inevitably, the debate on solutions to the present Asian crisis becomes a conflict of interests involving more than just awarding brownie points or penalties to participants. At stake today is the future property of Asia's capitalism, which has remained up to the Crash far more based on indigenous national lines than Europe's, or even America's. In other words, Asian capitalists – who are very real when they are Korean *chaebol* families or Indonesian tycoons, and a more fluid entity in Japan or Singapore – are not necessarily told to adapt *or* perish. They are really called upon to adapt *and* perish, as a final proof of their adaptation. Understandably, they are reluctant to take this step.

In fact, the chief contradiction in the global advice flowing to Asia from the IMF, the US Treasury and Europe, remains the focus on separate, national crises rather than on the strong wind sweeping the region. Putting out the fire in each economy is not possible unless some sense of regional coordination is restored. And in many cases, it really remains to be invented. The direct investment and market liberalization revolution that swept Asia from the mid-1980s usually bypassed the issue of region-wide regulation and organization. Asian capitalism and foreign investment created some elements of a region-wide industrial workshop. Capital markets were swamped by deregulation and by the huge role of offshore markets, including for example the infamous Bangkok International Banking Facilities (BIBF).[11] This has countered the national excesses of statism and monopoly firms. But the present situation neglects the prominent role that regulatory authorities play both in America and to some extent in Western Europe. Perhaps Asia does not need at this stage the equivalent of the US Justice Department's antitrust division. Throwing open the capital markets has in effect weakened national champions and big firms that always relied on their domestic backyard to fend off competition and raise capital. The Asian economic model has been thrown off balance by this change. No other model has replaced it, nor is there in many cases any effective regulatory system overseeing banks or some of the region's capital markets.

For these reasons, it is unreasonable to expect a quick fix to Asia's economic troubles. The question of renewed growth is inextricably caught up with the issue of deep, structural and region-wide reform. This issue unavoidably leads to a second question: how stable are the Asian developmental states, whose legitimacy had rested in no small part on their ability to deliver economic growth and to redistribute it according to customary and collective ways? Even more importantly, is political stability really desirable, at a time when the obvious inadequacy of public policies leads to a cry for reform? Listening to Western commentators from the media and markets, it often seems as if Southeast Asia's post-war generation of political leaders would serve their nations best by vanishing from sight. As for Japan, a key reason for widespread Nippo-pessimism is the awareness that the Liberal Democratic Party remains as unavoidable as bad weather at the Nagano Winter Olympics. In the urgency of the crisis, subtle answers such as a regional preference for gradual reform or the issue of regulation in the semi-voluntary transition to free market economics are often lost on outside actors. 'Everything, now!' seems to be the clamour from the outside world.

In the process, political leaders and economic bureaucrats often stand indicted for the very real sins of graft and nepotism. Indeed, the case of Indonesia's presidential family serves as an obvious illustration. Graft at the top has become the symbol of economic mismanagement throughout the region. Yet the question of how to reshape societies traditionally based on personal relationships rather than on public compacts remains a harder one to solve. Few, for instance, stop to ponder why one of Korean president Kim Dae-jung's first acts of power was to reinstate the practice of anonymous bank accounts that his predecessor had outlawed. In Asian societies, trust and transparency do not always go hand in hand; and in Asia, as everywhere, political leaders are made by their own societies as much as they shape them.

This book aims to provide an answer to these large and sometimes unmanageable issues. In a previous work originally published in 1993, I have tried to depict the many facets of the Asian renaissance.[12] The coming of age of post-colonial Asia was not a purely economic event.

I underlined at least some of the obstacles to the formation of a genuine region in the historical sense. Chief among these obstacles was Japan's growing aloofness, behind the veneer of post-war policies and economic diplomacy. Japan was no longer the abnormal post-war state locked in its relationship with the United States, nor had it the will to translate its status as the regional economic powerhouse into political, or even monetary responsibilities. I believed that the call of Asianism was more imaginary than real, although it served a useful notice on the need for a culturalist approach in understanding Asia's societies.

Nowhere, of course, had I foreseen an upheaval on the scale of the 1997 Crash. It is now revealing or confirming existing weaknesses and strengths throughout the region. This is a severe test for countries that had just begun to practise a cooperative approach to regional relations. But it is harshest for the Asian poor, who had started to benefit from the lift-off during the previous decades. They are the first to suffer in the fall back to earth.

A test for global cooperation

Finally, the Asian Crisis is a test of the new global order. One-third of the world's economy, and by and large its dynamo in the past two decades, does not come to a standstill without serious consequences for the rest of the world. True, the crisis has remained surprisingly regional. It first spread like wildfire among the emerging economies with frailties like that of Thailand. Growing regional interdependence, which was the most positive feature of Asia's economic development since the mid-1980s, turned into a trap. Since more than 50 per cent of East Asia's trade is now among East Asians themselves, the roof has collapsed on regional exports, with a major recession under way in 1998. Meanwhile, capital flight towards Western markets, along with reduced export and commodity prices are benefiting America and Europe. It is only in a second stage, hardly reached as of mid-1998, that the missing dynamo in East Asia will start to slow down the rest of the world's economy.

Even before this happens, Americans and Europeans have an obvious reluctance to accept more Japanese or Asian trade exports as a way to help them out of the crisis. Renewed growth of Asia's domestic economies is therefore held to be the key. Meanwhile, stringent austerity and falling domestic consumption are already creating large commercial and current account surpluses for Asia. For historical and political reasons, Japan has declined to lead Asia's economic growth in more prosperous times. It is now being asked to use its domestic economy as a dynamo of last

resort for Asia. But the Japanese consumer or saver's mood canno
be decreed. In a newly opened context of capital liberalization, ther
is a great risk that money created by Japan's government and th
Bank of Japan will simply fly out of the window towards more attrac
tive foreign capital markets. It is therefore highly doubtful that Japa
will commit its own domestic policies to 'saving' the region, as Prim
Minister Ryutaro Hashimoto bluntly put it to his regional colleagues o
15 December 1997.

The Crash of 1997, and the strategic, cultural or industrial clashe
we have discussed above, should not be the cause for an East–West rif
Western solutions to the region's problems are brought up by man
Asians but, apart from the United States' inexhaustible desire to lea
the region, Western powers are remarkably uninterested in the region
power balance, provided it remains stable. The Crash has taught a hars
lesson to all believers in weak, voluntary and informal cooperation. Th
logic of regional integration and institution-building is even mor
compelling today than yesterday. Yet the strength of the regiona
economic implosion, and the very high profile that Westerners hav
taken in prescribing or interdicting solutions, through the IMF or some
times directly, are disquieting. The optimistic talk about an Asia-Pacifi
era, the hopes for an Asia–Europe dialogue, the theories implying
global triad are now questioned. Naturally, sentiment is a factor lurkin
close to the surface in many judgements made about the Asian crisi
Asian nationalist frustrations, jingoist triumphalism in America and
measure of *Schadenfreude*[13] in Europe, are obvious impediments to futur
relations.

They are also misplaced sentiments. I do not believe in the Asia
chorus trying to sell the region's strong fundamentals, as these funda
mentals count for nothing if the right policies are not in place; policie
capable of withstanding the inevitable changes that go with the adven
of global integration. Asia can no longer claim political and economi
uniqueness and national leaders must become accountable to the
people. Yet the resilience of Asian societies, the solidity of their famil
structures and the quest for educational opportunities are genuin
cultural assets even if they do not constitute Asian values *per se*.

The drawbacks of globalization, long known to Europeans an
Americans with their rust belts and employment problems, also caugh
up with Asia. Through their extraordinary success – and the pyramid
financial constructions that gave them clout – many large Asian corp
rations became world-class operators. The comparative advantage
backwardness had exhausted itself, with Asian societies facing the typ
of global pressure the West had known for several decades. At the en

of 1996, a symbolic clash occurred in France between the supporters and opponents of a major take-over by Daewoo Electronics of the Thomson consumer firm. Many French people resented the loss of the family jewels, Daewoo essentially paying for the acquisition with the promise of future investments. More to the point, Korean unions, who knew how high Korean wage costs had risen, were worried about the loss of industrial jobs to France.

The game has therefore become more complex for rising economies and societies that competed successfully in the global marketplace during the first phase of their growth. Today, they need more brains than brawn to keep moving forward. Politics will dictate whether their societies adapt to this new requirement. The West can play a role in so much as it can ease some of the pain during the transition. At the grassroots of Asia's diverse societies, the instinct that may propel this change is already countering unavoidable trends towards a retreat from globalization and social revolt. To make the change compatible with the powerful force of tradition – still the binding glue for most Asian cultures – is the most difficult item on the agenda, and the one which foreign actors rarely perceive. The reformation of Asia will be a milestone in Asian history alongside the Asian renaissance of yesteryear.

2 An explanation of the 1997 Asian Crash

There are two views of reasons for the Crash. One is the conventional wisdom which is of course that no one saw it coming. The second view, which is also conventional wisdom, is that it was unavoidable and easily explainable by major deficiencies in Asian economies and markets, wrong government policies and the basic structure of Asian societies.

The rationale for the view that no one saw it coming is usually financial. Trust in markets cannot be decreed; panics can overwhelm rational thinking and destroy healthy projects. Even today, there is an enormous part in the unfolding of the Asian crisis that belongs to the psychology of its leading actors, whether they be market players, individual citizens or governments. My own explanation for the Crash and its aftermath fully recognizes the role of these human factors, which involve conflicts of interest between debtors and creditors, issues of face-saving, cumbersome economic doctrine leading to rigid courses of action, and the celebrated herd instinct that can drive all participants in the market towards a steep falling cliff.

At the other extreme, the rationale for the second view rests on a long-term structural diagnosis of what was wrong with the so-called Asian miracles or fast-growth economies. This long view can unite almost anybody who ever found a fault with the Asian economic (or political, for that matter) model, leading to retrospective judgements made with the benefit of hindsight. Asia's supposed reliance on cheap labour, the waste of environmental resources, the lack of spatial or social planning and redistribution in the era of fast growth, the heavy hand of government guidance and the cronyism associated with it, the growing preference for financial speculation over long term investment: you name it, anything is now liable to be called a cause for the 1997 Crash. We find here many previous critics of contemporary Asian societies for political, cultural and sometimes international reasons: to name but one example, the end of the Suharto era in Indonesia was an obvious question mark, with or without the Crash. However, 99 per cent of these critics had never previously come up with an economic rationale for the eventual end of Asian fast growth, much less a forecast of the Crash. On the other hand, the many economists who formulated one reservation or another have seldom gone as far as to predict an end to the Asian miracle on these economic grounds (again, some may have had political reasons to be sceptical of Asian trends).

Paul Krugman stands out as the sole exception who can claim prescience regarding the event. His provocative 1994 *Foreign Affairs* piece, entitled 'The myth of Asia's miracle'[1] came close to a diagnosis of what might stop Asian economies on their tracks. He cleverly acknowledges, however, that the reasons he cited are not those that actually caused the Crash. 'I was 90 percent wrong about what was going to happen to Asia. However, everyone else was 150 percent wrong – they saw only the "miracle", and none of the risks.'[2]

My view of these long-range explanations for the Crash is that they mostly miss the point, and particularly so when they are used as an indictment of the Asian model. First, before you start to criticize this model, you need to recognize the extraordinary path of high growth that Asian economies followed. That path extends over nearly 50 years for Japan, over 35 years for the Four Tigers (Hong Kong, Singapore, South Korea, Taiwan), over a generation for every other non-socialist economy in Asia except the Philippines, over the last two decades for the formerly socialist economies that have started the transition to market economies.

Second, the major event in East Asia's economic life since the mid-1980s has been the world's largest wave of deregulation, economic liberalization and opening up to global forces. In Japan, decades of hard-nosed bargaining by the West over its trade surpluses have changed policies, structures and relationships inside the economy. Indeed, all Asian emerging economies have competed against one another to raise capital, becoming the world's first destination for foreign direct investment, and freeing their capital markets in the last stage of this competition. Ironically, the only economies that have not changed policies or structures a great deal are Hong Kong and Singapore – Asia's free ports. They have profited immensely from the movement of liberalization around them.

On balance, most causes for the Crash are to be found in the recent monetary and financial history of Asia faced with globalization. The rush for foreign capital has created new weaknesses and a basic dependency, alongside the obvious rewards. This need not be a financier's view of the Crash. On the contrary, monetary and financial relationships

carry with them a very strong political meaning in international relations. In essence, they may have become the main area of contention
for power among nation-states, even more so since the end of the Cold
War.

Among long-range views of the Crash, one explanation does stand
out, however: it is the theory that Asia's quantitive growth did not come
with a significant rise in productivity. This chapter will explore this
theory, which sums up all other indictments of the Asian miracle or
model. The argument of a qualitative stagnation of Asian economies is
in deep resonance with Western judgements of Asia from the past. Views
of Asia as a static empire, non-developmental, culturally impaired and
mysteriously missing on the industrial revolution are nothing new. Paul
Krugman has predecessors, of whom I will cite the most dignified.

Another explanation commonly stands out – the role that Chinese
trade competition played in undermining Asian economies. China's
devaluation of the renminbi by a massive 34 per cent in 1994 is always
cited to support this explanation. I believe the explanation is a
sham, and belongs to the general category of contemporary publicity
that credits China with much more influence than it actually has. Of
course, this can become a self-fulfilling prophecy. In the political arena,
the belief that China is a world-class boxer leads to a situation where
China actually begins to look like that world-class boxer. Fortunately,
although economics are influenced by political perceptions, they cannot
be derailed for long. Wars seldom break out, but economic competition
is relentless.

Now that this important popular misconception has been disposed of,
this chapter moves on to the largely short- or medium-term monetary
and financial decisions that led to the 1997 Crash after Japan's own
speculative bubble burst in 1990. At the time of writing in 1998, a major
crisis that originated in Japan is moving back there. Yet I strongly believe
that apart from the obvious deficiencies in Japanese economic policy-
making, Western policies or lack of policies, and particularly those of
the United States, carry a good part of the responsibility for the Crash.
This is not meant to exonerate the tigers or the cubs whose careless
march forward prepared the ground for the Crash, or the European
financiers who imprudently loaned money to Asia. But the myth of
liberal market economies collaborating to launch the Asia-Pacific century
often overshadowed regulatory concerns, and deterred Asian states
from a more serious effort at regional construction.

Indicting Asia

A productivity gap?

Paul Krugman and the studies he cites anticipated major productivity problems for Asian economies, attributing them to poor asset allocation in the absence of open markets. The prognosis rested more on long-term educational and technological bottlenecks, as well as failed urban and environmental policies, than on the existence of a financial bubble. Authoritarian states had relied on perspiration, not inspiration. They had drawn on a vast pool of uneducated and poorly paid labour, bene-fiting from the one-off bonus of rural emigration and demographic transition. They competed largely through pricing and low wages, neglecting the huge effort necessary to move forward in terms of tech-nology. Their reliance on economies of scale – increasing production and exports to conquer world markets – led them into a trap. While developed countries, and especially the United States, worked hard to take the lead in innovative technologies and occupy exclusive market niches, Asia produced mass-market, banal, interchangeable goods, with the prospect of decreasing returns and a production glut.

Nothing seems to illustrate Krugman's thesis better than the huge drop in electronics exports from Asia in 1995 to 1996. In particular, the RAM[3] and other semiconductors, which go into every computer and are a main staple of the Asian electronics industry, saw their price fall incredibly low. In economic terms, they are now the industrial equiva-lent of coffee beans, whose producers are left to compete with one another on the sole basis of pricing. Southeast Asian economies in particular are now driven by the ups and downs of the global electronics cycle.

Can one generalize from this type of glut? A look at available research and statistics, even those that Krugman himself used, does not bear out the hypothesis of an Asian productivity gap. Other, more recent studies are much more upbeat on Asia's achievement on the technology scale, and emphasize the role that increased productivity has played in its economic growth.

The Crash of 1997 has in fact led no one to further question the technical ability of Asian producers. The Korean *chaebols*, or Malaysian electronic subcontractors are not inferior. The question behind their success was whether they could financially sustain a breakneck pace of investment that now threatens to bankrupt both the firms and their countries. A leading example is the Daewoo group, whose corpo-rate indebtedness was more than five times the value of its equity. Daewoo has consistently pursued a worldwide strategy of acquisition and expansion at the lower end of the consumer market. As I write, those Asian countries whose exporters have not lost the short-term capacity to buy materials and finance export trade, such as Japan, Korea, Malaysia and China, now have rising global, if not regional, exports. They will keep registering a trade surplus in the midst of the financial crisis.

'Total factor productivity' or TFP as economists call it,[4] has indeed risen continuously in almost all Asian economies. One of the main sources of Krugman's analysis was an earlier study by Alwyn Young.[5] He does not conclude that Asian productivity has been lagging behind the overall quantitative achievements of the region but merely notes that, with the exception of Singapore which according to his findings has had a disconcertingly low productivity growth rate, the Newly Industrialized Economies (NIE)s' post-war performance has been 'average' in historical terms. Other studies point to much more comforting results for Asia. Japan, of course, made giant strides in terms of productivity in the post-war era. This rate averaged 6.3 per cent from 1954 to 1973, and still 3.4 per cent from 1974 to 1990: the equivalent figures for the United States are 1.1 per cent and a negative –0.7 per cent for the same periods.[6] At the other end of the spectrum, China, after a long period of productivity stagnation, has experienced fast productivity growth in the 1980s, according to a 1997 IMF study.[7] The authors of this last study attribute it, however, more to the shift of labour force from agriculture to other activities, and to the impact of recent small and private firms and service sector enterprises, than to large-scale and state industry progress. The Chinese case, if we believe this study, is the closest illustration of Krugman's hypothesis. Yet he barely touched upon China in his thesis.

Between Japan and China, who were chronologically the first and last of the Asian high-growth performers, other studies are appearing that demonstrate the NIEs have enjoyed even more significant productivity increases than previously thought, along with their quantitative expansion. Singapore's apparent and startling non-performance, (–0.7 per cent decline in annual productivity over several decades, according to Alwyn Young's findings) are now attributed to the Singapore government's own overestimation of its capital stock. According to a well-researched recent study, Asia's NIEs have had performances that range from the remarkable (Taiwan, 3.7 per cent per annum over the period 1966 to 1990, Hong Kong, 2.7 per cent over 1966 to 1991) to a respectable average (Singapore, 2.2 per cent over 1972 to 1990 and South Korea, 1.5 per cent over 1966 to 1990).[8]

Debates among economists about productivity are endless. One need see only the recent upwards revision of US productivity figures, based itself partly on a downwards revision of price inflation over the last decade and a half, to have doubts about studies that deal with much less transparent Asian economies. Arguments about 'catching up' and 'one-off increases' are tricky when applied to contemporary cases, since they can only be verified retrospectively. Yet common sense should make us remember the region's entry into the ranks of world trade's top performers (leaping from 6 to 25 per cent of world trade in 30 years), coupled with the strong educational bias that exists in most, if not all, Asian cultures. Does not this suggest that a structural productivity gap is unlikely to become a long-term obstacle? Financial speculation, bubble economics and wrong choices may result in a temporary waste of assets. But here we are already much closer to short-term variables and to policy-based explanations. Neo-liberal economists believe that only the market allocates investment efficiently, while most developmental economists believe in a public guiding hand combined with market criteria: that has nothing to do with the so-called productivity gap any more.

A high-level equilibrium trap?

The underlying assumption that coolie sweat drives Asian economies is more interesting at the meta-economic level, where it encounters a tradition in the history of Western ideas. Describing the reasons why the China of the Ming and Qing dynasties [9] failed to utilize its huge market, efficient bureaucracy and merchant culture in order to initiate an industrial revolution, the historian Mark Elvin also cited a contrast between quantitative growth and qualitative standstill. He explained it by what he called the 'high-level equilibrium trap'.[10] Elvin evidences the high entrepreneurial level of imperial China, with increases in firm size and structures allowing for a larger number of employees, and the 'symbiosis between bureaucrats and merchants'. Yet 'the methods of organization tended to separate those in commerce from those in production'.[11] Elvin shows indigenous technologies, which had reached a ceiling in efficiency, cheap water transport that was a disincentive to road improvement, cheap and even cheapening labour, that encouraged economies of scale over labour-saving inventions, and a civilization that erected shrines to historical inventors but failed to develop patent laws. Ultimately, he falls back on the Malthusian balance between scarce food resources and a population kept in check by this as the limit to growth. Thus, according to one learned historian, did China forgo a Western style industrial revolution in the nineteenth century.[12]

Much can be said today to refute Elvin's founding paradigm on imperial China. Recent demographic study suggests that families, not the

Malthusian trap of limited food resources, controlled the number of the offspring. Rural imperial China generally lived above the subsisten level, not around it: the pattern of involution appeared only in the la nineteenth century and persisted in the first half of the twentieth centui just as it did in Java and Burma in the same period. The failed indu trialization that Elvin identifies in eighteenth-century China is actua very similar to Europe's proto-industrialization in the same century, a possibly more widely spread. Merchants and craftsmen with improvi economies of scale are in both cases examples of Adam Smith's class division of labour. While Elvin thought he had discovered the reas why China did not undergo a European style industrial revolution the nineteenth century, he put the finger instead on the rise of China economy along lines very similar to Europe's in the eighteenth centui China was not backward; it was more advanced in demographic a economic terms – and lost this advance over the course of the nir teenth century.[13]

The Southeast Asia of the late twentieth century bears little reser blance to Ming–Qing China. Up to the early 1960s, after the onset demographic revolution without any attendant economic growth, tl was truly the land of overabundant people and unchanged producti methods that Clifford Geertz portrayed in his classic study.[14] Since th date, the revolution of foreign direct investment has already propell Southeast Asia's economies far beyond the point to which their indig nous technologies and high savings rate would have taken them. T arrival of foreign capital also implies, immediately or as a result of tra negotiations, the opening up to competition of of key sectors. Squea clean factories with imported machines and transplanted labour nc predominate over courtyard sweatshops. What is more, the cost of labo has constantly risen, particularly over the last decade: Korea, Singapo Hong Kong, Taiwan and potentially Malaysia were bridging the g with Western industrialized countries in that respect. It is capital, n labour, that became increasingly cheap to emerging Asian economi Indeed, with cheap capital at hand, many governments and societ made irrational sectoral allocations. This is illustrated by the bubble real estate and construction, the wage inflation process common to mc Asian emerging economies, the explosion in imported luxury consum goods and the use of public money to satisfy clans and clients or to b votes.

Ultimately, much of the criticism aimed at Asian economies rea does not concern the fundamental factors of Asian economic growt but the political economy of redistributing this growth. Cronyism pe verting the relationship between state and market, corruption, nepotis and conspicuous consumption have undermined the sound fundamentals of Asia. Those who jumped from a bash-the-Qing movement in latter-day China to an overall indictment of the Chinese bureaucracy and statecraft made a historic mistake. Those who jump today from cronyism and corruption to a similar indictment of the Asian model are making a similar mistake. There are a few examples of Mark Elvin's 'high-level equilibrium trap' in contemporary Asia. These are the failure to make forward planning for infrastructures and the geographical redistribution of production that would put a lid on production costs. Wasting natural resources without concern for the environment is another example. In Sumatra, Borneo and peninsular Malaysia, the search for tropical hardwood, the pressure of slash-and-burn agriculture and the speculative fever around plantations have resulted in the world's largest forest fires. With the dry weather occasioned by El Niño, the entire region came under a blanket of smoke which threatens to become a regular event. Yet neither the smoke from Borneo, nor the exhaust fumes from Bangkok caused the Crash. Unlike God, economics does not punish sinners.

Indicting the Asian state

Another version of the notion that the Asian miracle was made up and largely the result of one-off economic factors is the purely political explanation. Why Asian market economies held for so long during the Cold War era is a question whose real answer is seen by some in the area of international relations. As *Business Week*'s senior editor Bruce Nussbaum writes, US post-war support for mercantilist policies (Japan) or strong military states fostering fast growth 'secured strong allies in the region and cheap products as well'.[15] Gullible international investors kept the model alive for some time after the end of the Cold War by pouring in hundreds of billions of dollars of international investment. Nussbaum stops short of recommending pulling the plug on Asia; but that is because he believes Asians pulled the plug on themselves, without any help. Instead, he suggests this is 'a second chance to create democratic, *laissez-faire* societies across the Pacific'. If that is indeed the case, the only service that present Asian governments, with very few exceptions, can render to their people is simply to disappear. If there are politically based explanations of the Asian Miracle, then there could well be politically based explanations of the Asian Crash. Nussbaum's wholesale indictment of Asian states is the Western cultural equivalent to Asian conspiracy theories of the Crash as the design of the West, or its heartless financiers.

There is some truth in the idea when it is applied to purely military regimes such as the Burmese junta or to unmitigated crony states such as Marcos's Philippines. It becomes irrelevant when applied to postwar Japan, a nation that has mostly relied on domestic economic growth over the long term and that incidentally contributes 4.5 billion dollars a year to the presence of American troops in the Asia-Pacific. It is irrational when applied to modern Singapore, whose infrastructures and efficiency were built to lure multinationals, and not the reverse. It is wrong even in the case of Indonesia, in spite of the bloody origins of the New Order put in place by General Suharto in 1966. Let's face it, President Suharto actually built even more than he and his family appropriated, he was not a Southeast Asian version of Mobutu of Zaïre.

Behind the consignment of contemporary states to the dustbin of post-Cold War history, there lies not so much the defence of democracy, but still the old-fashioned, time-honoured indictment of Asian state and bureaucracy, *any* Asian state and bureaucracy. That indictment is mostly wrong-headed. The twentieth century in Asia has seen its share of warlord states and squeeze bureaucracies, not all adverse to development. Conceptions of the state vary between Southeast Asian sultanates or feudal lords who fancied themselves as the legitimate owner of all surplus, and the sinicized world, where taxation on subjects was seen as an unavoidable levy that was best kept to a minimum. Historians are in many cases re-evaluating their views of the main traditional Asian states in a much more positive light. The Chinese imperial state of the last centuries, for example, is now thought to have been an example of *laissez-faire* and limited economic intervention. Its fiscal resources were largely inelastic, China's bimetallic currency system mostly escaped its control, the state kept for itself very few monopolies, and even in the latter case leased them to private entrepreneurs. The main areas of intervention are remarkable examples of seeking the enhancement of natural resources, the preservation of order and the protection of social balance: hydraulic works (usually left to others for management after construction, in a striking example of ancient build, operate, transfer (BOT)[16]), food granaries and famine relief.[17] Just as the Qing dynasty Chinese state has been caricatured, the efforts of East Asian states on the road to development are being either cast as a miracle, or seen merely as a hindrance to market forces.

What does this historical allegory tell us? That there is far from one Asian Model, and that even the most celebrated of Asian bureaucracies, the Chinese empire in its heyday, was a complex operation that associated, in modern terms, public overseeing with market mechanisms. The Asian miracle has been eulogized excessively during its long phase of success as a model of guided and even authoritarian development. In the new phase of economic fall that we are now witnessing, this same model gets blamed for nearly everything one can think of. Yet if one considers the alternatives, most Asian policies have been unmitigated successes. This was the case for the major historical states and for the Confucian bureaucracies that inspired them. In Southeast Asia, the British-inspired tradition of civil service (more than the Dutch and French colonial institutions, which left no legacy behind them) have provided another excellent tradition. The communitarian policies of Malaysia, often criticized by investors, have actually preserved that country's social and religious stability, without smothering economic initiative.

Today's Crash need not lead to a general rewriting of Asian history. To understand what caused this crash, we must first exclude from consideration the factors that did *not* cause it. Culture, communities, bureaucracies and even authoritarian states do not engineer financial meltdowns; markets do. The basic cause for the Crash must be identified in the confrontation between global market forces and local institutions which have not adapted well enough to new realities. Since market liberalization really started in Asia only in the mid-1980s, immediately resulting in a frenzy of foreign capital investment, this is perhaps not surprising.

Obviously, Asian states will have to adapt their policies and institutions to the requirements brought by internationalized finance. But there is no economic law or historical hindsight allowing us to predict that Asian states must fade away in the face of Westernized financial markets. Asian states have run markets in the past, or have let them function in an equilibrium that is well worth today's neo-liberal prescriptions. They have also run, or in some cases let alone, very efficient economic policies and practices. To indict them in sum for the Crash is as extreme as to pretend that they single-handedly engineered the preceding Asian miracle. Across the board arguments against Asian economies remain sweeping generalizations that fail to pinpoint the actual causes for the Crash.

Did China wreck the store?

More often than the argument about failed US–Japan financial leadership for the region, the finger has been pointed at China for being the basic factor, if not necessarily a conscious actor, in the Crash of 1997. This is the proverbial tale of the elephant wrecking the china store, with a new twist: charging forward, the Chinese elephant tramples the Asian tigers. The rise of China's economy and its entry into world markets obviously disrupts existing positions. Could China have displaced the Asian maritime economies and precipitated the Crash?

The theory has a lot of attractive facts going for it. China's surge in regional and global exports, the speed at which it has sucked in available international investment capital, its practice of competitive devaluation for the renminbi from 1978 to 1994, the well-documented cases of dumping by state exporters with almost no bottom line to worry about, took the floor from under many Asian commercial competitors. If indeed some of the economies of Asia have lost their buoyancy as a result of increased financial drag or diminishing returns, there is no reason why the Chinese juggernaut could not gobble up the laggards in the pack, on its slow progress to the top.

This argument, however, carries its own penalties. First, it requires thinking of the regional and global market as a zero-sum game, where newcomers inevitably crowd out the oldtimers, and where increased interchange with the Chinese economy does not lead to wealth creation at the regional level. That is not exactly what international statistics suggest. Although the rise of China's exports is impressive, it barely exceeds a similarly fast pace by Korea, Taiwan and the leading ASEAN countries' foreign trade. Second, it requires us to assume that while Asian tigers and emerging economies lag behind in productivity increases, or cancel out these productivity increases with outrageous labour and other factor costs, China is the lonely and massive exception that escapes this trend. Although economists usually view China as a country of infinite cheap labour resources, in other words a bottomless market, the reality is otherwise. Geographical distance, transportation bottlenecks, overcrowding of maritime and urban centres, disparity in educational resources between regions, and the sheer unattractiveness of sending expatriates, even overseas Chinese, to the pits of rural China, all point out to a somewhat smaller Chinese elephant. China's economic reforms add another important emerging economy to Asia, but do not change the overall scale of Asian economy.

When we look at the available data for the years preceding the Crash, we find a buoyant Chinese economy. It was running at the same pace as Asian economies, but it was not really catching up. Paul Krugman's arguments on technological backwardness and the productivity gap are much more easily applied to China (which he fails to do) than to the Asian tigers. The transfer from agriculture to industry, the one-time benefit of creating a service sector, and huge infusions of foreign capital plant, explain China's productivity rise. But with less than three million university students (or 3 per cent of recent demographic age groups), and an even smaller pool of human resources from the past, China has huge disadvantages for the continuation of this growth.

Of course, China's relative position looks particularly impressive when compared to Japan's stagnation in the 1990s. It is also particularly satisfactory to its American partner because, in exchange for a robust trade surplus, China recycles much of its current account balance in dollars, or even directly into the US financial system. Laura d'Andrea Tyson, President Clinton's former chief economic adviser who earlier tried to impose sectoral targets in order to manage US–Japan trade figures, now eulogizes China's rise, calling for its emergence as 'the dominant economic power in post-crisis Asia'.[18] But the comparison is meaningless from a genuinely economic perspective. Japan is a mature economy which, in the best of situations, cannot retread its two-digit growth track of the post-war decades. China, which entered the race from a much lower starting point in 1978, has yet to prove it can keep running for as long or longer than Japan did. Meanwhile, it suffers from some of the same financial woes of infantile financial capitalism as its Asian neighbours, and it has yet to get rid of much of its senile bureaucratic socialist system.

The authoritarian edge

China does have the edge, however, in terms of the financial and trade policy pursued by the central government. This may at first sound strange. The Politburo members of a communist party which has not made up its mind on how to treat its own totalitarian past, have turned out to be better economic strategists than the other governments of fast-track Asia. Part of this has to do with the so-called Chilean model of political authoritarianism backing the transition to a market economy. An authoritarian regime has the potential to step beyond narrow group interests and to maintain order during an inherently unstable transition. It can establish elements of a legal system while retaining arbitrary power at the top, in the interest of stability. Furthermore, foreign investors and lenders believe in this proposition. Political observers have noted that international financial institutions often have a soft spot for these regimes, which they believe to be more efficient on a cost-price basis than democracies, where special interests often overshadow markets.[19] The World Bank in particular has devoted more time, reports and money to China than to any other country since the late 1970s, and it has consistently eulogized the Chinese process of economic reform, which it is politically careful never to call a transition. Investors are perhaps more hesitant. They also like the stability, yet they fear the comparatively low priority for rule of law, resulting in corruption and decisions that can always be reversed. With the right connections, they generally hope that they can endure. They too can bend the rules. For example, thanks to a continued flow of new investments, foreign firms can actually under-state their profits to Chinese authorities, swapping the proceeds with investors who are themselves bringing in dollars. The first rule of the China game is that you never announce a profit, for fear of losing it. *Pour vivre heureux, vivons cachés* (To live happily, it is better to hide). On balance, investors worry more about political breakdown or failed liber-alization, and neither of these have seemed likely for China since the Tiananmen crisis of 1989.

China's leaders, partly because of the inner conflicts between conser-vatives and reformers, partly for more objective reasons, have maintained dual policies that emphasize state control and centralized rule as much as opening up to the outside world and surrendering control to market systems. They have kept strong mercantilist incentives to maintain the state enterprises' domestic market share. They practise the dumping of export goods, they limit capital markets to a minimum, never creating a national stock market and keeping a close watch on the swap markets that trade the renminbi used in real commercial operations. From 1994 onwards, they have built up the central budget by regaining control, or the appearance of control, over taxes. They have also reinforced their control over currency reserves, forcing state firms to declare their hold-ings and, at least in theory, to surrender most of them. Much of this remains more facade than reality, and would not stand up to a finan-cial storm. But the appearance of control and the impeccable statistics – almost no nominal budget deficit, huge currency holdings – matter more than the real picture of huge public deficits and poor central control over currency and financial resources.

The price to pay for this appearance of central tidiness has been in the runaway deficits of state enterprises who exchange their debt among themselves, in a poker game called the 'triangular debt'(*sanjiao zhai*). But apart from this process of spontaneous money creation, the money has come from the state banking system. While virtually every banking reform in China since 1978 has affirmed the need for using risk and profit as criteria for lending, Chinese banks have remained self-service counters for loans to the politically connected, or hospitals for the ailing state firms. All of this explains why China has much in common with the crony capitalism, bureaucratic tampering in markets and political management now denounced in Southeast Asia. Just like the most difficult countries in Southeast Asia, the games China plays are prof-itable to all when they are done quietly, either with strong and immediate mutual interest, or with large export loans or investment guarantees as a safety precaution.

Competitive devaluation is not the key

Chinese policy makers have also pursued, from 1978 to 1994, a path of successive devaluations which represent a process of perpetual adjustment to domestic inflation and overheating of the economy. Devaluation also enhances the international competitiveness of goods made in China (of which 60 per cent are produced in association with foreign firms). The last time it was done in 1994, the renminbi lost 34 per cent of its value on the dollar, and between 1978 and 1994, the Chinese currency lost nine-tenths of its value against the dollar. One obvious sign that it was undervalued at this point lies in classical, unweighted estimates for China's *per capita* GNP. While it stood at 280 dollars in 1978, it had barely passed the 500 dollar mark in 1994, after 16 years of feverish economic growth. Undervaluation allows China to retain the benefits of the least-developed economies in terms of international aid, and also to claim membership of the World Trade Organization on the same basis. Meanwhile, the preservation of a central government investment budget and the multiplication of local government levies on the economy has allowed huge infrastructure investments in the Special Economic Zones created to attract foreign firms. Tax rebates, preferential treatment for overseas Chinese together with these basic investments funded by the Chinese state have made China a competitive production base in many areas. The Chinese export surge is really a rise in exports by joint ventures with foreign capital.

Has this competitive process bankrupted other Asian economies? The Chinese government was sensitive enough to the argument to run a lengthy denial in its official press.[20] But Chinese arguments do score several points. First, the 1994 devaluation applied only to the official rate of exchange: for years, the commercial rate, used in 80 per cent of all transactions, was already much lower. Second, after an extraordinary statistical export boom of 36 per cent in 1994, much of which was really a consequence of a change in reporting, China's exports in 1995 rose at the same rate as Southeast Asia's. In 1996 they actually stagnated, like Thailand's. To further the comparison, Chinese sales to Thailand fell by 28 per cent in 1996, while Thai exports to China rose by 18 per cent. Competitive trade pressure from China is undeniable, although its markets also offered new opportunities to the rest of Asia. But the 1994 devaluation was not the trigger that sparked the 1997 crash. It is far less important than regional financial factors or the impact of changes in global demand on regional economies.

Hollowing out is for everybody

Industrial delocalization and the hollowing out process, long thought to be the preserve of rich and decaying industrial economies, has hit the economies of maritime Asia with a vengeance. Textiles (there is no silk industry to speak of left in Thailand), shoes, toys, household appliances and low-scale consumer electronics have migrated towards the Chinese mainland, with China exporting a significant part of its industrial goods to neighbouring Asia. This is indeed job displacement, which has forced Asian economies to go upscale in order to continue their growth. But going upscale means technology transfer and acquisition and high investment levels in plants, machines and human beings. South Korea and Singapore have been prime examples of a publicly led move towards high technology. In this area, they find themselves suddenly pitted against much larger developed economies with available pools of higher education and management resources.

China, however, has suffered from hollowing out more than any other Asian economy. Like the former Soviet Union, it possesses an immense 'rust belt' of state enterprises based on Soviet-era machinery, poorly managed technological imports, and an oversized labour force. Some cities in Northeast China approach the 30 per cent mark for urban unemployment,[21] while the gigantic plants of the military-industrial complex in Central China are sometimes the only employer in large cities. The Crash has suddenly thrown a harsher light on China's trend towards large-scale unemployment.[22] By April 1998, China had entered a phase of outright economic deflation, with its official price index registering a decrease for several months in a row.

China has no past record of economic cooperation in the region, a fact that is strengthened by its late membership in almost every regional forum. The high-profile gesture it made in the early weeks of Thailand's monetary crisis, offering to contribute 1 billion dollars from its central bank to prop up the Thai baht, has been repeated only once, towards Indonesia. The early offer to Thailand was probably made in the mistaken view that the crisis would remain contained. It is debatable whether China's leaders would imperil their own economy to help their neighbours, for example by holding on to an overvalued level for their currency. The record of the past decades indicates that China follows its own economic and trading interests. On the other hand, the slower export growth and financial imbalance that appeared in 1995 to 1997 in the region are not the consequence of China's actions, or even of its underlying competition for exports on the world market.

A financial crisis of global proportions

We should therefore resist both the temptation to ascribe every event to the much-hyped Rise of China, and the snap metaphysical judgements on Asia which present themselves in the wake of the stunning developments of 1997 to 1998. The Crash was not a celestial retribution for faults and sins in the Asian miracle. Instead, it is useful to place the Crash in the perspective of past global economic crises. Many observers have fruitlessly tried to make analogies between the 1997 Asian crash and the Mexican debt débâcle of 1994, or the Latin American crises of the 1980s. The Asian crisis is on a much larger scale, and it involves many more factors. It is neither the simple product of a market imbalance resulting in a panic, nor a straightforward cyclical event.

Instead, the 1997 Asian Crisis can only be compared with a few major historical precedents, of which the 1929 World Crisis and the ensuing Depression of the 1930s is the best example, although not the only one. It is also possible to find a precedent in the British commercial crisis of 1847 to 1848, which resulted from railway overinvestment, business failures and a monetary panic. According to Charles Kindleberger, both crises 'represented failures at a transitional stage from one set of institutions and forms to another'.[23] As we shall see, this is perhaps the best shorthand description for the 1997 Asian Crash, which followed years of trade and capital market liberalization, and a major 'change of rules' crisis for Japan's economic system. The 1929 crisis shared other factors with the present – contested economic or monetary leadership among nations, misjudgement and mismanagement on the part of major public actors, at the time limited to national governments, but now also including international financial organizations. In the following sections of this chapter there are representative examples of the causes Kindleberger pointed out in connection with the onset of the Depression. A tug-of-war between Japan and the US mirrors the Britain–US financial relationship of that era. Major decisions to cut spending in order to conserve reserves and firm up currencies caused the 1929 to 1930 monetary crisis to turn into a fully blown recession. Smaller countries without an effective anchor in the international system contributed to its dislocation by desperately trying to fend for themselves, e.g. to bet against each other. Trade relations (which were as important in relation to GNPs as they are now) broke down. Creditors insisted on being paid at all costs (France's insistence of getting on with the German war reparations being a major example of financial and, one might add, political folly).

The major difference, of course, is that the Asian Crash and recession happened and is happening in an apparently closed regional context.

Will it last? It seems obvious that a crisis which is inextricably linked with global capital flows to and from emerging markets, and which involves a historic reversal of Japan's major economic trends, cannot be called a regional crisis. Asia occupies a far more important position than any other emerging region in the global economy. In the first year, the world's other developed economies have felt more positive than negative consequences from the Asian Crash of 1997. These effects include reduced interest rates, fewer risks of renewed inflation, and above all an immeasurable boost to the Western *homo economicus'* morale, long threatened by the rise of Asian economic models. A positive linkage is still a linkage. Other effects, such as renewed export competition and reduced capital availability will also come.

The leader of the flying geese falls out of the sky

The most evident precursor of the Crash is Japan's own bubble economy of the late 1980s, which was deflated by the Kabutocho crash of 1990 to 1993, and a real estate bust in 1991.[24] Changes in monetary and credit policy, initially engineered to cool off speculation, ushered in a decade of stagnation for Japan's economy. This is not only a financial or economic event, but also a major challenge to the post-war Japanese political and social model. The crisis of confidence has shaken a country that had been adopting Western market rules over the preceding years, and where a political transition to genuine bipartisan politics had been under way at the same time.[25] The crisis also reverberated over Asia, where Japan is usually both an implicit economic leader and a role model. It is easy enough to forget that Japan alone accounts for two-thirds of East Asia's GDP. Or, in even more graphic terms, that its *pachinko* (parlour game) industry's annual sales in the early 1990s were equivalent to South Korea's GDP in 1992.[26]

Japan's stock market crash of 1990 is tied to a sudden change in monetary policy by the Bank of Japan and the Ministry of Finance. Worried by the ever-increasing financial bubble, these authorities decided to hike interest rates – which is indeed the standard orthodox prescription in these circumstances. Monetary creation was suddenly reduced from 13 per cent per year to 3 per cent. It was 'too much of a good thing', as Milton Friedman, the world's ultimate monetarist, dryly commented.[27] A voluntary credit squeeze sent real estate and share prices sky high, while flagging international demand deepened the downturn of Japan's economy. The sudden deflation of real estate and stock prices created a mountain of bad debt, held by Japan's finance and insurance institutions. On 29 December 1989, the Nikkei-225 index had reached an all-time high of 38,915. By August 1992, it had fallen under the 15,000 mark, a marker below which most of Japan's financial establishments run the risk of bankruptcy because the value of their assets also falls below legal requirements.

Meanwhile, the Japanese consumer's mood understandably turned sour. Back in the bubble days of the late 1980s, oddities such as the three-generations, hundred-year real estate loan had been introduced. Obviously, the homeowners and their offspring who are now stuck with these loans, combined with a 40 per cent decline in their home's value, are not going to be seen shopping around for some time.

The combination of asset deflation, yen re-evaluation and stagnant domestic demand now made it almost unavoidable to pursue a cheap money policy. With very low interest rates on the yen, Japan's financial establishment could afford to roll over its bad debts. The consumer, in spite of sagging confidence, might perhaps be induced to buy and to borrow again. And the cost of successive government demand stimulation programmes, which have increased Japan's public deficit to the highest current level among G7 nations, was seen as sustainable since a huge current account surplus from commercial exports kept the financial markets supplied.

But the beauty of Japan's painless cure for its speculative bubble of the 1980s is that it seemed to require only conjunctural action to solve a structural problem. With time, the huge bad debt problem, now eased by low interest rates, might fade away, thanks to a new cycle of growth that would bring back confidence. Meanwhile, the sacred cows of Japan's economic establishment (insurance and security firms, construction and public works companies) would escape the inconvenience of outright bankruptcy, and the need for a bail-out would remain limited.

Japan – the mirror of France

Japan's credit mountain is not uniquely Japanese, although perhaps its scale befits the size of Japan's economy itself. Nor is it uniquely Asian. There are appropriate international parallels. One of the closest analogies lies in the management of France's burst real estate bubble after 1991. France's property bust was no larger than Britain's or other European countries. But France's financial establishment, with one foot in the ministries and public entities that were supposed to oversee the financial sector, and the other foot in banks, behaved very similarly to the Japanese. In the late 1980s, banks outdid one another in the pursuit of market share and real estate profits. Real interest rates shot up after German unification in 1989, and began to hurt borrowers, however.

Instead of reducing their engagements some of them became even more adventurous internationally. Among them the celebrated Crédit Lyonnais, whose cost to the French taxpayer has now passed the 30 billion dollar mark, managed to sweep its bad debts under the rug for some years. Exactly like the Japanese, its losses rested on a familiar trinity: the real estate bust, failed Hollywood designs (in the Crédit Lyonnais case, it was with Metro Goldwyn Mayer), and even Asian losses before their day. Few observers recall the following anecdote. Some time before the roof fell on the Crédit Lyonnais, and years before the Asian Crash of 1997, the French public bank had already been implicated in large speculative loans to gain credit market share in Taiwan, and dubbed 'Crazy Lyonnais' for the losses of its Taiwan branch.[28] The mechanism that would inflate the 1995 to 1997 Asian bubble, was already there in a nutshell: a large bank trying to make up for lost money overextended its loans in a golden Asian territory. Incredibly, by early 1998, Crédit Lyonnais, which received a huge bail-out from the state, is again Europe's most exposed bank to the Asian risk, with bad loans to Asia reportedly reaching 145 per cent of its equity.[29]

The reasons for this repeat situation are the same as in Japan. The cosiness of high financial civil servants with their former classmates and colleagues in the banking sector has certainly contributed to a lack of control and safeguards on lending; it also served to sweep the bad debt problem under the rug. Even the mentality of high civil servants and politicians is very close. France's president Jacques Chirac (who has 43 recorded trips to Japan) has been the political demigod of Corrèze in Central France for three decades, covering the area with public works, as the celebrated Kakuei Tanaka did in his own time for the remote district of Niigata. When public planners needed money in the early 1980s to finance the Channel tunnel, they found Japanese banks enthusiastic about the project. By early 1997, these banks had to unload their worthless Chunnel debt paper at 40 per cent of its face value. In both cases, banks managed to avoid the sudden purge and bankruptcies normally associated with a bursting bubble. Successive government relief actions, sometimes financed indirectly by the proceeds of privatization in the French case, have enabled these establishments to roll over the debt and to avoid a crisis of confidence with depositors.

The economic consequences of this refusal to face reality have been similar in France and Japan. While other European property markets have recuperated some years after the 1991 bust, France has suffered a stagnation of demand through most of the 1990s. So long as every potential buyer knows there is an overhang of bad debts and unsold real estate, he is unlikely to enter a market which could fall even lower if financial bottom lines were put out to dry on the clothes line.

The analogy, of course, stops there. Far from being a mirror of Japan, France now exists in the European environment, where stronger forces prevail. After 1995, many choice real estate lots were bought at a discount price by American investors, and the stock market has been bailed out by foreign investors, who now own more than 40 per cent of the Paris Bourse. French interest rates are decided largely in Frankfurt, or rather, the autonomy of decision of the French is merely a choice between sticking with a policy that will ensure German-like interest rates, or embarking on a fancy of their own which will quickly land them in trouble. The European Union, in the name of equal competition, has forbidden any further subsidy to Crédit Lyonnais (these subsidies might otherwise have continued forever). For France or any other individual European country, belonging to the European Union forces some rational behaviour on otherwise eccentric practices. Japan, which has no Asian region to integrate itself with, because it would immediately become an overpowering economic leader within that region, misses out on this chance to liberate itself from its own irrationalities.

The price of inaction

A stock decline leading to mushrooming bad debt is the best description of what happened to Japan after 1990 to 1991. The model would apply as well to Asia's 1997 financial Crash, with a difference: loans issued in domestic currencies, but repayable in dollars to issuers who themselves had more often than not taken forward positions in yen, would become the trigger for the explosion of bad debts all over Asia. The mechanism itself was the same as the one which had fuelled a capital explosion on the Tokyo market prior to 1990.

The consequences for Japan and Asia are important and far reaching. Of all developed countries, Japan will have the lowest average growth rate for the 1990s. That fact was obscured for some time by temporary rebounds in the Japanese economy, and also by its sheer scale. For instance, when Japan's GDP experienced a temporary rebound of +3.5 per cent in 1996,[30] this increase alone constituted two-thirds of Asia's overall economic growth for the same year. Japan also maintained huge trade and current account surpluses throughout the period, remaining a net contributor to world capital needs. Therefore, the protracted domestic slump remained largely unnoticed abroad.

The Japanese themselves tended to focus on a succession of unforeseen events. They included the many financial scandals, the 1995

Hanshin earthquake, the Aum Shinrikyo sect nerve-gas incident, a 1996 food poisoning episode which in itself is said to have cost 1 per cent of the GDP in lost *sushi* and other eat-outs, and a rise from 3 to 5 per cent in sales tax in 1997 which was enough to turn consumers away from the shops. But other analysts, and also some Japanese reformers, blamed the Japanese economic model. In the 1970s, Japan's industrial public policy, guided by the prestigious MITI (Ministry of Industry and International Trade) had become obsolete in the face of Japan's multi-national firms' worldwide push.[31] In the late 1990s, the Ministry of Finance and the Bank of Japan are finally suffering worse indignity for their failure, or unwillingness, to stick the knife into the financial sector's mountain of liabilities and corrupt practices. Economic history was on the side of the civil servants, who merely repeated what they had done in other circumstances, distrusting market mechanisms and trying to engineer an orderly and collective rescue of Japan's big financial names.

The bureaucrats merely overlooked a new factor. The blind trust of Japan's citizens, with their huge spending and saving capabilities, was suddenly missing. The Japanese would spend no more on big ticket items implying faith in the future. In 1997 they also began to hoard their savings, or to seize on the opportunity of Japan's Big Bang financial deregulation to move abroad. By the first quarter of 1998, Japanese savings reached 32 per cent of disposable individual income, an extraordinary rise that only partly benefits Japan's financial system. Japan's engine of post-war growth, whose fuel had long been collective behaviour and government corporate ties, hiccuped on the new market-based economic rules introduced in the past decade. It is now stalled, and the economy falling. The event has obvious implications for Asian countries that had also adopted the Japanese model of policy guidance from government and hand-in-glove relationships with big business.[32]

Is it worth a yen?

Meanwhile, Japan's vibrant exports and the resulting commercial quarrels with the United States maintained an upward pressure on the yen, until it broke all sustainable levels for the average Japanese company. In 1990, the year when the Nikkei index started its plunge, the yen still had an average value of 145 per dollar. At the top of the spiral in 1995, its average value had climbed to 94, and even reached 79 yen per US dollar in early April 1995. This re-evaluation went far beyond the restoration of international competitiveness levels, and put Japan in the absurd position of having by far the world's largest per capita income at 38,000 dollars, when every available measurement of purchasing power parity (PPP) indicated this was not a realistic assessment.

There are many theories that strive to explain exchange parities between currencies, and they give very different results. In its June 1998 annual report, the Bank of International Settlements estimates that on a purchasing power parity basis, the dollar should be at 169 yen. According to a trade-weighted average, it should be at 95 yen (the dollar was trading at 140 yen in June 1998). Since the trade surplus with the United States has been the element that both politicians and markets watch most avidly, it makes sense that the trade-weighted estimate should usually prevail.

In the case of the yen, however, the psychological pressure of influential declarations, as well as threats or predictions regarding commercial sanctions, can exercise a major influence. Sudden swings in the yen–dollar exchange rate do not come any longer from relative productivity changes. They do not even result from the herd-like judgement of money traders, or from the scholars' or gurus' declarations. Exchange rates are no longer the consequence of financial fundamentals or market equilibrium, but rather the result of a 'political paradigm',[33] as Kenichi Ohmae calls it. 'Politicians and high-ranking government officers have made the turns and accelerations'.[34] The market tries to second-guess the decisions of major political actors. Kenichi Ohmae, who wrote months before the exchange rate suddenly turned around in May 1995, blamed US officials for these declarations: indeed, the previous year had been a festival of discordant remarks by US Treasury officials and Japanese government figures. Yet in May 1995, a sudden meeting (with a content that has never been disclosed) between Japanese and American monetary officials resulted in this 180-degree turn in the exchange rate.

In retrospect, a sober assessment is that when the US and Japan agree about their mutual economic relationship, the exchange rate can be kept under control and even managed by political statements. An absurdly high re-evaluation in April 1995 threatened to bankrupt most of Japan's industries, save for a few internationalized giants. Belatedly, the US Treasury arrived at an informal Plaza agreement in reverse (after the historical 1985 Plaza Accord to re-evaluate the yen). With carefully orchestrated declarations reversing earlier predictions, and by careful coddling of the markets together with the Bank of Japan and 'Mister Yen', Vice-Minister of Finance for international affairs Eisuke Sakakibara, they engineered at last a downslide of the yen. Japan's cheap money policy and the lust to delocalize industry facilitated it. From a historical high of 79 per US dollar, the yen was back to a healthier average of 115 per dollar in the first half of 1997.

The point, however, is that commercial or monetary agreement between Japan and the United States has been rare since 1971: commercial disputes are the normal condition of the relationship. Kenichi Ohmae is sometimes dismissed as an Asianist friend of Dr Mahathir. Independent research substantiates his viewpoint. A recent study of the yen–dollar relationship points out that the US has consistently applied mercantilist pressure on Japan's economy, staging up the value of the yen and thereby forcing Japan's monetary policy to neglect its domestic needs in favour of a hugely deflationary policy.[35] One of the criteria for making this judgement is a close look at the timing of yen re-evaluations over the past two decades. If the exponents of market theories are right, the adjustments in the value of the yen, designed to re-establish the trade weighted value, should happen *ex post*, e.g. after a new peak in the US–Japan trade balance has occurred. McKinnon and Ohno's study finds on the contrary that the adjustment often happens *before* a new and major imbalance sets in. We are indeed reminded of the old adage once forged by John Connally, secretary of the Treasury in 1971: 'Our currency, your problem.'[36]

The implications of these findings are stunning. Japan is an industrial power and the major source of surplus capital in the world, yet it is not a true financial power since it has demonstrably no control on the value of its currency. The United States is not an exporter commensurate with its economic weight, and it is the world's greatest debtor: yet it is the pre-eminent monetary and financial power, thanks in part to its ability to influence major exchange rates. That ability does not lie solely in the markets, but also in the confidence of others in the continued strength of America, and finally in America's political influence on international relations and the world order. Being a strong political power has significant side benefits.

The Nordic Track exercise

The back of Japan's financial system was broken in 1995, when it became clear that any further advance in trade competitiveness would only result in a further disastrous hike of the yen. This is the monetary version of the Nordic Track exercise. The faster you walk forward, the faster the treadmill brings you backwards: the exercise can become quite discouraging after a while. For the first time since 1971, when the United States' decision to abandon the Gold Standard led to the end of the post-war fixed parity between the yen and the dollar, it became impossible to anticipate any profit in holding on to the yen. It equally became evident that Japanese export policies were running into the wall of monetary re-evaluation.

Expectations have thus reversed themselves, with money to be made by betting steadily *against* the yen. By the last quarter of 1996, a more reasonable exchange rate again propelled the Japanese trade surplus upwards. Yet the yen has not stabilized, the domestic economy has not been buoyed, and has in fact begun since that date a slow descent to hell. Can it be that Japanese market operators, private citizens and politicians alike know a little secret that does not appear in economic textbooks? There is no future for Japan in following its previous export path, because a swing in the monetary exchange rate will immediately 'punish' it. For decades since the Second World War, the psychology of the Japanese has been boosted by the elation they feel at economic and commercial success. Even if the domestic economy is actually much more substantial, future expectations of international eminence are a major factor of confidence. The doom and gloom in Japan's collective psyche does not only come from the burst bubble of 1990 to 1991 and its lasting effects. It is also a feeling of international defeat.

Inaction as the best course of action

Of course, part of the blame must be placed on Japan's own doorstep, and especially in the lack of imagination of successive governments facing this novel situation. Seven successive emergency spending packages designed to revive the domestic economy have failed. They were closer to Herbert Hoover's public works projects than to the Keynesian spending programmes of the Roosevelt era. Aimed largely at the construction and public works sector, which was threatened by bankruptcy because of the downturn, they have resulted in a spate of useless rural highways, empty harbours and other profligate projects entrusted to local authorities. Meanwhile, Japan's Ministry of Finance officials, seeking to preserve an orthodox balanced budget, have done their best to cut ordinary spending or delay special work outlay. The result is that ever since 1991, Japan's economic bureaucracy has combined a succession of emergency spending packages mostly tied to special construction programmes with austerity budgets relying on taxation to keep the public deficit in check. In other words, they have been stepping on the gas pedal and the brakes at the same time.

Meanwhile, the absurdly low interest rates, dipping under 1 per cent for short-term money (and under 0.50 per cent as of June 1998) have had a perverse effect on capital flows throughout Asia. Not only did Japanese firms export capital in order to delocalize production: this was a smart move between 1985 and 1995, since they set up factories in Asian countries whose currencies were mostly pegged to the dollar, therefore ensuring stable pricing for their key export market, the United States. The move was indeed exceedingly fortunate in 1995. It became less so in the years that followed, as the dollar edged up against the yen. But Japanese financial institutions and foreign banks working on the Japanese market soon sought to take advantage of the sliding yen and its almost free borrowing rate. The recipe for disaster was created at that point in time, when speculators began to borrow short-term money in yen in order to loan on a longer-term horizon in dollars or, even better, local currencies tied to the dollar. The move created instant profit, since the dollar, and even more Asian currencies pegged to the dollar, carried much higher interest than the yen. For example, Korean government and corporate bonds routinely carried interest rates of 15 per cent per annum in the mid-1990s.

The move also followed tradition. Internationally, Japanese firms, like all their counterparts in countries with abusively high taxation rates, have always liked to locate part of their profits in off-shore subsidiaries, and therefore create a large credit supply in centres such as Hong Kong or Singapore. So do the Germans and French, who appear in the Bank of International Settlement statistical reports as the world's main suppliers, together with Japan, of off-shore credit. Japan's move also followed a domestic tradition. The Bank of Japan and Japan's main banks have always used a large amount of short-term yen loans as a domestic commercial and financial instrument. These practices hark back to the Japanese tradition of 'overloaning', e.g. financing firms without attention to actual reserves or risk, but by relying on customary relations. They have been an essential feature of the *keiretsu* group relationship, providing cheap capital with control.

Bubble economics 101

During the years of Japan's bubble economy, huge rises in real estate and equity prices meant there was a source of instant, free and profitable monetary creation in the hands of the market itself. After 1995 and the simultaneous decline in the value of the yen and its interest rates, Japan's bubble has been exported to Asia. Borrowing at 1 per cent on three-month terms while the yen stands at 100 to the US dollar, and immediately lending at 6 per cent for one year in a currency tied to the dollar is the first part of the trick. Paying back the initial loan after the dollar has climbed to 110 yen, or even better, loaning again the money while rolling over the short-term yen debt, is the second part. It is a sure-fire method to turn a profit without any initial outlay. The trick soon became a classic of off-shore markets, and is in fact recognized as a trigger to the disaster by the Bank of International Settlements' July 1997 report that sounded the alarm – too late, of course. Another effect of this was to create a permanent outflow of yen, lowering Japan's current account surplus and increasing the downward pressure on the yen. In the 1980s, Japan's financial markets had created a huge domestic speculative bubble from low interest rates and a soaring currency. After 1995, the international financial community created a huge regional bubble in Asia from an even lower interest rate combined with a falling currency.

Europe's financial establishment had long bickered over the high interest rates forced after 1989 by German reunification and the Bundesbank's conservative hostility to monetary creation. From 1995 onwards, these interest rates also fell. The money that banks would not loan to a stagnating European economy began to flow in huge quantities to the ebullient Asian economies. Europe invited itself to the party that Japan had started in Asia. Only American banks, absorbed by US domestic growth, largely abstained from it.

The impending catastrophe

It was in the first few months of 1997 that Japanese financial and monetary authorities got an inkling of the coming crash. There had already been isolated signs of debt failure in the most vulnerable Asian economies: the Korean Hanbo steel group defaulted on its loans in January 1997, and Thailand's leading financial real estate company, Finance One, became insolvent in February. Both countries showed a rising external account deficit, and a high, mainly short-term external debt, with a very high proportion of Japanese lenders. Two things happened at the end of the first quarterly period for 1997. Japanese banks and subsidiaries had been content up to then with 'rolling over' – or renewing – short-term credits to their usual customers. They suddenly began to pull the plug on these borrowers, in an effort to jack up the level of their own assets towards the end of the fiscal year, compensating for large stock market losses. The yen also firmed up suddenly, making short-term borrowing in yen less attractive. This sign, as we shall see, was unfortunately misunderstood by a number of large European banks. They were only too happy to step into the shoes of their departing Japanese competitors, and thus acquire an immoderate amount of Asian debt paper at the worst possible time in this century – the second and third quarters of 1997.

The Japanese financial authorities expressed their own concern in a more direct way. In March 1997, the representatives of finance ministries and central banks from six key Asia-Pacific economies[37] met for the first time. Mentioning the potential for a serious monetary disturbance in Asia, the Japanese representatives suggested the setting up of collective mechanisms to prevent and contain such crises. They were not listened to by the United States, as would remain the case during the entire year of 1997. This was, before the crisis actually flared up and not after it, Japan's first attempt at what would later be called an Asian Monetary Fund – in other words, a reserve facility on which embattled central banks could draw on in case of speculative attack. The proposal would be formulated again in a more detailed way in July 1997 at a meeting in Shanghai with central bank governors from Hong Kong, China and six ASEAN countries. It was finally repeated at an emergency meeting in Manila of finance ministers on the eve of the APEC summit in Vancouver of November 1997.

US officials have mostly refrained from comment about these Japanese proposals. They did not take any action on them. Privately, administration sources may comment that Japan's proposal was nothing more than a gimmick to rescue their own banks from all the bad loans outstanding in Asia.[38] That goal, however, is precisely what the IMF on a larger scale is currently attempting to achieve for the international banking community, as a prerequisite to renewed lending and capital flows. On the record, some noted pundits of the Asia-Pacific and APEC circuit make no bones about the reasons why the United States was not interested in a regional emergency rescue fund. As former US Treasury official and economist Fred Bergsten put it:

> Japan's proposals for an Asia-only 'Asian monetary fund' . . . would exclude us from the most crucial area of cooperation with the world's most dynamic economies. . . . The costs of any such outcome to the broad national security as well as economic interests of the United States, would play out over many years and could be huge.[39]

Bergsten also noted at the time that the proposal had been rejected by every other Asian country. This was a serious misrepresentation, since several meetings in Asia had positively endorsed the idea, and several ASEAN countries clung to it even after Japan stopped voicing the proposition publicly. Later, there would be great praise for China's economic cooperation in order to prevent the crisis from worsening, and financial *op-ed* pieces praising China's future economic leadership in Asia. But at the critical juncture, the United States and Japan had once more parted company. Much more realistically than Fred Bergsten, Chalmers Johnson, the dean of so-called revisionist studies on the Japanese model, later commented:

The Japanese ... proposed a new multi-national financial institution led by Japan and instructed to make loans to Asian countries. The American instantaneously objected, correctly sensing that Japan was about to try its hand at long promised but never delivered international leadership. If the Japanese had succeeded, they would have slipped the leash of the US Cold War system. Moreover, they would have started using their surplus capital to help countries in Asia rather than continuing to send it to the world's number-one debtor nation, the United States.[40]

Is there a pilot on the plane?

At this point, the lack of cooperative leadership in financial and monetary matters between the United States and Japan suggests again the ghost of the 1929 world Crisis. Kenichi Ohmae had already noted in 1995 that the surge from one extreme to another in the yen–dollar exchange rate had a historical precedent. 'The history of the pound–dollar relationship before and during the pre-Great Depression era is almost as "wild" as the recent dollar-yen relationship.'[41] And indeed, in his masterful explanation of the Great Depression, Charles P. Kindleberger writes that the failure of cooperation between England and the United States was the key factor explaining the severity of the crisis:

> The international economic system was rendered unstable by British inability and United States unwillingness to assume responsibility for stabilizing ... In 1929, the British couldn't and the United States wouldn't. When every country turned to protect its national private interest, the world public interest went down the drain, and with it the private interests of all.[42]

No historical analogy is ever perfect, of course. Although the economic symbiosis between Britain and the United States before 1929 played an essential role, Britain was already in relative decline and more concerned with preserving its Commonwealth economic space than with global leadership. The United States at the time was an international lender, not a borrower as in the 1980s and early 1990s. Arguably, the lack of international financial institutions in 1929 made a direct intervention by the leading countries more essential than in 1997 to 1998. However, Kindleberger also mentions in the contemporary context an IMF inside joke to the effect that 'If the United States does not move, nothing happens'. In retrospect, it is an apt comment on the IMF's role in 1997 to 1998. The main cause of the Great Depression after the crash of 1929 was the US failure, under President Herbert Hoover, to take the lead, while Britain receded into her own problems. Optimism and procrastination from 2 July 1997, when the Thai *baht* broke lose from its mooring to the dollar, until South Korea's sudden plunge towards national bankruptcy in late December 1997 are a short take from the Herbert Hoover era.[43]

The bubble bursts in Southeast Asia

There are two ways of looking at the Asian emerging economies' situation on the eve of the financial crash. The first, of course, is to judge them with the benefit of hindsight. This, as Joseph Stiglitz ironically notes, 'leads many to the fallacy of believing that any problem that existed prior to the onset of the crisis is automatically a cause of the crisis'.[44] There has been no shortage of I-told-you-so latecomers in this vein, with some former ideologists hoping for the best, which, in this case, meant the worst.

Why the dog didn't bark

A more sober view starts with a peek at Asia's real economy – e.g., the GDP growth rate, industrial investment and production, exports and consumer demand (see Table 2.1). None of these indexes would indicate a crisis in the making, and in fact the economies that crashed in 1997 had maintained robust growth during the first half of the 1990s. As to the GDP per capita growth rate, Asian tigers and emerging economies crowd the world's first rank over the longer-term 1960 to 1995 period.

Nor would a superficial examination of their public budgets have revealed anything amiss. One of the traits that the World Bank hailed in the Asian miracle, and which compared favourably not only with other emerging countries but also with the Organization for Economic Cooperation and Development (OECD) zone, was the pattern of balanced budgets and conservative public spending in Asia. This, obviously, was a major difference from Mexico and Latin American countries that had produced earlier financial crises. It explains why Asian governments were seen as models of wisdom, and generally trusted by foreign lenders and investors. The only exception was Malaysia, which had an oversize public investment programme – although important infrastructure work was needed for the Malaysian Peninsula. Much infrastructure work could be justified by the country's vibrant growth. However,

Table 2.1 Emerging economies, growth rates 1990 to 1995

	Real GDP growth	Growth in exports
South Korea	7.8	12.6
Indonesia	7.1	13.3
Thailand	8.9	19.1
Malaysia	7.1	19.9

the new airport project, the gleaming Petronas towers that were the highest in the world and other projects were already considered as white elephants. But so long as fast growth continued, these countries were all in the textbook situation of economies going through their first phase of growth. During that phase, large amounts of capital are needed, with promising returns. Asia's Newly Industrialized Economies (NIEs) were not, like Mexico, importing capital to finance profligate consumer spending or public deficits, but simply because domestic savings, however high, could not meet the demand for new investment. This was investing in the country's future, as economic theory recognizes.[45]

In retrospect, bankers and international institutions may regret not having had at their disposal the proverbial barking dog who warns of an impending crisis. At this stage though, it is probable that the dog would have slept soundly. Fiscal policies and budgets were conservative. Exports were still growing. Current account deficits could be explained by the need for infrastructures and technology, and therefore categorized as an investment. Certainly, growing amounts of foreign capital were directed towards emerging Asia. At 33 billion dollars in 1994, the four ASEAN emerging economies (Malaysia, Indonesia, the Philippines and Thailand) still received no more foreign capital under various forms (direct investment, loans, bonds and equity) than China took in foreign direct investment alone for the same year. In the case of Thailand though, the dog should have been barking every night since the early 1960s. With the single exception of 1986, Thailand had been running a yearly current account deficit, and was none the worse for it.

Korea goes for broke

A different version of the same tune holds true for South Korea, the other leading casualty of the Crash. In spite of enormous domestic savings, Korea had relied on foreign capital for its fast-paced development, and ran a worrisome current account deficit in 1991. A somewhat slower pace of growth had cured the problem and by 1994, the Korean economy was back on the fast track. With the rise of the yen, foreign capital flowed easily to Korea, whose industries gained in competitiveness against Japan.

Then the tide turned in 1995. The yen started its decline against the dollar, lowering the profit margin for Korea's large export – *chaebols*. Korea's capital markets, however, were thrown wide open by a government deregulation of finance. Its aim was largely political. This was the price to pay in order to get Korea into the 'rich man's club', the OECD whose only non-Western member was Japan. The *chaebols* at this point could afford to ignore high domestic interest rates, and borrowed even more heavily in foreign currency. Rather than retrench and face a recession at home, they decided to go for broke, acquiring market shares all over the world. From 1994 to the third quarter of 1997, Korean direct investment abroad grew at an astonishing pace. Korean firms also plunged into speculative market activities from their foreign subsidiaries.[46] By the end of 1996, the 30 largest *chaebols* had an average debt that was almost four times higher than the value of their equity, with Daewoo topping the list at five times its equity value. Incestuous relationships with Korean banks meant that they always found the intermediary who came up with funds: in most cases, these were now short-term infusions borrowed in turn from abroad. Not to be outdone, in fact, many Korean banks and financial institutions also grabbed at international market share, extending loans wherever Korean industry went, and in particular to Indonesia. At the end of 1996, the Korean current account balance was back in heavy red ink. To hold steady the receipts from unit exports, the Korean government kept the won almost pegged to the dollar – thus endangering the competitivity of Korean exports. Korea was now an accident waiting to happen. But lest we should blame the Koreans alone for their reckless interpretation of financial deregulation, we should remember that Moody's, the international ratings agency, for example, still had an A1 rating for Korea's sovereign debt in January 1997.

The currency reserve illusion

Concern about the growing Thai need for foreign capital or the appetite of the Korean *chaebols* for external financing did exist. It was enough, for example, to push up interest rates in Korea. But the money, in both cases, seemed to go to promising ventures, and few drew a line between these scattered points of concern, or with the Mexican crisis that had worried other emerging economies in 1994 to 1995.

Since 1994, in fact, most analysts had been concerned primarily with the overheating of the Chinese economy, which many saw headed for a tailspin. The gradual cooling off in China, arguably the least transparent of Asian economies, had a soothing effect on investors. Both China and other emerging Asian economies had another answer for the wary. Their central banks maintained large, even oversized currency reserves, which were supposed to act as a buffer in case of a failure of confidence. This was another measure of the robust conservatism of central monetary authorities. Thailand's level of reserves at more than 30 billion dollars was comparable to that of France's. Over all, the region had a huge share of the world's currency reserves, at more than 500 billion dollars in 1995. The highest amounts were held by Japan, China, Taiwan, Hong Kong and Singapore, and indeed helped them throughout the Crash. Observers duly noted that this level was in fact an added cost on the economy, and a drag on potential investment levels. These reserves were largely sterilized, while the countries needed to borrow for their huge infrastructure and modernization programmes. The critics also noted that more transparent capital markets with better accountability would have permitted Asians to dispense with such levels of reserves. Why should Thailand, with a foreign trade one-fifth of France's, maintain the same level of currency reserves? At least this high level seemed to lower the risk of a monetary meltdown. These were the years when Asian equity, with a low starting point, offered huge returns to international investment. In retrospect, the rush of pension funds towards the Asian tiger economies was overstated. When the crunch came in 1997, fewer than 2.5 per cent of US mutual funds assets, for example, was invested in the region. That, however, was already a large amount for markets in their infancy.

The loan addiction

Much of the money flowing to Asia has been in the form of loans rather than equity. This is true of every Asian emerging economy except Malaysia and the Philippines. There is almost no market judgement for loans, which are more dependent on the rating of borrowers, and can be influenced by the backing of public or government authorities. International rating agencies are new to Asian emerging capital markets. The ratings they produce are paid for by the borrowers, rather than by potential lenders. The same situation applied to Chinese state enterprise, whose shares were issued in increasing numbers on the Hong Kong market, where they are listed as 'red chips'.[47] Prestigious international accounting firms now certify the surrealist practices of China's state firms. They have survived for decades by disregarding accounting and profitability (a taboo, in fact, in Maoist China), preferring instead to lobby for more budget allocations. Since the advent of reforms, they have become masters at advertising losses to the ministries that rule them, often placing profits in quasi-private subsidiaries or abroad. In other words, they are masters at juggling the books. The expectations of high gain fuelled by astounding growth rates were enough to dispel doubts, and their prices skyrocketed on the eve of the Hong Kong handover to China in July 1997. In a well known case, Beijing Enterprise, a municipal company best known for its tourist stands near the Forbidden City and the Great Wall, was oversubscribed 260 times. By the end of 1997, and often within months of their first listing, Hong Kong's 'red chips' crashed by 75 per cent from their high point. Should not the accountants who had certified their books at the time of offering be held as much responsible as the gullible investors?

Viewed from the vantage point of the so-called red chips, it is not certain that a more substantial equity market would have saved Asian finance. If professional expertise from major international firms can prove so misleading, would even more substantial equity markets have saved Asian finances from its excesses? Emerging capital markets are often a glorified lottery to outside investors, but they seldom reach Asia's level of capitalization. A watershed was passed in 1997 with a formidable Indonesian gold mine swindle. A company had apparently discovered a gold mine in East Kalimantan, and an international mining giant, Bre-X from Canada, sped to the scene and formed a joint venture which drew thousands of investors. In early 1997, the gold mine was declared non-existent. The Jakarta stock exchange suffered badly from the incident, in which government authorities had evidently been implicated. The swindle signalled the retreat of international investors from Jakarta's stock market.

But much of the money that was invested did not have the protection that comes with the existence of a financial market, even if that market remains less then transparent. A lot of the lending and borrowing took place through convenient off-shore capital markets – starting with Hong Kong and Singapore. Statistics from the Bank of International Settlements (BIS) reveal that at the end of 1996, almost half the capital lent to Asia by banks within the BIS's area of reporting (e.g., for practical purposes, from the Western and Japanese financial system) passed through off-shore capital markets. Within these off-shore centres, Hong Kong and Singapore come second and third, immediately after the Cayman Islands.[48] Even these statistics are largely defective. They do not take into account, for instance, lending by Korean financial institutions to other Asian economies, since Korea is not a member of the BIS reporting system. No mention is made either in the BIS data of the new off-shore markets created by countries such as Thailand, which functioned as an unguarded back door for investment in the Thai economy. Encouraged and protected by Thailand's leading financial institutions, the Thai off-shore market became a source of huge and unpublicized short-term money for speculation in the country's boom economy. But even in Hong Kong and Singapore, it was often the case that no one really knew who was the borrower of last instance.

There are clear signs that these deficiencies are being recognized in retrospect. In May 1998, the BIS set up its first foreign office in Hong Kong, a move clearly aimed at more efficient supervision of the Asian financial system, or of the lack of it. But in 1995 to 1996 the occasional dog who woke up and barked was rarely, if ever, listened to. In the fateful fall of 1997, many risk analysts would find themselves thumbing back issues of *International Finance, Euromoney* and the like. They looked for paid advertisements by loan syndicates in these magazines, trying to 'guestimate' who had really borrowed what. And, perhaps more importantly at that point, from whom. The search for a lender of last resort had begun.

A tale of coffee and chips

Two things happened in 1995. First, global demand for electronic and computer components made in Asia suddenly peaked, and the prices dropped for these parts, which had become a mainstay of Asian industry. The movement still goes on, with 16 megabits random access memories (RAMs) of the type used in every computer, retailing for hardly more than a dollar. Producing the basic and standardized electronic chips is like entering the coffee bean business: there are huge swings in the demand cycle, and long-term deflationary pressure. In this sense, countries producing these elemental electronic components are little more than glorified primary material producers. There has been a lot of talk about the New Economy in the United States, fed by demand for computers and chips, enhanced by the increased productivity that they bring, and guaranteed by lower purchasing prices that promise endless inflation-free growth.[49] Much of emerging Asia has been sucked in by the New Economy, and turned into a component supplier, assembler or subcontractor for the global electronics industry.

It is no coincidence that at the APEC's 1996 summit in Manila, the focus of US trade liberalization pressure on its Asian partners was a demand for immediate and total liberalization of trade in the computer and electronics sectors. When global demand is pulling the market, this is a bonus for Asian growth: Singapore, where the leading private employer has for a long time been the French electronics firm Thomson, or Malaysia, where Matsushita's local output alone represents between 5 and 7 per cent of the GDP, are cases in point.

The downside is that the electronics cycle now has a direct influence on Asian economies. In 1995 to 1996, when the demand for semiconductors and electronic parts suddenly dropped, overall exports began flagging in a number of countries around the region. All Asian countries except the Philippines saw their export growth rate fall back to one-digit; Japan's overseas sales actually fell by 7 per cent (in dollar terms) and Thailand's by 1 per cent. This meant that the regional capacity to finance growth and investments was also constrained. The export slowdown of 1995 to 1996 should have resulted into a slower rate of investment and cancellation of projects, even outside the main export industries. It should have resulted in reduced economic growth in 1996 and 1997.

Not to worry, however. Another development occurred simultaneously. Lost export receipts were quickly made up with an increase in loans, especially on a short-term basis. The flow of cheap Japanese capital or of forward contracts in yen increased markedly, while several governments around the region thought they could sustain their growth rates with increased public spending. This was especially the case for Malaysia, whose public projects became gigantic. The Bakun Dam and its hydroelectric station, a new airport and a new administrative capital were launched while PM Mahathir energetically backed the 'national car' Proton company. In Indonesia too, a 'national car' company was started by President Suharto. Who better than one of his sons could manage this project? And why not name it the Timor, after the rebellious island province that Indonesian nationalists held so close to their heart? History does not record whether Suharto thought that naming his first car the Timor would improve its chances of a successful launch on, say, the Australian market. But since he had several sons, and there were also several Korean firms vying for the car joint venture, he soon created another one. Meanwhile, technology tsar B.J. Habibie, already famous for buying the entire fleet of the former German Democratic Republic in the hope of retrofitting it for the Indonesian navy, had a commercial jet plane in his sights: he had long been the German aerospace MBB[50] group's scientific adviser, after all. There is a reason why these projects happened, apart from the Randolph Hearst-like dreams of their progenitors. Cheap capital was available, but direct foreign investment was flagging and economic activity threatened to slow down. Contracyclical Keynesian spending was the polite name of the game, much as in Japan where special spending plans succeeded one another. In fact, the rescue of public work, construction and real estate firms with the right friends in the right places had begun, and politically tied firms were making the mistake of fighting the tide of international markets instead of riding the trend. In the later words of Malaysian think-tank chief Noordin Sopiee, 'The tiger economies of East Asia have been first rate in their management of the economic fundamentals in the real economy. They have been second rate in the management of market fundamentals.'[51]

Cronyism: but we always did it...

Everyone has heard the story of the explorers and priests who try to convince a man-eating tribe in Africa that eating human flesh is actually a sin: 'Why, we always did it', they chant back. The barrage of critics against crony capitalism is reminiscent of this. In a downbeat interview with *Asiaweek*, M. Mahathir remarked: 'We have been doing the same thing all this while. We haven't changed ... whatever you find under the microscope has been there all the time.' And when faced with a question about cronyism, he replied: 'We make it a public policy that this is Malaysia Inc. ... We work with all the capitalists in this country ... Everybody is our crony, every single one.'[52] As often with Dr Mahathir, the words are both self-deprecating and infuriating, but also revealing of a deeper intent. He does not really answer the charges but he politely points out the hypocrisy of the situation. Furthermore, the past implication of foreign firms and businessmen in the pattern of corruption makes many protests sound hypocritical. Viewed from a distance, is it not hilarious to see Japan's government threaten Indonesia with a complaint to the World Trade Organization because two Korean firms had been awarded well-protected auto factory deals? The past history of Japan's business dealings with Indonesia is after all replete with intermediaries, shady deals and the pursuit of official protection. When Suharto fell in May 1998, huge multinationals began counting their losses from past associations with the First Family. Indicting crony capitalism for the crash of 1997 is like blaming the Roman empire for its fall: in that case, you should also praise it for its long success. It took all the energy and willpower of Lee Kuan-yew to stamp out public corruption in Singapore, and decades of energetic action by Hong Kong's anti-corruption team under British rule to achieve some of the same results. And these are major financial markets that could not build up confidence without this basic reform. Every other Asian country has had its share of major money scandals, often with well-documented accusations against political rulers, their families and associates. If anything, there was probably more clean-up going on in several of these countries in 1995 to 1997 than at any other point in history. In Japan, nearly every major politician save the last two prime ministers (the ineffective Socialist Murayama and, to this day at least, the current prime minister Hashimoto) has been incriminated at some point for money politics. In Korea, president Kim Young-sam made the fight against the corruption of his predecessors a major feature of his administration. For the first time in Korean history, two former Korean rulers, General Chun Doo-hwan who had other sins to contend with, and General Roh Tae-woo who had had the good grace to usher in political democracy in 1991, were sentenced to death. The implication of several Kim Young-sam relatives in questionable deals probably saved the lives of the two generals. In Taiwan, public and electoral graft, connections with the underworld, bribes for public contracts are not new. But they have become the hottest topic in journalism and parliamentary debate. In the Philippines, worry about public honesty is high – popular newspapers hound police and even government officials who are suspected, sometimes wrongly of being responsible for the lucrative kidnapping business. In a country where the word 'cronyism' was actually coined to describe Ferdinand Marcos's style of government, President Fidel Ramos's term has been unusually free from such accusations. In Malaysia, where Dr Mahathir has on occasion sued British newspapers after allegations of shady foreign deals, corruption is an open tug of war in the national press and among political parties. Clearly, there is room for improvement in a political system where the UMNO[53] is dominant. Only Indonesia seems to have shown a steadily worsening trend. Bribes, protection money, official rackets and ethnic Chinese businessmen serving as money bags for high military officers are nothing new in the archipelago. But its growing riches and President Suharto's incredible fondness for his clan clearly tip the scale. Meanwhile, China provided an interesting backdrop, where honest economic and financial cadres living on less than a hotel bell boy's wages can be found alongside totally corrupt local administrators and public firm executives.

Corruption and crony capitalism never stopped international money flowing in. Nor did they chase it out in 1997. A return of major international capital to Asian markets, however, will require more transparency and a rules-based environment. The crisis has exposed more fundamental defects than corruption itself, such as financial market control and regulatory supervision. The next phase in Asian growth will require much better financial management, besides stamping out corruption, than was needed in the first phases.

Herd instinct and the liquidity crunch

Once the background from 1995 is understood, the Crash of 1997 becomes easier to chart, since it essentially unwound the springs that had been tightened to the limit. Of course, one must take into full account the human comedy, including mistakes by several political leaders and major financial players. No one has a monopoly on these mistakes. Leading European banks decided in early 1997 to step into the leading position of their departing Japanese competitors. Had they not done so, however, the Crash would merely have started a few months earlier. President Clinton spoke in November 1997 of 'glitches' in the Asia-Pacific economies when an unprecedented panic was under way. The International Monetary Fund, as we shall see, worsened the Southeast Asian crisis during the autumn of 1997 when it insisted on budgetary discipline and bank closures in Indonesia, at a moment when deflation was in full swing and a wave of depositor's fear was hitting the financial establishments.[54] Southeast Asian policy mistakes do stand out. Thailand's central bank spent several months denying both the true amount of indebtedness of the country and the low level of actual currency reserves. When the dam finally burst on 2 July, the flood swept away the Thai economy.[55] Dr Mahathir initially practised an exercise akin to standing with arms raised in front of an incoming freight train. Every time he spoke out against speculation, the market reacted with another onslaught, until he eventually changed his tactics. Each time Dr Mahathir railed against speculation or decided on a measure to slow the market Malaysia's finances were dealt another blow, often by panicking domestic investors themselves. The coincidence of a Korean presidential election in early December 1997 paralysed decision-makers in Seoul, while the different candidates outdid each other with patriotic statements. But the first prize should be given to President Suharto, whose evasive and undecipherable tactics have brought Indonesia to the edge of a precipice from which it has yet to climb back.

It is possible to chart a myriad of wrong policy decisions, to picture the rising swell of panic that carried the financial stampede from one market to another throughout the region. But unfortunately, it is impossible to know who did what to whom on the market itself. Even on the best of open markets, where applied mathematicians now put ticker tape vibrations into instant equations, there is no historian of financial war. At best, we have rumours, or confirmations when takeovers are under way: there is no obligation to publicize a sell order, however. In the case of Asia, we will probably never know who the key actors were at any given point. In one of the most interesting phases of the Crisis, these rumours contradict themselves. Hong Kong saw a major attack on its currency between 23 and 25 October 1997. This triggered an instant decision to raise overnight interest rates to 200 and even 300 per cent, and this decision itself caused a precipitous drop in the equity market. To this day, the local real estate firms, whose indebtedness level was too high, have not recovered from this rise in the cost of money. Who really started this move? Was it international mutual funds bailing out in a hurry? Or were some of the very same targetting the Hong Kong dollar to shoot down the Hang Seng index and buy on the cheap later? Or was it mainland China firms running to the escape hatch from a frightening regional crisis? Or perhaps even China teaching a lesson to would-be speculators? The same question applies to the strong buy back that pushed the index up two days later. Hong Kong is the biggest Asian financial market after Tokyo. One should not forget, perhaps, that during the October 1987 Wall Street crash, the president of Hong Kong's stock exchange sold his personal shares abroad while shutting down the market for several days (and was later fired for this action). Events elsewhere are even murkier. International speculators were most often blamed during the first months of the Crisis, but after a while the role of domestic savers, starting with the large regional fortunes, became much more important. By early 1998, Korea and Indonesia were bled dry of any foreign currency on the local market, so much so that the panic fed upon itself with very little capital. On some days, the Indonesian rupiah could fall by 10 per cent with less than 30 million US dollars actually changing hands: this in a world where the daily trade volume averages 5 trillion US dollars.

The sheer opacity of the financial markets, or the tight-lipped attitude of the various organizations supervising them, is a major reason for political sniping at either speculators, foreign governments or the IMF and its brethren. Much has been made of the so-called herd instinct, a compromise formula that recognizes the psychological factor, but implies also that there are really no leaders, only followers: the market decides, and humans follow suit. Since the market is the grand sum of all moves, it is always right. A winning speculator is someone who anticipates the truth, a loser is one who has gone against this truth. When Malaysia or Korea tried to buck the trend with the financial equivalent of speed bumps (by capping daily sales or index declines), they were seen as hindering the freedom of market forces (thus provoking investors to bail out as quickly as they could). Yet Wall Street's own stop measures (such as a limit on the hourly moves of the indexes) are well accepted, because they are seen as technical moves to ensure the fluidity of the market.

A definitive history of the Crash will therefore have to wait until its protagonists step forward and record their roles and understandings of the situation. To a large extent, only political leaders and bystanders have expressed themselves so far. It is highly probable that such an investigation will show market play is not a polite game that softens relations of brute strength. It merely serves as a meter registering decisions that proceed from animal instinct, greed and fear. The problem with opponents of the market at times of crisis is that they cannot have it both ways. Emerging economies cannot hope to accept international capital flowing in with the hope of supplementary profits, yet deny that self-same capital's elemental instincts and basic freedom when things go awry.

In the wake of the Crash, policies aimed at limiting short-term capital movements have become fashionable in some quarters. Dr Mahathir first touted the idea to considerable international scorn, but it has been taken up under various forms by political forces as diverse as France's neo-Gaullist party and US senator and Democratic leader Richard Gephardt. When Alan Greenspan suggests that interbank short-term lending is 'a significant source of systemic risk', and ponders the possibility of 'increasing the capital charge on lending banks, instead of on borrowing banks',[56] it means the idea has arrived on high ground indeed.

From day one, however, the basic problem with this type of proposal has been the need for the universality and comprehensiveness of any restrictive measure. So long as the global market remains a reality that is beyond the reach of existing states and institutions, these proposals will look like storm-breakers on the edge of a raging sea: they may end up kicking sand and silting up the shores rather than restraining the high waves.

Conclusion: shared responsibility for the Crash

My basic explanation for the Asian Crash indicts neither the Asian model nor the role of international speculation. I believe that the transition from guided developmental states with closed capital ownership and guided allocation of assets to wide open market economies has never been successfully achieved. Not even Japan has adequately passed the 'change of rules' stage that in fact implied a complete overhaul of its political, administrative and economic structure. I also believe that the United States has unwittingly had a hand in the Crash. It played a very rough game in monetary policy towards Japan, trying to win back in this area what Japan's industrial policies were gaining in the United States, pushing for free capital markets everywhere in Asia without adequate warnings about improper use. Japan's burst bubble of 1990 to 1991 coupled with intense monetary pressure on the yen led to a second bubble, exported to the Asian emerging economies that were liberalizing their capital markets at the same time. Europeans joined the fray for their own reasons, turning this into a global casino. When the Crisis broke out in 1997, the US stuck to a neo-liberal view, whereby the market is the only teacher and pupils only learn by their mistakes. Non-intervention by the Asia-Pacific's first economic power, whose currency swings called the shots, made Asia's debt pyramid unstable and unmanageable. Finally, the applying of IMF prescriptions usually designed for emerging economies at a far less advanced stage, but suddenly inflicted on full-blown economic and financial markets, blew up the entire regional system, or what passed as a system. Even a mountain eagle could not have sailed through.

3 Asia, meet the rescue party

Has there been an efficient response to the 1997 Crash from the global financial community? Obviously not. By May 1998, 10 months after the Crash originated in Thailand and spread around the region, a second wave, or aftershock hit the region. Not only has the rally in currencies and capital markets that occurred in early 1998 petered out. A recession is hitting Asia's real economy, making a nonsense of all economic forecasts and particularly those made by international financial organizations. Worse, a new downslide is originating from more complex causes – the ever-increasing bad debts in the hardest-hit economies, and the impact of Japan's own domestic recession and self-doubts are triggering new losses around the region. Unquestionably, the economic and social situation of the three countries 'assisted' by the IMF – Thailand, Korea, Indonesia – has gravely deteriorated. In addition, major changes have occurred in international rescue agreements that can be read as positive and pragmatic adaptations to the new emergency. Yet they also reflect the mistakes made during the second half of 1997. Global financial institutions at best failed to prevent an escalation of the crisis, and at worst may have fuelled it.

This chapter therefore seeks to unravel the tangle of actors who have influenced these rescue plans, and to explain their various concerns and motivations. Basic explanations for the Crash differ (as discussed in Chapter 2), and it is therefore not a surprise that prescriptions differ, too. There are different economic doctrines at work, most obviously in judgements about the balance of market freedom and public intervention, including in the rescue process after the Crash. The reactions of Asian national actors – governments and public – is equally fundamental, with likely political outcomes a key concern. More fundamentally perhaps there is a dividing line between the many who see Asia's Crash as a string of separate and discrete crises in emerging economies, and the few who see it as a global capital market phenomenon. Finally, and most importantly, there is the question of how the main industrialized countries have perceived their own economic outcome to be affected by the Crash. For although most observers are having a field day today at IMF-bashing, the IMF is really a proxy for the large industrialized nations.

We will take the reader through an Asian economy increasingly strewn with debris, while tackling the above-mentioned issues in the following order: 1) the basic ·Western (and to some extent, Japanese) attitudes to the Crash which were, and remain, a fundamental factor; 2) the IMF's arrival in Asia, its policy assumptions and the varying skill with which it has tackled three country cases in a region-wide crisis (never calling it that) that will become a classic of international public finance courses; 3) the hurt reaction from Asia's often long-standing national leaders,. the unravelling of political order when economies crashed which constitute a series of short stories in their own rights.

The Western reaction to the Crash

The day of reckoning for Asia unfortunately arrives at a moment when it is no longer the sole, or even the main, engine of global growth as it was during most of the 1980s and the early 1990s. The present moment is a phase of extraordinary financial optimism in America, while Europe enters the final stage of monetary unification.

Granted, the jury is still out on some aspects of the New Economy in America. It is possible, as some assert, that the present phase of strong US economic growth without inflation still pales into insignificance, when compared to the golden Eisenhower decade of the 1950s, or even to the New Society optimism of the Lyndon Johnson era. But it certainly does not feel small when the average US mutual fund owner checks the value of his portfolio. After decades of talk about an impending American decline, the US economy has entered a self-centred era of growth where Wall Street gains provide a new fuel, while a rise in productivity clears the risk of inflation from the air.

To some, the Euro is less of a surefire success. Yet in Europe, the prospect of a genuinely unified single space for industry, trade and financial transactions now boosts optimism, after a long drought of investment. America's permanent need for foreign capital somehow figures as a sensible form of investment for the rest of the world rather than as a worrying current account deficit. Europe's top-heavy social and retirement costs are now viewed merely as an entrance fee to do business in the mega-market that has just been created.

Europeans and Americans have in common a huge economic base, with 70 per cent of US multinational direct investment going to Europe, against 9 per cent to Asia. 'Most US multinationals have more to worry about the smooth introduction of the Euro than about another round of competitive devaluations in Asia',[1] concluded one analysis of the repercussions of the Asian financial crash. Trade and investment between Europe and America, seldom talked about in the past decade, are intensifying. Is the Asia-Pacific century over before it even started?

While several Southeast Asian economies were drowning in market panic during the summer of 1997, the orchestra never stopped playing on the upper deck, that is, in the Western industrialized countries. Certainly the event immediately caught the attention of Western institutions, such as banks, who were caught on the hop because of loans or other capital commitments. It attracted vengeful comment about the validity of the Asian economic model or of Asian values from those interested in theoretical debates. But to the real-world investor sitting in Wall Street, Omaha or Frankfurt, the Bangkok, Jakarta and even Kuala Lumpur equity and money markets are just pocket change. Only the region's larger capital markets – Tokyo, Hong Kong, Singapore and perhaps Seoul – really qualify for global attention. The issue of outstanding loans is the only pressing cause of direct concern to the West, as we shall see. Even Tokyo's Kabutocho, which had passed Wall Street in terms of daily turnover during the late 1980s, saw its capitalization drop behind London's in April 1998.

Next door, the Chinese-led economies of the region have done their best to remove themselves from the scene, emphasizing how much better run they were. Yet Singapore and Taiwan have committed large amounts from their own reserves to the regional rescue. Even China and Hong Kong have chipped in modest amounts of support. These amounts are far from justifying, however, the hype that has been generated about China for resisting the temptation of devaluation. To this day, lack of regional solidarity remains a striking feature of the crisis, with ASEAN figures such as Fidel Ramos, Chuan Leekpai and Mohammed Mahathir often doing their best to point the finger at their neighbours. This is, after all, consistent with the definition of a panic, but it may also be a recognition on their part that they have no solution apart from the market itself. As usual, Dr Mahathir may be franker than most when he gloomily confides that 'we no longer have any power over our economy'.[2]

Windfall profits from Asia

The West, however, was not gripped by this panic. Far from it. It is significant that the subtext of what was said by several of the West's foremost economic leaders indicates that the Asian crash has also its positive side. When Alan Greenspan, the chairman of the Federal Reserve Board, expressed himself first on the Asia crisis, it was to emphasize that the event could serve to dampen the enthusiasm that was carrying Wall Street to dizzy new heights. Even in February 1998, his declarations still carried a sense of the positive consequences of the Asian crisis:

> The key question going forward is whether the restraint building up from turmoil in Asia will be sufficient to check inflationary tendencies that might otherwise result from the strength of domestic spending and tightening of labor markets.

Marginally, Greenspan worried that the forces from Asia might dampen the US economy 'by more than is desirable'.[3]

This is a different position from the doctrinaire market liberalism that inhabits a Republican majority in Congress, which precludes committing taxpayer's money to the salvation of Asian sinners. But to the most powerful economic official in America, a moderate and long-enough period of financial turmoil in Asia was not a source of discomfort in itself.

Almost a year of debate over an American special contribution to the IMF, marked by partisan politics on Capitol Hill, has taken its toll. It has often isolated Clinton's administration officials, especially those from the US Treasury, who wanted to move forward quickly. A group of moderate Republicans ready to back a Democrat administration appeared in the first weeks of 1998. It included such celebrities as Henry Kissinger and former president George Bush. Some of these Republicans, such as Douglas Paal, former Asia adviser to the Bush White House, explained early on that 'there was an urgent need for a bargain between the international creditors and their Indonesian borrowers'.[4] That deal, indeed, would emerge two months later. A business lobby formed in February 1998 to work the Hill on the subject of the IMF. Helped by Treasury Secretary Robert Rubin, and encouraged by Alan Greenspan, the coalition was essentially made up of export firms.[5] Mainstream Republican figures, however, stayed with their ultra-conservative indictment of the IMF. In a scathing attack, former Secretary of State George P. Shultz and former secretary of the Treasury William E. Simon asked: 'Who needs the IMF?' By interfering with the market, they argued, the IMF was encouraging future crises. They also borrowed a leaf from the progressive book, noting that 'when the IMF intervenes, the governments and lenders are rescued, but not the people'. And they concluded that the IMF was 'ineffective, unnecessary and obsolete'.[6] We know the old saying which proclaims: 'I didn't steal the pan, and it sticks, too'. Very often, when critics look for reasons not to intervene in the financial crisis, one finds side by side mention of liberal/conservative and progressive/radical arguments.

By mid-June 1998, Congress agreement for an 18 billion dollar supplementary contribution to the IMF rescue was still lacking, with political support waning. House Speaker Newt Gingrich, Republican chairman of the Joint Economic Committee James Saxton as well as the bipartisan House Banking and Financial Services Committee were in fact attacking the IMF on its entire track record of recent years.[7] The very limited actual intervention that the IMF had in fact conducted none the less became a political liability, with mainstream political figures veering towards financial isolationism.

Europe offline

Europeans, by nature, are even more diverse in their reactions. Up until the beginning of 1998, literally no stand had been taken by either the European Union or the heads of government. At a Europe-Asia meeting of Finance Ministers in September 1997, only three out of 15 principals from Europe actually showed up,[8] while almost all their Asian counterparts were present. The previous record of no-show had been set at an ASEAN–Europe Foreign Affairs Ministers meeting in February 1990. A few months after the fall of the Iron Curtain, seven out of 15 Europeans had understandably not found the time for ASEAN.[9] This time around, the coming Euro kept them busy at home. As late as January 1998, European Commissioner Jacques Santer delivered a speech in Singapore whose message could be summed up in three sentences: the Asian crisis was mainly cyclical, and the right policy mix could solve it. Europe was already contributing to the solution through the IMF, and 'by keeping our markets open'. And the Euro coming after 1 January 1999 would 'strengthen, stabilize and diversify' the financial system.[10] According to press reports, even EU diplomats on the spot were 'disgruntled with the vague rhetoric', contrasting Europe's silence with the growing involvement shown by the United States in the previous weeks.[11]

European public opinion has been brought up on heavy doses of Asia-bashing medicine, starting with blaming Asia's cut-throat competition for hollowing out European industries and creating the record unemployment level we now experience. The overall balance of trade between the European Union and Asia has run in Europe's favour since 1995. Ironically, that is as much a consequence of runaway Asian spending and European recession as of a conscious policy. The fact itself has not fully registered with European public opinion. Also ironically, Europe's overall economic relationship with Asia is replicating America's in some respects. European exports have been expanding at the average pace of 17.5 per cent per year since 1980, reaching the same absolute level as the United States' in 1996 (roughly 140 billion dollars in each case).[12] As high as it seems, this figure is not enough that a variation has a significant influence in the short term, except perhaps on Germany or the Netherlands, who send a higher proportion of their exports to Asia.

Meanwhile, the influx of capital fleeing Asia's markets produced a historical record of low interest rates in every European currency except British sterling. A few months before the transition to the Euro, this is a windfall profit that cannot be ignored. Europeans could well ratify Alan Greenspan's judgement. As 1997 drew to a close, the European stock markets embarked on a meteoric rise that mirrored Wall Street's earlier trend. In the United States equity market itself, 1997 saw a net influx of 66 billion dollars, or as much as in all of the preceding nine years. Japanese flight capital and overflow cash from China's currency reserves,[13] not doctors from Toledo, are driving up the Dow Jones these days.

Europeans have a stronger downside, however. According to every published figure, loans from European banks hold the first place in Asia. At the end of June 1997, figures from the Bank of International Settlements indicated that European Union banks alone held almost 40 per cent of Asian debt, and 50 per cent of debts contracted through Hong Kong and Singapore.[14] The same figures revised for the end of 1997 went even further: European exposure had grown to 47 per cent of Asia's debt, with Germany, France, the Netherlands and Great Britain most exposed. Japan held 30 per cent of outstanding loans, and the United States only 10 per cent. Were these figures to include Swiss banks, the total would be even more impressive. Apparently, US banks that had gone through the Latin American and Mexican crises became more cautious as a result. But there is significant concern that European private banks might suffer greatly from a default by any Asian country. Publicly, several banks chose an early write-off of some of this debt from their books as a gesture to maintain confidence: Deutsche Bank announced, for example, a 770 million dollar provision on losses from Asia in 1997.[15] Its outstanding loans to the region still weighed 5 billion dollars at the end of the year, a commitment that was pared to 4.2 billion dollars three months later.[16]

With their own past involvement in mind, European banks were engaged in a behind the scenes effort to broker IMF agreements and avoid default by a debtor country. Although they can easily encourage the IMF, governments and ultimately taxpayers to pay for the rescue of Asia, private bankers are much more hesitant about committing their own resources to the same task.

This is perhaps why some European governments have been somewhat softer than the United States in their expression towards Asian countries resisting the IMF's conditions. A prime example is former Chancellor Helmut Kohl's call to President Suharto of Indonesia, which was said to be an expression of sympathy and support. It was followed, in January 1998, by a visit from a special envoy who promised technical assistance from the German government. When the French saw the deadlock in talks between IMF's Camdessus and the Suharto government, they certainly backed the IMF's conditionality. But they also suggested a more political attitude towards Indonesia by sending Jacques Delors, the former EU president.[17] Although the project did not materialize in this form, British Foreign Office Minister of State Derek Fatchett took a swing through the region for this reason. At the ASEM summit of April 1998 in London, Europeans also took a more benign public stand towards Asia, and especially Japan, than American leaders. The difference reflects frustration at the way America tries to gain a maximum leverage from leading the process. In February 1998, Netherlands' Finance Minister Zalm strongly complained that his country had not been asked to contribute to the IMF rescue of Indonesia and Thailand. He criticized the United States' taking over the role of the monetary fund by 'making promises off its own bat',[18] and warned against 'a competition between the Americans, Japanese, and the Europeans to take on the leadership'. But he was also strongly supportive of the need for equivalent conditionality in the IMF's agreements with different Asian countries.

For German, French and Japanese public authorities looking at Indonesia, the dilemma was simple: too much *diktat* from the IMF could result in either a chaotic breakdown, which alarmed everybody, or more simply a full moratorium on private debts, which would hurt primarily the heavy lenders. Only Bundesbank president Hans Tietmeyer, ever the guardian of Bundesbank orthodoxy, complained that the IMF had actually done too much and encouraged future delinquency by debtor countries.

Europe pays, America decides

In sum, while European governments and the European Union have been criticized in the Southeast Asian media for indecision and even indifference towards Asia, they were much more directly involved in the risk of financial default throughout the region, and therefore inclined to soften the terms of a deal. The United States, although directly implicated in the ultimate geopolitical stability of Asia, were much less involved in the short-term issue of financial survival of many Asian borrowers. They could therefore afford to drive a much harder bargain, while minimizing their actual supplementary commitments to the rescue packages. By April 1998, the United States still had not committed more than 3.5 billion dollars over their quota obligations to the IMF, or to the other international institutions involved such as the World Bank and the Asian Development Bank. They ended up deciding more, and paying less, while Europeans paid more but had less influence on the bargaining process.

There is a perception, particularly in ASEAN quarters, that Europe has been hanging back from the rescue effort while the United States have been forthcoming. While that perception has some justification in the disorganization and poor language of European-wide diplomacy, it is not justified by facts. As of May 1998, the real obstacles to a stronger outside rescue effort were to be found much more in Congress than in Europe, and actual disbursements by Europeans were well beyond America's own contribution.

Indeed, the US abstained from any additional commitment to the Thailand rescue plan. It committed less money than tiny Singapore to the IMF rescue of Indonesia. Although its participation in the Korean rescue has been larger, it is still well under the consolidated contribution from the European Union,[19] or even from Japan.

The IMF's role under scrutiny

From August 1997, the time of the first planned rescue of Thailand, to December 1997, when the Korean financial system broke apart, the IMF has been sent into the breach with two contrasting mandates – the first was to deliver strongly worded policy advice to the leaders of Asia's ailing economies. The second, however, was to keep a tight rein on the actual disbursement of funds committed for the rescue plans.

These mandates fit the pattern of the IMF's bitter prescriptions for its patients. But they were made necessary, in Asia's case, by the extreme difficulty of obtaining any bailout funds from the US and by European reluctance to actually produce the sum committed on paper.

In effect, the IMF was supposed to restore confidence by its mere presence and by the policies it prescribed.

Shoot the director!

On any movie set in Hollywood, there is a moment known to the cast when tempers flare and the collective mood inclines to shooting the director. Unquestionably, Michel Camdessus, the IMF director who found himself in world news as a result of the pressure on his institution, went through this phase. One could even point a finger at the exact moment when this happened – a picture, indeed, caused it. The 15 January 1998 news photo of Camdessus standing, arms crossed, above President Suharto signing the terms of his country's IMF agreement went around the world. To Asians, and in particular to Indonesians or Malays, it mostly recalled the colonial era and its permanent humiliation of native pride. The feeling united reformist economists such as Faisal Basri, Islamists such as Amien Rais, the chairman of Indonesia's second Islamic organization, and Suharto cronies such as his own son Tommy who denounced 'a new form of neo-colonialism'.[20] Yet to neo-liberal Westerners, the second IMF agreement was another flagrant case of wasting public money. And in retrospect, it was a particularly premature ceremony since, as the next months showed, the IMF had to backtrack on some of its conditions.

IMF-bashing for everybody

The IMF does not quite qualify as a secret or Mafia-type society working to subvert honest countries. Since its main objective, as defined by founding members, is to ensure trust in the world currency system, it has a lot to gain by being transparent about its analyses and the factual data that lead to them. Just like rating agencies, in fact, the IMF has grasped the usefulness of quick and equal access to news about the financial data it processes. Its 'Dissemination Standards Bulletin Board', now posted on the World Wide Web,[21] is a model databank on economies and institutions under its supervision. But the other side of the IMF is indeed closely tied to the priesthood of international finance market economists and high civil servants seconded from finance ministries and central banks all over the world. Debates among insiders, kitchen recipes for IMF operations and most of the actual hard bargaining with debtor countries who have to ask for the Fund's assistance, remain largely hidden from public view. It is notable that among the 2,000 decisions or so the IMF Board has reached over the past five years, only 12 were made by voting.[22] Harvard economist Jeffrey Sachs, who has had his earlier tussles with the IMF over policy towards Russia and the Ukraine, emphasized this secrecy with great effect, since this particular grudge unites the nationalist, radical or Third World critique of the Fund with neo-conservative, liberal and pro-market viewpoints. 'Anyone who has met with IMF executives has sensed the haughty, We-are-the-masters-of-the-Universe atmosphere', noted the Washington correspondent of the *Singapore Business Times*, who must have known the feeling at first hand from his paper's hometown.[23]

Criticism of the IMF's technocratic and antisocial·recipes is nothing new. Scores of Latin American or African governments, and more importantly their citizens, have experienced first hand what an IMF austerity programme feels like. Third World militant literature has always denounced the IMF as a tool of the world's club of rich banks and countries.[24] In a new twist of the same old story, it now comes under attack for 'practicing double standards in favour of international banks and creditors, and against local financial institutions, companies, depositors and shareholders'.[25] In the space of a generation, Third World advocates have indeed become streetwise *vis-à-vis* financial issues.

The IMF dealt with Mexico after 1994 by means of an overall 52 billion dollar bail out, and routinely advises post-Soviet Russia on financial reforms and regulation. Yet not much had prepared it to intervene among some of the world's most dynamic economies, whose economic policies had been hailed by every international organization, including the IMF, as a triumphant success in the preceding years. Nor was the Fund the only international organization caught unprepared. The World Bank, which had been a much closer observer and participant of the region's large investment plan over previous years, seemed to believe in its own analyses about the Asian economic miracle. By the summer of 1997, it had, for example, decided to put up its Bangkok local headquarters for sale, as it did not expect to intervene any more in Thai financing needs. 'We hadn't intervened in South Korea for six years, we had not done any macroeconomic study or financial analysis of Thailand since 1985, and we were leaving this country for good',[26] commented one vice-president. In contrast, the IMF had actually published a fair amount of warnings about the possibility of a Mexican-type crisis in Southeast Asia, particularly concerning Thailand.

Ensuring adequate insurance coverage without encouraging accidents to happen

Originally, the IMF was created in 1944 to restore confidence at times of monetary breakdown by disbursement of special drawing rights (SDRs) against the Fund's reserve quotas. Obviously, disbursement was supposed to be quick and was a form of insurance policy, buttressed by previous contributions to the Fund's reserves. Almost all Asian countries today, whether they actually need a disbursement from the IMF or whether they are self-sustaining, did not contribute to the Fund's reserves to anything like the level of their national currency reserves. While the United States maintains 18 per cent of the IMF's reserves, and the countries of the European Union 30 per cent, Japan, China, Taiwan, Hong Kong and Singapore, with the world's largest holdings of currency reserves, maintain only a fraction of the Fund's reserves. Perhaps in exchange, the average European country does not bother to maintain reserves on a par with, say, Thailand or Malaysia, even though its GNP is much larger.

Of course, absolute levels can be a fragile index, as demonstrated by the virtual disappearance of reserves in the three Asian countries that were hardest hit. They point, however, to a fundamental imbalance between Asia's dynamic growth and high capital availability of the previous decades, and the very low premiums it has paid to a global insurance system. In effect, like some homeowners, Asian countries had chosen to self-insure their own house, obviously creating a larger risk for themselves. In this light, the debate between critics of the IMF becomes secondary. Certainly, as was pointed out, there is a need for a lender of last resort at times of financial panic. Since the IMF only disburses what it has been entrusted with, it cannot be a lender of last resort. Only participating countries, starting with the United States, which is the world's *de facto* creator of currency reserves, or a club of the world's industrialized countries, or a more collective insurance group involving all members, can assume that role. One should remember that at the time of the October 1987 Wall Street crash, and during the savings and loans crisis, the Federal Reserve Board placed massive amounts of liquidities at the disposal of private financial actors to avoid a liquidity crunch.[27] Obviously, what a central bank will do on its own domestic turf, it may not be prepared to repeat on international ground

And certainly, full coverage insurance leads to moral hazard, as the neo-liberals quickly pointed out. Houses will be set on fire to collect on insurance premiums, cameras will be left on coffee tables because they are fully insured in any case. In the Asian case, moral hazard is evenly split between lenders and debtors. Banks that have indulged in an orgy of short-term loans can hardly be expected to walk away from the scene without losses. And rescue funds for financial systems should not be used to bail out bankrupt financial establishments and insolvent firms, but to help governments and central banks recreate liquidity in markets that have been bled dry by panic, and encourage healthy firms to take over the remaining assets of failed enterprises.

Understandably, many Asians and some of their governments have tended to shoot the messenger, rather than address the behind-the-scene principals. The IMF is not a lender of last resort, but a proxy for the countries who define the international financial system. Only national central banks can ultimately provide an unlimited supply of funds to cut off a crisis of confidence or a panic.

Those who see the Asian crisis first and foremost as a problem of confidence also believe that the true guarantors behind the IMF system should have acted directly to restore confidence prior to reforms by Asians themselves. Conversely, those who believe the Asian crisis is structural, and who warn against throwing good money after bad, wish to limit the IMF, or any other intervention, to sound advice on the assumption that the market itself will act on news of successful Asian restructuring.

The two phases of the IMF intervention

There is an element of truth in the often heard criticism from Asians. By February 1998, the three IMF-led rescue operations for Thailand, Korea and Indonesia amounted, if all the money being committed was indeed used, to 109 billion dollars,[28] of which 45 billion would be drawn from the Fund itself. This exceeds the amount set aside by the IMF for this type of contingency. But Asian critics maintain that it is still too little, too late. Another school of thought, which has been adopted both in the ranks of Western economists such as Jeffrey Sachs and among Asian governments asking for a rescue, also maintains that the IMF plans came, especially during their first phase, with the wrong type of conditions attached.[29] Asians usually add that the United States, or more generally the West, has remained largely uninvolved in the event. Jeffrey Sachs's own anti-IMF critique is peculiar in that the United States and Japan hardly play any role in his explanation for the Crash, and therefore in its solutions. Old fashioned panic, and the IMF's warped politics in addressing that panic, are the only variables in this story.

Timing, therefore, has been crucial in discussing solutions to the Asian crisis. Much of the financial débâcle is self-propelled, not only by the subjective panic factor that creates an investor stampede to the emergency exits, but also by a chain of events. Falls in currency result in a revaluation of all foreign debts, whether public or private. A steep rise in private debt renders insolvent many firms that were previously thought to be safe. A new, and sudden revaluation of real, and previously hidden or unpredicted, debt levels provokes a chain reaction of no confidence. Risk analysts and rating agencies extend their new appreciation of risk to other countries, causing institutional investors to automatically reduce their exposure. At every stage, delay in stopping the damage results in a wider and deeper crisis, that becomes increasingly difficult to solve. There is no need to blame speculation, or even the celebrated herd-like behaviour of fund or loan managers. In a relatively free capital market environment, or when many opportunities exist for capital flight, domestic savers and middle-class wage earners join the stampede.

It would seem that in the first few months at least, the Fund did not take its cue from its earlier record of consideration for Asian achievements, but from the much more brutal operating manual reserved for the poorest, most debased economies. Yet the conditionality of its programmes involved not only the standard austere, belt-tightening programmes which are the Fund's trademark. The most striking conditions raised by the Fund for actual disbursement of the rescue plans were really, as Martin Feldstein[30] has noted, major structural reforms that implied market liberalization and the opening up of capital markets in the countries concerned. Ironically, he noted, the IMF was created to defend the fixed exchange rates that are now judged to be the origin of the financial Crash in Asia. His criticism was not directed so much at the Fund's large disbursement as at the confusion between monetary rescue on the one hand, and taking over the management of national economies on the other. Unconditional aid, applied earlier, with pressure on banks to reach agreements on the short-term debt that was owed by Asia, would have served the same purpose with less financial chaos and less cost to the international taxpayer. Another well-known monetarist, Bundesbank president Hans Tietmeyer, took the same view on the need to strictly separate the Fund's short-term rescue operations from the longer-term aim of managing and reforming national economies.

Martin Feldstein's criticism is convincing in pinpointing the extraordinary changes in the prevailing winds of economic policy. His orthodox monetary views coincide with more radical criticisms by pointing out that the Fund would hardly use the same yardstick for the main industrialized countries – Europe's many labour market rigidities and corporative arrangements spring to mind. However, his view simplifies the job of fighting a currency crunch to an extreme and overoptimistic degree. Indeed, for the Latin America of the 1980s, an agreement among private banks to rescue debtors took years to establish, until the first Brady Plan. In the meantime, Latin American economies went through a slump that would have even worse consequences if it happened in Asia.

In its role as fighter against the breakdown of financial confidence, the Fund initially expected standards almost as high as those of mature capital markets from Asian economies. Not all Asian countries can complain about this treatment. After all, they drew in record amounts of international capital, and some of them claimed an increasingly high status on the international economic scale. Yet, one must recognize that the Fund has also served as either the provider or the conduit for injecting funds into the most troubled Asian economies.[31] The scale of the genuine rescue effort has been much smaller than was publicly heralded: once you deduce 'second line' commitments that have remained virtual, and once you factor in the IMF's heavy conditionality imposed on debtor countries, the 100 billion plus IMF plans become something of a *soufflé*. That, however, has more to do with the basic attitudes of the countries running the IMF. Indeed, what the Fund has been administering to Asia since July 1998 is a striking example of creditors' justice, where the interests of the international lending community are far better insured than the debtors'. In any case, the IMF has remained their only option.

This phase in the IMF's role started to wane in December 1997, when Korea's débâcle began to register with the leaders of the global financial system. Here was a country that had just succeeded in entering the OECD,[32] whose membership remains a symbol of the achievement of fully industrialized status. Yet it was evident that Korea's financial system was on the verge of disintegration. The IMF could neither administer an orthodox prescription as a cure nor pretend a major structural overhaul could be undertaken without huge external support. It could not deny either that the issue of private debt had to be tackled directly and at the same time as the country's public solvency. It was over Korea that the IMF began a turnaround in its policies that would apply to Indonesia in April–May 1998.

The IMF began this second phase by fighting a battle on two fronts. In G7 countries, and the US in particular, fund officials countered the neo-liberal argument that it was squandering taxpayers' money to help insolvent or delinquent borrowers.[33] The other front in this battle was the decision to push private banks into compromises with their private debtors. In December 1997, the IMF's negotiations with Korea began to implicate the international banks which, together with the country's authorities, hold Korea's largely private short-term debt. Although the banks needed the IMF's authority over the situation to justify a regaining of confidence, the IMF (and Korea) also badly needed them to fill the huge gap between the IMF's bailout of 57 billion dollars, and the pile of bad debts that had spiralled, panic-aided, to almost 200 billion dollars. Certainly the banks were also interested in a solution, yet they could on occasion work at cross-purposes when it came to bargaining over the terms of rescue. The stricter the conditionality imposed by the IMF, the higher the chances of private banks seeing their debtors default. In a typical case of what game theorists call the prisoners' dilemma, Japanese banks also called on their Western counterparts to begin the rollover in order to act themselves, after a government-inspired meeting of the 10 largest creditors led by Bank of Tokyo-Mitsubishi.

Individual Western governments, and in one reported instance the Bank of England,[34] put some pressure on their banking establishments to roll over their short-term loans to Korea, and resist the temptation of leaving the scene quickly with the IMF money in hand. In the United States, the Federal Reserve Board urged a private bank meeting with their Korean debtors at J.P. Morgan's headquarters. The format was enlarged to include other Western creditors.

Political stability as a concern in rescue efforts

In a striking difference from the world of the 1930s, regime stability, if not strict personal continuation of leadership, has been sought by all other protagonists. This is perhaps the clearest indication that Asia may pull through without a political earthquake, not so much because of regional or global conservatism, but simply because there is much more to lose than to gain in sudden political change coming on top of the Crash. In a bid to further this stability, key international organizations such as the World Bank are involved alongside the IMF in social aid programmes that do not come with the same type of conditionality. The World Bank has committed 16 billion dollars to what amounts to an Asian social rescue package that is meant to ease the IMF's own terms. The Asian Development Bank has earmarked twice its average yearly amount (10 billion instead of 5 billion dollars) for the same purpose, although its spokesmen try hard not to give in to IMF bashing. Neither organization, one might add, had made much disbursement by early April 1998 (see Tables 3.1 and 3.2).

Indeed, the World Bank's chief economist Joseph E. Stiglitz notori-ously clashed with IMF deputy director Stanley Fischer in the first months of the Crisis. Housed side by side in Washington, the two institutions are both complementary and competitive. The conflict highlights a different sense of mission: the IMF aims to ensure the safety of the inter-national financial system, while the World Bank deals with a wider range of issues that involve social and political stability in emerging economies. It also underlines a world of policy difference. The World Bank had accepted the guided economy that is a feature of Asian growth. The

Table 3.1 International community financial assistance to Thailand, Korea and Indonesia: chronological highlights

Thailand

20 August 1997	Financial support approved
25 November 1997	Letter of Intent on additional measures
8 December 1997	First review of the stand-by arrangement
24 February 1998	Letter of Intent on additional measures
4 March 1998	Second review of the stand-by arrangement
May 1998	Third review of the stand-by arrangement

Korea

4 December 1997	Financial support approved
18 December 1997	First bi-weekly review of the stand-by arrangement
24 December 1997	Letter of Intent on intensification and acceleration of its programme
7 January 1998	Memorandum on the economic programme
8 January 1998	Second bi-weekly review of the stand-by arrangement
7 February 1998	Letter of Intent on additional measures
17 February 1998	First quarterly review of the stand-by arrangement
May 1998	Second review of the stand-by arrangement

Indonesia

5 November 1997	Stand-by credit approved
15 January 1998	Memorandum of Economic and Financial Policies on additional measures
10 April 1998	Supplementary Memorandum of Economic and Financial Policies on additional measures
To be announced	First review of the stand-by arrangement

Source: *The IMF Response to the Asian Crisis*, International Monetary Fund, April 1998

IMF set out to level the ground for market competition, without much regard for the consequences. On political issues, the World Bank did not hesitate to act, and played a restraining role in Indonesian politics. Tom Wolfensohn, the World Bank's president, threatened Indonesia with a refusal of aid if the Suharto regime carried its anti-Chinese ethnic campaign any further in the first weeks of 1998. The World Bank was far less doctrinaire about imposing structural economic changes in the midst of the Crisis. Once under way, the World Bank's programmes were largely designed to soften the edge of the IMF-inspired reforms, and provide some measure of protection for millions of impoverished Indonesians. Ironically, there was no way to achieve this in the short term except by having dealings with President Suharto and his entourage, 'swindlers'[35] and all.

Table 3.2 International community financial assistance to Thailand, Korea and Indonesia: commitments and disbursements (US $ billions)

	Thailand		Korea		Indonesia	
	Commit-ments	Disbursed[1]	Commit-ments	Disbursed	Commit-ments	Disbursed
Multilateral Aid	6.6	3.8	34.9	23.1	17.9	3
IMF[2]	3.9	2.7	20.9	15.1	9.9	3
World Bank	1.5	0.5	10	5	4.5	0
ADB	1.2	0.6	4	3	3.5	0
Bilateral Aid	10.5	6.4	23.3	0	22	0
Japan	4	2.7 *	10	0	5	0
The United States	0	0 *	5	0	3	0
Australia	1	0.7 *			1 *	0
China	1	0.7 *			1	0
Hong Kong	1	0.7 *			1	0
Malaysia	1	0.7 *			1	0
Singapore	1	0.7 *			5	0
Indonesia	0.5	0 *			5 *	0
Brunei	0.5	0 *				
Korea	0.5	0.2 *				
Total	17.1	10.2	58.2	23.1	39.9	3

1 Disbursements as of 10 April 1998, except for bilateral aid (as of 31 March 1998)
2 The European Union's contribution amounts to 30 per cent, the United States' to 18 per cent and Japan's to 6 per cent

Sources: *The IMF Response to the Asian Crisis*, International Monetary Fund, April 1998.

* According to Steven Radelet and Jeffrey Sachs, *The East Asian Financial Crisis: Diagnosis, Remedies, Prospects*, Harvard Institute for International Development, April 1998.

Repentance from the IMF

Evidently, protagonists learned from their worst mistakes in the process. The IMF initially charged into the battle armed with a military surgeon's lancet and a list of instant recipes from previous crises in emerging economies. In common with military surgeons it finished off the wounded as often as it cured them. Alongside much criticism of the huge deflation that the Fund's requests had created in Southeast Asia, it has occasionally come close to self-criticism behind closed doors. A confidential report to its Board members explained that the Fund's requirement in November 1997 to close 16 insolvent banks in Indonesia, 'far from improving public confidence in the banking system, have instead set off a renewed "flight to safety"'.[36] This was an isolated retreat, however. The Fund has been trained to operate on South American or African countries, including emerging economies, where public budget deficit is a chronic habit, and a key factor in financial crises. As Jeffrey Sachs put it, 'the usual target of the Fund is a government living beyond its means, financing budget deficits by printing money at the central bank. The result is inflation, together with a weakening currency and a drain of foreign exchange reserves. In those circumstances, financial orthodoxy makes sense.'[37] Many of the early IMF requirements of Thailand, Korea and even Indonesia focused on cuts in budgetary spending, at a time when these countries' budgets were balanced or with minimal deficits. Just when local firms and banks needed a shot in the arm, IMF medicine further depressed economic activity and therefore bankrupted new companies. By June 1998, in the prevailing atmosphere of gloomy anticipation of a second Crash, IMF spokesmen began on the contrary to sound upbeat and almost cheerful. They had at last understood that their public criticism of Asian governments and economic policies, designed to strengthen the Fund's hands in negotiation, had inadvertently aggravated the crisis.

The Fund indulged in more self-criticism in May 1998, when it became clear that the stricken countries' private debt was still ballooning and leading to a second Crash. The Fund's doctrine is that it rescues economic systems, not private debtors. In fact, since the end of December 1997 it has stepped over that boundary, informally encouraging private creditors to reach a settlement. Renegotiated agreements by the Fund with Korea, Indonesia and Thailand have authorized these governments to at least partially back private debt consolidations with a public guarantee. Yet the initial failure to recognize the need for this has had dire consequences. Fund executives now speak of the need to 'establish more effective procedures to involve the private sector in resolving debt crises'.[38] This is the Fund's understated way of ackowledging the previous error in its ways.

As a consequence, another debate has emerged which centres not so much on the solutions to the Asia Crisis as on the reform of supervision and emergency mechanisms in the international financial system.[39] This debate holds little interest for Asians, as it deals mainly with the next crisis. But the IMF, like its protagonists in the region, learned as it went, and managed to reform or to hide its unmistakable air of technocratic arrogance, which to Asians is a symptom of the West's domination. By March 1998, although the world's financial media still reverberated with calls for strict reform programmes, transparency and conversion to market rules, the practical points of rescue in several cases – Korea, Indonesia and Thailand – were much more a matter of give and take, with hard bargaining but fewer overall indictments.

Moral hazard vs. effective rescue

In theory, the IMF injection of more than 100 billion dollars should have been equivalent to the drop of foreign direct investment in Asia of 92 billion dollars in 1997. The Fund's capital base, drawn from members' contributions according to statutory quota, has in fact been depleted after these rescue plans. Or rather, it would have been depleted if, by June 1998, the amounts committed had been effectively expended. In any case, these amounts can hardly reach the level of capital destruction brought by the mayhem in the markets. Overall, this destruction was put at 700 billion dollars by the Federal Reserve Board's chairman[40] in January 1998, an estimate obviously surpassed since that date. In relative terms, between early July 1997 and January 1998, Indonesia's stock market had lost 75 per cent of its value, Thailand's had lost 63 per cent, and Korea's went on to lose 67 per cent in little over four months. But the real story lies beyond these comparative figures, in the terms of agreement by the IMF and the actual rate of disbursement of rescue capital. This is where critics, right and left, liberal or interventionist, clash with the Fund. These critics include, perhaps, the World Bank, which took pains to show in the case of Korea (and only in that case, one might add) that its own commitments to the Asian rescue plans led to very fast disbursements. The 3 billion dollars it had earmarked for Korea changed hands within three weeks of the signing of the corresponding agreement.

From the first to the second Crash

The Crash of 1997, and its continuation through 1998, has had sudden stages of market destruction, followed by long phases of simmering crisis, and even rebounds that were always seen in the short term as the end of the tunnel for the countries involved. It has journeyed from Thailand in July 1997, to other ASEAN countries and especially Malaysia in August, an assault on Hong Kong in October that jolted the world's markets, and a crushing move on South Korea between early November and the New Year. Indonesia, already among the first group of economies that were hit, was sent reeling in January 1998.

Finally Japan, where the government had shored up the currency and stock market until the deadline of the fiscal new year on 1 April, came under siege at that very moment, sending shock waves again through Asia. The Crisis had originated with Japan's failure to deal with technically bankrupt firms and their bad debts after the bubble burst in 1990. It had journeyed throughout Asia, but it hit back at Japan with a vengeance in April 1998. The Moody's rating agency downgraded Japan's sovereign risk when it was still the first worldwide provider of excess capital. Sony chairman Nori Ohga and the OECD, announced that Japan was at the edge of a severe recession, and Prime Minister Hashimoto had to concede that the economic circumstances were the worst the country had seen since the end of the Second World War. The optimism that had lifted Asian currencies and markets in the first quarter of 1998 was blown away, with some seasoned observers dubbing it the 'suckers' rally'.

By mid-June 1998, the Crash was already leaping again from Japan, sinking currencies and markets throughout the region. The strongest centres – Taiwan, Singapore and Hong Kong – were now under attack, as it appeared that they could simply not maintain any pretence at stability in this atmosphere. China's currency was next on the list. A year of mutual refusal to take charge for the role of lender of last resort, by the United States, Europe and Japan brought on the catastrophe.

Asian responses to the rescue plans

The battle of Seoul

The model adopted for Korea in the final weeks of 1997 was dubbed IMF Alpha by insiders. Talks between international bankers and debtors were held, sometimes at J.P. Morgan's headquarters in New York, sometimes in Seoul. While the IMF had drawn up a minimal conditionality for Korea to receive its help, the bankers largely negotiated directly with their debtors the terms for a rescheduling of Korean debt. Thus, the rescue was evenly divided. The IMF released the first instalments of the money it had earmarked for Korea – never actually reaching the so-called second line of defence drawn up with European reserves. This provided cash for Korean state and public institutions to keep some liquidity flow, at a time when the won was literally burning the hands of those who held it. By rolling over short-term debts into loans with a maturity of one, two and three years, foreign private banks allowed the Korean government time to find money on the open market by issuing government-guaranteed bonds. If successful, this issue would help the country to avoid bankruptcy, since the amounts coming due in short-term debts were simply unmanageable: 15 billion dollars by the end of December, another 15 billion in January, and another peak at the traditional end of the fiscal year on 1 April. Almost as heavy was the top Korean *chaebols'* short-term debt, which was not revealed at the time.

Later, it would be announced that at the end of December 1997, the top 30 *chaebols* and the 150 firms they controlled had piled up a short-term debt of 58.5 billion dollars.[41]

Throughout this intense phase of negotiation, the Koreans treated this emergency as a struggle. Historical references to past Korean national battles appeared in the press. A popular campaign to donate and melt gold jewels and ingots for the country's central bank got underway, while the country's extravagant habits for private ceremonies gave way to 'IMF weddings' with a new frugality. An interesting and quasi-Marxist analysis of financial capital appeared in the Seoul press. It divided the financial community between 'an investment bank faction', led by J.P. Morgan and predominantly American, which had required interest rates over 10 per cent to roll over Korean debt, and a 'commercial bank faction', predominantly European with a large contribution by German banks, which reflected industrial capital and were 'closely linked with the real economy'.[42] It warned, therefore, against the mutual funds rooted in 'stock market capitalism', that might pull out of Korea again even before any long-term merger and acquisition by serious foreign enterprises could take place.

Yet the Koreans had also learned how to be flexible. All candidates for the national presidential election scheduled on December 19 agreed, for example, to the terms of the bargain set by the IMF. One of Kim Dae-jung's smartest moves, immediately after his election, was to call in George Soros for 'consultation'. The amicable meeting worked wonders in transforming international apprehension of what was seen as a nationalist and quasi-socialist politician into admiration for a smart market liberalizer. And indeed Kim Dae-jung went far – in the first week after his inauguration, he authorized the anonymous bank accounts that his predecessor, Kim Young-sam, had banned. Kim Young-sam's gesture had been a key rejection of black money in the Korean financial system, but it had been very costly. Since Koreans could no longer discreetly deposit any more the cash proceeds from shops, services and/or any form of corruption, they had taken the money out of the country, weakening the equity markets and forcing a rise in interest rates. Kim Dae-jung, the democrat, socialist and humanist, immediately reinstated the anonymous accounts that allowed black money to be laundered back into the legitimate financial system. By being extremely flexible on the reforms demanded by the IMF and by foreign banks – and in particular, by promising a nearly complete opening of Korean firms to foreign ownership – Kim Dae-jung may have appeared to his countrymen to be selling the future for the present. But at a time when other Asian economies could not get a penny in foreign financing, he secured extremely advantageous terms under the circumstances. 'Private banks will have to take a hit. Instead of lending at market rates, they'll do it at a level significantly lower than that,' explained Michel Camdessus.[43] European commercial banks, led by Société Générale of France, persuaded American counterparts to accept a 100-point reduction on the interest rate terms. In February 1998, Korea's new government-backed loans on the international market were set at an interest rate spread that was only 2.25 to 2.75 points above the London Inter-Bank Offered Rate (LIBOR), and denominated in dollars. At 7.61 per cent, the IMF loans were the cheapest; commercial banks lent between 7.85 per cent and 8.35 per cent, while previous short-term debt had been charged at 9.5 per cent or more. A won issue would have been much more costly, while the currency stood well below its purchasing power parity. Korea can therefore expect to get a lift from any upwards trend in its own currency. The first issue in early April 1998, for 4 billion dollars, has been oversubscribed three times in the market, in another sign that a modest dose of confidence is returning.

This confidence was still fragile. Korea's mountain of *chaebol* debt is far from resolved, and opportunities for a crisis abound as they come due, or as an important lender, such as Japan, might choose to attend first to his own needs for financing. In May 1998, the KOSPI, Korea's stock index, dipped again to its lowest level in 11 years.

IMF plus or IMF minus? Suharto's Indonesia

As fierce as the Korean struggle was to extract terms from the international community, it remained mostly quiet and behind the scenes. This was indeed a low-key struggle, compared to the extravagant theatre played by Indonesian authorities with the IMF and its supporting cast of rich Western countries.

Indonesia had been the prime victim of contagion from 'bahtulism' (Paul Krugman) in the early fall of 1997, but it had plenty to atone for on its own. Between July and early October, a 40 per cent fall in the Indonesian rupiah led to a cascade of bankruptcies, themselves snow-balling foreign debts that could not be repaid at the new exchange rates. The event also revealed that many of Indonesia's largest corporations and business families had quietly borrowed funds from off-shore sources, without listing them as debts. The nebulous organizational flowcharts of large Sino-Indonesian firms allow for much creative accounting. To a public debt of 100 billion dollars, one should therefore add a private debt of more than 65 billion dollars. Against this, of course, the presumably huge holdings stashed abroad by rich and/or prominent Indonesians should in all justice be counted. Deposits by these farsighted individuals in Singapore or Hong Kong are thought to run between 20 and 30 billion dollars. But it has become evident that earlier flight capital would never be collected back. On the contrary, the crisis and the authorities' behaviour accelerated the exodus.

By early October, the country was already on the ropes, and Suharto was a prime target for world-wide accusations of crony capitalism. His family and close friends, after all, dominated the entire economy, and had been involved very recently in extremely prominent cases. His sons Bambang and Tommy's various automobile pet projects and the protections afforded them had angered every competitor inside and outside Indonesia. His golf partner Bob Hasan's forest empire, at a time when loggers were thought to be responsible for Borneo and Sumatra going up in smoke, was a symbol of rampant cronyism. The Riady brothers, leading members of the Lippo group, who ironically do not belong to Suharto's court businessmen, had got caught in the business of seeking favours from the Clinton White House in exchange for campaign contributions. In addition to the usual human rights complaints against the Suharto regime, the slate was really full.

Suharto rose to the challenge in his usual style; with shadow boxing, evasive tactics, moments of humble contrition followed by almost his totally rescinding the needed reforms. He pushed the envelope very far indeed, implicitly threatening the Indonesian Chinese community for retribution if the IMF maintained its toughest requirements, and surviving the steepest currency fall in the Crash of 1997. The rupiah had been holding at 2,500 to the dollar until July 1997, but by January 1998, it had fallen to 17,000. Almost simultaneously, Suharto had tried a game of accommodation by calling to the rescue Indonesian technocrats from the early days of the New Order, survivors of the so-called Berkeley Mafia who were not on the best of terms with his own relatives and cronies. Widjojo Nitisastro was one, who had presided over the economy from 1966 to 1983, promptly returning his government-issued Volvo sedan to buy an unadorned Toyota, as observers noted. At about the same time, and for a matter of some weeks, Suharto seemed ready to push his eldest daughter Tutut forward for succession – progress of some sort since the other siblings were under the worst of clouds.

Unfortunately, Tutut herself (short for Siti Hardijanti Rukmana), an interesting character who is married to the businessman Indra Rukamana, and who had counselled moderation towards political opponent Megawati Sukarnoputri, soon came into the limelight for her own business practices. Not only was she the owner of a nicely arranged network of toll roads, whose employees wore uniforms without pockets so they could not keep motorists' spare change; she had also bought heavily into Steadysafe, the dubious cab company whose demise in November brought down Hong Kong's largest investment firm, Peregrine.

As for Suharto, his reforms were like lamp shadows on a windswept batik. On 20 September, he had cancelled a number of large public projects, in line with the cutback in investment that the situation – and the market – demanded throughout Southeast Asia. On November 1, a few days after the first agreement with the IMF, he reinstated those projects. On January 10, he stopped them again. The same pattern applied to other decisions, such as the foreclosure of 16 insolvent private banks, pressed on Indonesia by the IMF. Several months later, the banks, some of whom were owned by Suharto's son Bambang or his half-brother Probosutedjo, were still operating, sometimes by simply changing names.

The IMF had also exacted a key reform in the area of distribution, with the dismantling of a number of monopolies and cartels on key primary materials – flour, palm oil, plywood. This policy, enforced by the IMF, is in fact dubious. While these cartels in a key area of Indonesia's export economy undoubtedly act as a restraint on free trade and another occasion for political patronage, they also serve to regulate prices for the country's teeming peasant population. In the weeks following the crash of the rupiah and the suppression of controls on palm oil trade, for example, this basic commodity became a speculative resource for business intermediaries trying to procure foreign cash currency. To hold down the price of a product that is essential to the livelihood of ordinary Indonesians, Suharto's government suddenly banned exports, in complete defiance of IMF free trade orders. Other IMF requirements were just as devastating – lifting subsidies on oil, flour and other basic commodities would result in a huge surge of inflation. The man in the street, and even more the man in the villages, had hardly noticed the drop in the rupiah's value, since he could hardly afford imported goods in any case. But the huge price increases that would result from deregulation in a context of panic were sure to be perceived as the consequence of a Western plot to undermine honest and God-fearing Indonesians.

If Suharto could sometimes claim he was defending the peasant family's livelihood against international perils, it was probably not for that reason that he let other monopolies get by, long after the decision to abolish them. Apkindo, the plywood export cartel whose chief is Bob Hasan, also the owner of a maritime line transporting the wood for the cartel, was still open for business in February 1998.[44]

Scapegoating the Chinese

These evasive tactics were viewed by the IMF and its Western backers for what they were. Pressure began to build around President Suharto, who was on the receiving end of a 30-minute telephone call from President Clinton. The message was never described as sympathetic. And the IMF money remained on hold, while market conditions deteriorated. But Suharto had far more in store. On 20 January, five days after cringing in front of Michel Camdessus, he took his revenge. He announced informally he would appoint B.J. Habibie as Vice-President, retiring the discreet Try Sutrisno. The move sent the market reeling, since Habibie had been the flamboyant symbol of a new generation of technocratic high spenders, who sought to build national industries from scratch with largely public funds and an infusion of heavy investment. In fact, long before the Crash of 1997, observers had contrasted earlier Indonesian economic planners favourably with 'Habibienomics'.[45] But the move had other implications. Habibie, apart from his engineering endeavours, is a long-time proponent of Islam and *pribumi* promotion over the Chinese and Christian element. He is on record for criticizing in 1993 the presence of Christians in earlier Suharto administrations.[46] Without many known connections to the Indonesian military establishment, with which he has often clashed regarding weapon procurement and industrial interest, he has become the protector and middle man for many members of Suharto's own family.

Suharto's choice had the unique flavour of an elderly king finding a regent who would protect his children from harm. But it also had grave consequences, as it rekindled racial and religious conflict. Within days, *pribumi* businessmen, such as Aburizal Bakrie, the chairman of Indonesia's twelfth-largest group, president of the national Chamber of Commerce and Industry and a leading Golkar member, were issuing calls to 'redistribute the property of Indonesian firms on a wider base by allowing for a large share to native Indonesians'.[47] Stung by a barrage of international criticism, elements in Indonesia's vast security system began an intimidation campaign against the prominent Christian Chinese Wanandi family, who had indeed turned from their anti-Communist struggle of the 1960s to the advocacy of political liberalization and market transparency. Riots, which have been erupting again in parts of Sumatra and Java for some years against ethnic Chinese and Christian churches, were on the rise because of the sudden unemployment. They were now directed against Chinese shopkeepers in the name of Islam.

This nasty turn in the first two months of 1998 obviously has a far-reaching meaning in terms of Indonesia's identity. But it also proved to be a classic piece of strong arm tactics on the part of Suharto himself, who was now showing his steel. To his generation, blood is not something that flows only when stock markets fall. While expatriates flocked to the airports, and panic began to grip the wealthy Indonesian-Chinese community, the army protected local Chinese from physical harm, shooting a few demonstrators in the process. Suharto was serving notice to the West that there was, as yet, no alternative to his own rule, and that a bankrupt Indonesia could easily descend into chaos. Close neighbours such as Australia, whose agricultural and mining interests had grumbled against the IMF bailout and the increased competition from devalued Indonesian products on the world market, began to plead with the IMF and the West for softer terms towards a dangerous country. 'Indonesia, not Iraq, is the number one foreign policy dilemma for Australia', reported a realistic observer.[48] Indeed, as Olle Törnquist aptly summed up, what Suharto was suddenly pointing out to the West was a mirror: 'I'm still the beast that you enjoyed so much seven months ago. But if you try to fool me and take everything away, I will turn a much worse oligarchic nationalist beast.'[49] This tactic has the flavour of Saddam Hussein, who is a popular figure in Muslim Indonesia.

Taking the IMF for a ride on the currency board

Meanwhile, like everybody else, Suharto was desperately looking for an end to the accelerating currency crunch that was ripping apart the Indonesian economy and creating an explosive social situation. He began describing this quest as an IMF-plus solution for his country. In the search for an alternative solution to the IMF's slash and burn *diktat* against his own interests, Suharto hit on an unexpected ploy: the technically complex, but politically simplistic, idea of a currency board for managing the rupiah at a fixed exchange rate with the dollar. It is clear that the idea did not come from the technocratic management he had just installed as his economic advisers and put in charge of the central bank. Indeed, over the four months between December 1997 and April 1998, Suharto twice changed the top staff at the central bank to try and find some compliance with his own game plan. It is also doubtful too whether B.J. Habibie, an engineer with a distaste for financial calculations, had anything to do with the idea, which he finally disapproved.[50] Indeed, the *Wall Street Journal*'s persistent advocacy of tough monetary solutions, and Suharto's financially literate daughter Tutut, seem inadvertently to have been the prime movers, if somewhat inadvertently as far as the leading media of the global financial community was concerned. In another unpredictable convergence between neo-liberal and nationalist Asianist approaches, the *Journal* had begun an editorial campaign against IMF profligacy. In so doing, it uncovered the currency board idea[51] three days before Camdessus's fatal photo opportunity with President Suharto. The currency board had been applied in 1983 in Hong Kong, when speculation about the Sino–British negotiations had threatened the Hong Kong dollar, in Argentina in 1991, and in various East European situations.[52]

The currency board is a monetary regime whereby control of the local currency is fixed once and for all, for instance against the dollar. The value of the currency is therefore taken out of the hands of the central bank and monetary authorities. It is certainly revealing that the board's first salesman in January 1998 had earlier argued against the existence of central banks in developing countries.[53] For, with complete exchange rigidity, there are only two ways to ensure the safety of the plan. The first way is to back monetary creation with large reserves. In most cases, at least one US dollar is added to the reserves every time an equivalent amount of local currency is created. And the second way is to counter forward speculation against this local currency, which results in indirect monetary creation, by an iron will to infinitely raise the interest rates applied to the domestic currency. The real secret of the currency board, apart from the huge foreign currency reserves needed, lies in the complete subordination of the domestic economy to the foreign currency peg in value. Hong Kong's currency board, established on 15 October 1983, has worked because the territory's authorities have never used their currency as an economic management tool. In October 1997, when speculation struck again, they were willing to jack up overnight interest rates on the HK dollar to as much as 300 per cent, inflicting a huge deflationary blow to all those who had borrowed short term in that currency.

Soon, an astute professor from Johns Hopkins University, Steve Hanke, who had earlier been making prescient comments about the Crash of 1997,[54] gave the idea a lift. He certainly had an audience in Indonesia. While on a trip in Turkey, Suharto's entourage called him and by 2 February, he had been secretly taken to Jakarta to meet the king himself, and central bank officials as an afterthought on the following day. A little-known American associate professor was beating the IMF's highest officials at their own game. This apparently has not been forgiven and Hanke has been repeatedly denounced as a hack, perhaps most bitterly by Paul Krugman himself, his senior colleague from the Massachusetts Institute of Technology.[55]

But Suharto got what he needed from the plan. Fixing the rupiah at a rate substantially higher than its present low would immediately help

Indonesian companies to refinance themselves. In particular, heavily indebted firms, including many belonging to members of Suharto's own entourage, could repay their debts thanks to a boost in the rupiah's value. The much-needed dollar reserves could be procured by the IMF's injection of rescue money. In the short term, the currency board is a remarkable instrument for restoring forward confidence. Every time Jakarta seemed closer to adopting one in February–March 1998, at a level usually anticipated around 8,000 rupiah per US dollar, the Indonesian stock exchange got a lift.

A currency board presupposes extraordinary budget discipline, monetary and credit transparency and a willingness to strangle the domestic economy in order to kill monetary creation at times of speculation. It simply was not a genuine option in Indonesia's case. Most observers saw it as a short-term ploy to rescue privileged Indonesian debtors, and as a huge future risk for any international institution that would supply Indonesia with the level of US dollar currency holdings necessary to get started.

Perhaps this hardly mattered. By his combination of plaintive statements appealing to the old underdog anti-colonialist feeling in his country, his thinly veiled threats against the Chinese business community who were usually associated with foreign partners, and his remarkable dance around the IMF's orthodox envoys, Suharto successfully ran the gauntlet. Certainly, the prospect of social and political chaos was the key element in the West's change of heart. 'Suharto's Ace: He's the Only Game in Town', lamented the *Washington Post*,[56] and Yusuf Wanandi, a known critic of Suharto, concurred: 'We do not have a credible opposition that can replace him immediately'. In March 1998, EU envoy Derek Fatchett would counter publicly that the IMF was also 'the only show in town'.[57] While the army played a key role in channelling the new unemployed back to their native villages, lessening the chance of riots in the large cities, thousands of Sumatra residents had begun to flee towards Malaysia, where the authorities detained them and protested the sudden influx. Indonesia in 1998 had become a demographic, social and religious bomb waiting to explode. In a matter of weeks the context of the IMF negotiations with Suharto's government changed from a showdown between neo-liberalism and crony capitalism to an old fashioned rescue of a government that remained a key geopolitical factor in Asia's stability. Suharto, the wily peasant from Central Java, had won a reprieve against the silk-stocking aristocrats from the IMF. What's more, given the huge social costs of the reforms initially demanded by the IMF, Indonesia itself had actually gained more than it had lost from Suharto's struggle.

As appropriate, Japan served as the bearer of the good news. It had after all been most involved in previous loans, and Japanese firms had a lot to lose by Indonesia's collapse. Japan's large trading houses in particular have even more at stake in Indonesia than the banks themselves. The Hashimoto government's willingness to come with gifts to Jakarta served other purposes as well. On the surface, it satisfied Washington's constant pressure for more financial participation in rescuing neighbours from the financial crash. In fact, Japan had not done as much for Korea at the beginning of the year. On 17–21 March, the new Vice-president B.J. Habibie, together with Indonesian Chamber of Commerce chairman Aburizal Bakrie, toured Japan and pleaded for help from a 'true friend of Indonesia'. Habibie said after meeting with Foreign Minister Obuchi: 'We want Japan to explain the situation facing Indonesia at a meeting of the Group of Seven finance ministers and central bank governors'.[58] When Prime Minister Hashimoto visited Jakarta in early April, he brought an additional commitment of 2 billion dollars in loan and trade guarantees with him, as well as a food aid package that included 500,000 tons of rice. Announced before a final IMF agreement was agreed upon, these Japanese grants signalled the discreet return of the Asian solution to the crisis, and put pressure on the West to either match it or precipitate an even more serious showdown involving Japan. Although Hashimoto had delivered to Jakarta a standard follow-the-IMF lecture, he had not actually waited for the final agreement to fall into place, even if he immediately praised it. To further coax Suharto into acceptance, Australia's Prime Minister John Howard had promised by telephone on 4 April to chip in a further 400 million dollars, after another call to Chinese Premier Zhu Rongji.[59] By the time the new IMF agreement with Indonesia, the third in six months, appeared to be clinched on 8 April, the rescue package had grown from 37 billion to 43 billion dollars. China had committed 1 billion dollars in 'second line' support to the IMF package. On 12 April, China also signed a 200 million dollar bilateral export credit facility with Indonesia, augmented by 3 million dollars' worth of foodstuffs and medicine.[60] This was China's second contribution to the rescue operations, after its first 1 billion dollar commitment to the Thailand rescue plan in August 1997.

In the end, Suharto could not reverse the tide of a crisis that was impoverishing millions of his people and encouraging demonstrations against his New Order rule. But his obstinacy clearly won the day against international requirements. Perhaps, as the IMF's chief negotiator said, 'as many safeguards as possible [had been put] into the program to ensure a maximum degree of certainty that this program will not remain just mn paper'.[61] This meant, as previously, that the IMF money would be disbursed very slowly, a condition that also happened to satisfy most of the participating countries. Up to April 1998, indeed, only 3 billion dollars from the core IMF commitment of the previous month had actually been disbursed. But to Suharto and his associates, the agreement itself mattered almost as much as the money. It meant the restoration of trust on terms which they still hoped to mitigate. A key portion of the agreement involved a foreign bank rollover of interbank credits to domestic banks, a move also designed to restore trade financing.[62] Led by Deutsche Bank, Mitsubishi and Chase, these foreign banks began negotiating a Mexican type debt plan in April 1998, where local currency could be used to settle foreign denominated debts. The Indonesian government undertook to guarantee a fixed exchange rate for this purpose. On 10 May, unfortunately, the first round of negotiations between foreign banks and their Indonesian debtors ended in Tokyo without any solution.

In contrast with these important steps by the international financial community, the Indonesians merely retraced some of the measures they had already committed themselves to under the two previous agreements. Out of the 16 banks originally scheduled for closure, which included some properties of Suharto's close relatives, but not Bank Umum National, belonging to his golf partner Mohamad Bob Hasan, seven were said to have closed on 5 April. The oil palm embargo, imposed in total contradiction of the first IMF agreement, was scheduled for rescinding, but against a 40 per cent tax on exports of the precious oil. Though a lid was put on public interest rates and spending, provisions were made for social subsidies which the first IMF plan had not addressed. On the eve of the agreement itself, the government granted new licences on public grounds to Suharto's youngest son Tommy.

The survival of the Indonesian system, by early May 1998, rested on the following outcomes. Either the overall IMF agreement was enough to restore a modicum of business confidence: this would allow the most viable of Indonesian companies to refinance themselves, in which case foreign banks would then think it appropriate to strike a deal for the overhanging bad debt. Or alternatively, the momentum from the IMF agreement would remain insufficient. The quantity of bad debts would then keep increasing, as new Indonesian firms became bankrupt. In that case, Indonesia under new management would desperately need the actual disbursements from the IMF and not merely a commitment.

This dilemma worsened the political situation in Indonesia. The essential part of the IMF reform programme ultimately involved challenging the economic power base of the ageing president. His closest associates gave up on him in May 1998.[63] But every single problem remained to be solved. By early June 1998, the IMF stopped insisting that subsidies on basic foodstuffs be removed by 1 October, as had been prescribed by the agreement with Indonesia. On 2 June, Stanley Fischer, IMF's number two, had optimistic words for the negotiation of the country's private debt with international bankers.[64]

By 5 June 1998, a tentative agreement had indeed been reached in Frankfurt with a syndicate of Indonesia's leading creditors. Predictably, its terms were more favourable (and complex) than the terms granted South Korea only months earlier. Indonesia's indebted firms received a three-year grace period on the principal (but not on interest). Indonesian banks could spread their interbank repayments over a period of three years. An Indonesian Debt Restructuring Agency was set up, guaranteeing the availability of foreign currency and limiting the impact of exchange fluctuations.

Thus a new precedent was set. The cost of Indonesia's staggering private debt would be shared between the debtors themselves, the foreign banks, which would clearly have to cross their fingers and wait, and the Indonesian state, which was expected to pitch in. As many observers had predicted, there was just no way the repayment could rest only on the debtors' shoulders, and a complete default on these debts would have been even worse for international finance. Suharto's fall concluded the shouting match with the IMF. Pitched against the evasive dictator, the IMF had run an ignorant and cruel experiment on the Indonesians themselves.

A domestic IMF without the IMF

Not every government in Southeast Asia demands, as President Suharto did, to be saved almost exclusively on its own terms. But perhaps Suharto's defiant and unpredictable behaviour eased the way for other countries, notably Malaysia. Indeed, by April 1998 that country, whose leader had been demonized by the West's financial community, and vice versa, now came close to a mutual understanding. Certainly Malaysia's sound fundamentals – vibrant foreign direct investment and industrial exports, civil service tradition and adequate infrastructures – played a role. But Mahathir's policy of avoiding at all costs the midnight call to the IMF, and therefore embarking on a programme of reforms and belt tightening, are equally responsible for the turn-around. In essence, such reforms are not very different from those undertaken by Thailand's Prime Minister Chuan Leekpai. Even Singapore, which had not suffered directly from the speculative onslaught, took the hint and embarked on a financial liberalization programme. Yet in some aspects it went against the tradition of heavy-handed government intervention that has benefited the city-state so much in previous decades.

Malaysia, Singapore and Thailand share some common traits. To a large extent, the skeletons in their closets were uncovered early on in the chronology of the Crash. Singapore's only real weakness was its dependency on close regional neighbours for a living. For the first time in their history, Singapore's major banks have written off bad debts in sizeable amounts. To counter mistrust in the local financial establishment's management of assets, a further move towards transparency and market rule was necessary. It was a move that Singapore could well afford, although it promised to reveal less than optimal investment strategies on the part of local firms. But Thailand and Malaysia also differ from Korea and Indonesia in a key area. As bad as Thailand's private indebtedness and Malaysia's semi-public financial bungling has proved to be, it has not continued its deterioration since the Crash ran its full course. To some extent, this is due to a less advanced – and less ambitious – position on the international scale. While Korea's *chaebols*, saddled with huge debts, can neither afford to continue with their international investment plans, nor afford to cancel the strategy of market share capture that is at the heart of this plan, Thailand's private firms and financial establishments have always been more focused on the domestic market. Likewise, Malaysia's huge infrastructure and industrial expansion plans can be cut immediately. Retrenchment is hardly an option for Korean firms, who run the risk of immediate disappearance and cannot hope to climb down quickly from their 5.5 to 1 ratio of debt to equity.

The political context of these three countries is also much more favourable than Indonesia's. Capital flight occurred during the financial panic, but it does not hinge on geopolitical factors. Cronyism and corruption abound in Thailand, and exist in Malaysia, with community implications. But they have not turned into a permanent threat to a particular ethnic or religious group.

Probably the most convincing act that Malaysia's government could undertake in these troubled circumstances was to bring about an opportune *rapprochement* with Singapore. The gesture certainly did not come easy to Malaysia. Only a year previously, the two governments had been embroiled in a series of neighbourly tussles. An interesting but ill-advised remark on the part of Lee Kuan-yew, who had speculated that a weakening of Singapore's moral and political fibre might lead to a future reunification with Malaysia, had not been received kindly in Kuala Lumpur. There were commercial quarrels, friendly competition in advanced weapons acquisition, and a perpetual and unspoken rivalry to serve as a guide for ASEAN.

The weakening of ASEAN ties in the face of the financial emergency and the likely prospect of a political and social storm brewing in Indonesia caused a reversal of the history of the 1960s. Malaysia and Singapore, two former British colonies retaining an essential security tie with the Commonwealth, were then united to resist Sukarno's Indonesian encroachments. Indeed, the two countries have moved towards each other again under the realistic maxim of 'prosper thy neighbour', as one Singapore commentator put it.[65] Characteristically for the financial-minded Lion City, one of the best examples that he cited for this proximity was the fact that Malaysian shares would be allowed to be quoted in Singapore dollars on the local stock exchange – a situation envied by other 'foreign' shares. The timing for this example was well chosen, since it coincided with the sudden relaxation of Malaysia's strict ownership laws on business firms. Daim Zainuddin, financial moghul and Mahathir's preferred business adviser, announced the liberalization of foreign ownership rights, which also involved easing the rules applying to Malaysia's non-*bumiputra*, e.g., Chinese or Indian groups. Ironically, the real test of this policy, here as in Korea, remains to be seen. To this day, Malaysia has yet to approve foreign ownership including and above the 50 per cent ceiling for firms trading on the stock exchange. But the speeches directly addressed to Malaysia's Chinese, and the similar angling towards Singapore-owned businesses, have a soothing effect. During a widely reported visit by Singapore Premier Goh Chok-tong in February 1998, expectations were raised higher when he called for cross-holdings between Singapore and Malay businessmen. Although the six-page joint statement between the two governments touched on financial cooperation, the local press depicted more graphically Singapore's 'strong economy and large reserves',[66] which could serve to help neighbours in need. Some in Kuala Lumpur became unusually emotional about the shared past, mixing admiration for a Singapore compared to Israel for its 'human tenacity' with a call for reunification in the next 20 years.[67]

Meanwhile, each of these countries proceeded to attempt to put their house in order with financial reforms. Singapore was first, and had in fact appointed a committee in May 1997 to suggest proposals. Characteristically, Brigadier General Lee Hsien-loong felt the need to call for radical ideas. In spite of this encouragement, the result was somewhat moderate and gradual. Furthermore, the government turned down a key proposal to have Singapore's Central Provident Fund – the huge public retirement fund – hand over part of its management to private bankers. But in other respects, Singapore moved towards true financial deregulation. Singaporeans can now buy shares listed in foreign currency on the local exchange with their retirement funds. The government has decided, for the first time, to issue government debt bonds which would create an interest rate market for the Singapore dollar, and increase its potential as a regional currency. While Singapore had always maintained an extremely conservative attitude to its own monetary and financial affairs on the market, the Crash of 1997 has persuaded it to take a jump into the unknown in the interest of a stronger regional role.

It is an inescapable fact that those Asian economies that have not had to meet the IMF's initially stringent criteria for a bail-out have fared much better than their unfortunate neighbours. Of course, their neighbours were also the most deeply exposed to start with. Yet one cannot fail to point out that the key goal of any IMF intervention is to restore confidence and prevent any further financial downslide. Of course, as IMF executives point out, that goal applies first to the integrity of the global financial system, and second to the rescue of a particular economy. One can argue, as opponents of the rescue packages did, that a more comprehensive and less conditional intervention would only have spread Asia's financial ills to the global financial marketplace.

The argument does not really rest well. First, there has been, and there remains, an immense amount of politics and domestic political debate on the actions of Western G7 nations throughout the emergency. Why else would US Treasury Secretary Robert Rubin proclaim 'his deepest preoccupation – completely shared by the President – with the decline of public support for globalization at a moment when economic, national security and geopolitical interests of our country require the opposite'?[68] The American delay in recognizing this fundamental truth (between July and December 1997) and the ambivalence of many other Western nations, which also saw the crisis as essentially regional and hoped for continued windfall profits, are an important lesson for the future.

Second, this delay in addressing the initial currency and debt problems resulted in an enlargement of the crisis. Debts piled up as currencies crashed, the means to pay for them evaporated with the decline in export prices for several Asian economies (starting with world energy prices, a major factor for Indonesia and Malaysia), and a chain reaction of bankruptcies spread across Asia.

Third, there is a near unanimity among observers today that the IMF's prescriptions have worsened several national crises instead of limiting them.[69] Without going as far as the *Wall Street Journal*, which has editorially commented that the IMF 'has not been fighting financial fires, but dousing them with gasoline',[70] it is clear that the IMF's policies have suffered from three interrelated effects. By treating the Asian Crash as a series of discrete and unrelated national breakdowns, it has entirely ignored the contagion and panic that spread around the region. By blindly forcing severe austerity policies on the real economy to compensate for financial losses, it has started a new spiral, where the financial crises and the real economy's recession reinforce each other. By highhandedly dealing with the governments involved, it has in effect aggravated the crisis of confidence in these governments, effectively bringing about their downfall.[71] The IMF thus managed to combine the traditional secrecy behind its decision-making process with public controversy. In one case, the Fund's executive director Stanley Fischer berated Japanese economic policy, provoking a fierce retort by LDP general secretary Koichi Kato. The net effect of this public squabbling was to further deepen the atmosphere of gloom in Japan. There must be a better policy.

It is pointless to move from this conclusion to the hypothesis of a deeply entrenched Western interest in seeing Asia fall. True, jingoism sometimes takes extreme forms, such as when Rudiger Dornbusch, a Nobel prize-winning economist, explains about Korea that 'a moratorium on commercial debt service will teach both the country and its markets an overdue lesson'.[72] As in the case of the previous debate on Asian values, it is also not a surprise if some Asian trendsetters chose to believe that there is 'an increasing feeling among young intellectuals in Asia that the crisis was the product of a conspiracy by the US and other Western powers'.[73] More realistically, the essential lesson to be drawn from the Asian bail-out experience of 1997 to 1998 is that the West has weighed its own economic interests alongside the dangers stemming from the Crash. The West has certainly not seized the occasion to press for Asian integration, preferring to keep a strong hand in the region's monetary and financial arrangements. Yet, since Asians themselves gave a blatant show of their disunity, perhaps the West was simply not in a position to force events.

4 Asian values, minus the debate

The facts behind the myth

What relationship exists between a financial crisis and the value sys
of one of the world's principal regions? In principle, none. In fa
although Europe's long period of slow growth after the oil crises of 19
and 1979 gave rise to so-called 'Europessimism', few would be able
establish a relationship between the continent's economic woes and
fate of European culture. The issue is even less simple where
American case is concerned, since American values are so indeli
linked with hard work – and success. In Asia, the first casualty of
Crash was undeniably the aspiration to modern-day Asian values – a
for a good reason. The advocacy of these values has usually be
premised on East Asia's economic rise and renaissance as an influen
global player. It was not simply that Asian concepts and beliefs w
played out against universal values, but that the rise of the Asian r
of the Pacific was contrasted more often than not with a decline of
West.

My belief has always been that the rebirth of Asianism had more
do with the political goals of some Asian leaders than with a genu
cultural phenomenom.[1] The pendulum is now swinging to the ot
extreme, with Asian politics now being blamed for everything that I
gone wrong. In the meantime, anthropological and demographic stud
of Asian cultures have progressed from the mere recording of progr
in terms of modernization and transition to an in-depth approach t
takes Asian systems of beliefs and practices seriously. New evidence I
surfaced that in many cases implies a separate Asian route to mod
nity. This chapter charts the collapse of the Asian values debate si
the Crash. Out of the wreckage, I present the case to be made in fav
of Asian values – without the political bias that was present in the ye
of the Asian renaissance.

The collapse of Asianism

The Asian values debate is over. For more than a decade, aspirations to independence on the part of newly rising Asian economies, official frustration at interference from the West on issues of human rights and citizenship, the resurgence of a public neo-Confucianism competing with the civic philosophy of European tradition, and above all sheer pride among Asian officials and professionals, had built up the theme of Asian values as separate from universal values. Much of the debate happened in the media, more often than not by the English language opinion-shapers of global influence. Kishore Mahbubani, the affable secretary-general of Singapore's Ministry of Foreign Affairs, wrote his famously insulting piece against the American system of government for the *Washington Quarterly*.[2] In it, he argued that the American system of checks and balances had been devised to counter a long-dead British monarch. His words were to come back at him with a vengeance after the Crash, when the chairman of Goldman Sachs pointed out that the American Constitution had laid the ground for an independent financial system and public accountability by business as well as by government.[3] In other instances, former Oxbridge dons teaching at Singapore or Kuala Lumpur universities had sparred with the classics of political philosophy they had learnt. Strong exposés of neo-Confucian philosophy came, more often than not, from within prestigious universities. It is true that some China-based intellectuals and ideologues also joined the Asian values debate. In the late 1980s, they had discovered the merits of 'neo-authoritarianism' for post-communist China. This vogue, however, coincided with a popular and political swing towards the West under the guidance of Hu Yaobang and Zhao Ziyang, China's twin reformist leaders until 1989. In practice, most of the neo-authoritarian philoso-phers were really more attuned to rule of law philosophy and opposed to Marxism. In the 1990s, there were straightforward nationalists and rejectionists of the West emerging from China, who remain unswayed by the Crash. On the contrary, they see it as another example of the West's pernicious influence. These nationalists are important on the Chinese scene. But they are an exception in the wider Asian context. Much of the Asian values debate reads like a tiff between former colo-nial or Cold War protectors and irate former students and junior allies searching for their roots after decades of elite Western acculturation. Never in the 1980s or 1990s has there been in Asia a popular move-ment feeding on an Asian rift with the West, which was the essential basis of anti-colonial sentiment in the past.

Saint George slays the dragon

In any case, the Crash settled the public part of the Asian values debate. One might almost write that St George has slain the dragon. St George refers to George Soros, the speculator *cum* philanthropist who has shaken currencies the world over, while promoting political democracy and free markets thanks to his private foundation. Soros became famous during the 1992 European monetary storm, when he reportedly gained upwards of a billion pounds at the expense of the Bank of England. He was certainly not popular at that time. The part of the dragon in this story belongs unequivocally to Dr Mahathir, the leader of Malay destiny. From August to October 1997, Dr Mahathir reacted to the fall of the ringgit, Malaysia's national currency, with frustrated and angry outbursts against international speculators, and even the occasional jibe against the role of Jews in the financial crisis.[4] Mr Soros happened to belong to both categories, and Dr Mahathir called him a 'moron'.

In so doing, Dr Mahathir dug the grave of the Asianist ideology he had helped so much to promote in the preceding decade. At a moment when the exact nature of the financial crisis and its possible implications were hard to evaluate, many saw in the duel between Mahathir and Soros a convenient metaphor for the situation. This was a case of market forces allied with the moral cause of democracy. They were bound to triumph over Asian models and values fraught with economic inefficiency. Markets could not be wrong, *ergo* Asian leaders could not be right, and Dr Mahathir's wrongful jibes provided the needed confirmation. Free marketeers rallied democrats and everything that was good on their side, while the bad and the ugly were systematically assumed to rest with the hand of the state in economic affairs. Never, in fact, had economic liberalism been turned into such a systematic political philosophy. This way of thinking gripped many Western observers, at least until South Korean markets were blown apart in December 1997. At that point, views began to be moderated by the discovery that the world's eleventh-largest economy, a political democracy at that, was threatening to collapse and send shock waves throughout the global system.

It is probably useful to point out that not even the symbolic struggle between Mahathir and Soros was representative of their own actions. In February 1998, George Soros's fund empire was said to have lost 12 billion dollars as a result of mistaken currency deals during the Asian financial crisis. Soros himself denies having gambled against the Malaysian ringgit, and it is entirely possible that he got caught in some paradoxical countermove. Like nearly everyone else, he misjudged the severity of the crisis and the strength of the panic. Malaysia's and Dr Mahathir's actual return on investment is harder to assess, of course. In 1992 and 1993, Bank Negara, the Malaysian central bank, had lost 5.7 billion dollars, reportedly in ill-advised short-term currency operations, most of it during the European monetary storm.[5] Apparently, Malaysia's leaders were not averse at the time to a bit of public short-term speculation. But on a more theoretical plane, Dr Mahathir sometimes finds himself in good company. His proposal, made in early September 1997, to tax short-term currency transactions not only mirrors an earlier proposal by Nobel prize winner, James Tobin; it has since been taken up by his colleague Lawrence Klein, and latterly by none other than George Soros, presumably chastized by his own losses. The tax on short-term currency transactions may still remain an impractical idea, but at least it is not a lonely flight of fancy on the part of Mahathir.

See what we do, not what we say . . .

Even more importantly, skilled politician that he is, Dr Mahathir plays a far more subtle game than some of his verbal excesses suggest. In a spirited defence of the man's record, a *Bangkok Post* writer has remarked that Mahathir does more to squash Islamic fundamentalism in his own country than any US administration at home.[6] The prophet of an East Asian caucus without Caucasians,[7] who occasionally encouraged his defence establishment to buy some Migs in order to prove his independence from the West, leads the most open ASEAN country, after Singapore, to frequent US navy visits and informal exercises. The Asian friend of the Arab League did not react when the brother of Malaysia's nominal sultan visited Israel in 1994. Malaysia has received high-level visitors from Israel in recent years, and is now open to commercial relations. The same capacity for pragmatism is also shown in other areas. Mahathir has been in the past Asia's strongest champion of non-involvement in another country's internal affairs, often criticizing the arrogance of lesson-givers from the West. Indeed, his government threatened Europeans with a boycott of the ASEM London summit in March 1998 if they did not invite Burma. But when the time came, he lectured the Burmese junta on 'certain standard practices or values that had been accepted by the international community' in March 1998,[8] and sent his foreign affairs minister on a visit to Aung San Suu Kyi. While strengthening Asian or Malay bondage against the West during the financial crisis, Mahathir tersely notes about Suharto's fight with the IMF that if Indonesian leaders 'want to make a mess for themselves, they have a right to'.[9] Meanwhile, Malaysia is busy strengthening business relationships with Singapore, and opening up for the first time the doors of *bumiputra* firms to ethnic Malayan-Chinese.

It is therefore no wonder that Malaysia found itself after some months of regional crash in a better situation than most commentators had anticipated. The decline in currency and stock markets was halted by early 1998, and the country avoided calling in the IMF. Instead, it is giving advice to its neighbours in Indonesia and Thailand, and even lending money to bolster Thailand's dwindling currency reserves. True, it is debatable whether these results have much to do with Dr Mahathir's speeches, or with his own prescriptions. For months, he has acted on the international scene as a Dr Jekyll and Mr Hyde together with his heir designate, vice-premier and Minister of Finance Anwar Ibrahim. If Dr Mahathir is the nemesis of financial markets, the astute and articulate Anwar is undisputedly its darling. There was much speculation regarding the true relations between the two men, or the division of work they may have agreed on, with Dr Mahathir catering to Malay and fundamentalist sentiment, while Anwar courted the international community and the middle classes.[10] Whatever the case, Mahathir was smart enough to set aside some of his more outlandish political insights, and to instigate a long list of courageous structural reforms and policy moves that halted Malaysia's downslide. He also clearly began a regional policy turn to prop up Malaysia with increased cooperation from a financially-sound Singapore, overcoming a long history of personal competition with its leaders.

Privately, it is likely that Mahathir perceives this pragmatic turn as an unfortunate but necessary concession to the market forces that the West could unleash against Malaysia's economy. After all, much obscurity remains in his country's financial sector, and most notably in the support that public banks gave to firms and finance establishments tied to the UMNO[11] party's politicians. In all probability, Mahathir, like many other Asian leaders, sees the events not so much as a defeat of Asianism, but as a process of give and take. This is essentially another stage in the contest of strength between the developed West and the emerging Asian powers.

Facts, therefore, do not completely coincide with the myth of the market crusaders defeating Asian values. The fight took place on two very different planes – the economic market place and the public opinion debate. A fundamental truth has emerged, however. Whatever their inner reservations and assessments of responsibilities, most Asian leaders fight the market crisis with market tools, or at least adopt a politically correct attitude towards the international organizations that might rescue them. Instead of shutting themselves off from the market, and trying to partly or temporarily insulate their economies, they go along with its rules. Or at least, they pretend to. President Suharto's long hesitations did not prevent him from paying humiliating lip service to the IMF, which he now despises so much. 'We will never enjoy again an economic growth such as we have experienced for more than the past quarter of the century', he said darkly during his inaugural address to the Indonesian rump parliament on 11 March 1998.[12] But whether he accepts an agreement with the IMF's Camdessus or tinkers with the notion of an 'IMF Plus'[13] policy, the perspective is now limited.

China changes gear

Even China's leaders have gone against the grain and moved further towards the conventional financial wisdom of their command economy. They are certainly aware that the very archaism and semi-isolation of their financial and monetary system has saved them from the contagion of panic. Yet they are also quick to adopt at least surface reforms shielding their domestic economy from blame. They streamlined their government on the eve of Prime Minister Li Peng's replacement by Zhu Rongji in March 1998 and they announced the issue of 35 billion dollars' worth of public bonds to plug the gaping hole in the nation's domestic banking system. Socialism is turning to be closer to capitalism in this respect too. In China, just as in the giant American Savings & Loans bankruptcy of the late 1980s, the average tax payer or individual saver is required as a bail-out of last resort. Basic financial institutions, that are private in America but public in China, cannot be allowed to go bust, and a public guarantee has to replace evaporated trust. For China, where the formerly all-powerful state enterprises disgorge even more red ink than so-called 'red chips', this move is meant to signal that policies based on the bottom line have finally arrived.

The state keeps the upper hand

Yet here, as in Malaysia, Indonesia or Thailand, the state, rather than the market, has remained the arbiter of solutions to the crisis. Public accountability and transparency are minimal, and what is really required from the Asian state and the former guiding hand of development is nothing short of self-reform without major political change. In Thailand, the return of Prime Minister Chuan Leekpai, a respected civilian technocrat who had already taken charge once after the political disaster of the Bangkok military repression in 1992, does not really end the nexus between politicians, bureaucrats and leading businessmen. It has merely helped to deflect public anger at the sudden austerity and rising unemployment resulting from the financial crash. Singapore itself, a leading regional advocate of further market liberalization and opening up of Asian economies, has adopted several important measures of financial transparency to improve trust in the Singapore stock exchange and the city-state's role as a regional financial headquarters. There is no implication of any imminent political reform, however, and in fact no public demand for any such reform. Indeed, the Singaporeans are mesmerized by the rising threat of political chaos and ethnic strife inside the neighbouring Indonesian giant.

Here lies another paradox of the Asian crisis. The Asian developmental state has risen to the fundamental challenge of the marketplace by enhancing market mechanisms and responding to the demands of international institutions and foreign governments. If the Asian way of doing business is thus weakened, the response does not go so far as to accept a complete separation of power, even in the field of capital markets. A few days after the handover of Hong Kong to China on 1 July 1997, chief executive Tung Chee-hwa quietly took to his own direct responsibility ultimate decisions in monetary affairs. In December 1997, Lee Hsien-loong, senior minister Lee Kuan-yew's eldest son, became the head of Singapore's Monetary Authority.

Kim Dae-jung's peace with the chaebols

Nor of course are governments ready to dismantle the political superstructures of Asian states. This is of course obvious where autocrats or one-party systems prevailed. Where a democratic process has allowed for a change of government, the new leaders themselves immediately seek a natural balance with the forces of the past, and with the prevailing culture. Thus, President Kim Dae-jung, the prophet outcast of South Korean politics, has reversed himself shortly after his election. He campaigned against the nexus of compromises and corruption between the large Korean *chaebols*, the Korean bureaucracy and the ruling party. He also railed against the external humiliation of IMF requirements, vowing to consider himself free from earlier agreements made by the Kim Young-sam administration. He thus appeared simultaneously as the champion of national independence and of the Western conception of democracy, proclaiming the futility of Asian values.

Once elected, however, he immediately set out to ratify his predecessor's agreement with the IMF, although the Korean negotiating team is skilled at obtaining the best possible loan terms under very poor circumstances. He has also prevented a parliamentary vote of no confidence, and he has installed as Prime Minister the former arch-conservative Kim Jung-pil, who is, ironically, one of the founders of the KCIA, Korea's secret police agency, and was also a key backer of the Park Chung-hee dictatorship in the 1970s. For the Ministry of Finance, President Kim has selected Lee Kyu-song, a technocrat who held the same job under General Roh Tae-woo, and who ordered in 1989 a huge bailout by Korea's central bank of the three leading investment houses in the stock market.[14]

Kim Dae-jung's real originality and success has been to persuade the unions to accept the flexibility and austerity policies they refused from his predecessors. Kim, the outsider from Cholla province, who was supposed to chase the powerful elite from Seoul, has realistically made his peace with the traditional fabric of Korean society in the name of a sacred union against dire circumstances. After all, there is more of the Asian than Western way in his behaviour. By March 1998, several of the large Korean firms that had gone into bankruptcy are as active as ever. Kia, the auto manufacturer allied to Ford, is still busy acquiring dealerships in the United States. Korean competitors to the Hanbo steel-making company, whose bankruptcy in January 1997 actually predates the Asia-wide financial crisis, complain that the group has merely been put in a position where it does not have to service its debts, and can therefore afford to undercut prices.

There is life after bankruptcy

The same story has been told about the simultaneous bankruptcy of Peregrine (Hong Kong) and Steadysafe (Jakarta), respectively creditor and debtor. While the offices, furniture and artworks of Peregrine's headquarters were immediately seized under Hong Kong's tough bankruptcy rules, business is still going on at Steadysafe, although it is also legally bankrupt. There has been an Asian way of economic success. There is now an Asian way of foreclosure, and it is just as distinctly original, if somewhat more debatable. Suharto practised it clumsily, Kim Dae-jung with an eye on international opinion. Undoubtedly, the quick conclusion of two overall rescue agreements between South Korea and its international creditors led by J.P. Morgan and the IMF are largely due to president-elect Kim Dae-jung's pro-market stance. The Korean bankers, financial officials and *chaebol* representatives' willingness to agree with just about anything that was required of them in the early weeks of 1998 stunned their counterparts. As business negotiators, Koreans have a reputation for toughness. There was, of course, more to this than met the eye. Would-be lenders to Korea soon learned that behind the blanket acceptance by shell-shocked Koreans, there remain layers of passive resistance. Many Koreans feel that these changes undermine the basic economic system that earlier gave them the status of a developed country. Not only does the government try to support failing *chaebols*; the ordinary and otherwise law-abiding citizen occasionally vandalizes imported cars in Seoul streets, as a gesture of defiance to the outside world and to Koreans importing luxury goods. This, after all, is only an extension of the 'frugality' campaign designed by the previous administration to curb the current account deficit.

Adapt or perish: the argument for chameleons (Taiwan and the Philippines)

In other words, those Asian countries and leaders who deal most adequately with the crisis subscribe, either completely or at least outwardly, to market philosophy. In principle this means also the priority of due process and a rules-based environment over custom, personal relationships and the guided economy. In fact, vocal acceptance of market rules makes it easier to strike a deal with foreign creditors and international financial institutions, while preserving at least some special or customary interests and practices. Polemics against the tyranny of international finance only defeat that purpose.

In the first group can be found Taiwan and the Lee Teng-hui government, which basks in the light of its financial results and its democratic system. The gangland scandals that severely marred Lee Teng-hui's popularity less than a year before, publicizing the connections between many elected politicians and gangsters, are conveniently forgotten, so strong is Taiwan's high-tech entrepreneurial sector and its financial management. Taiwan's good reputation enables it, in fact, to take measures to limit the freedom of capital movement and foreign investment that, everywhere else in Asia, would be considered an affront to market philosophy. The Philippines and President Fidel Ramos are also a case in point. The purging of the corruption of the Marcos era, and the privatization programme was been enforced while the country remained under permanent IMF watch and guidance, have proved to be extremely useful. Although the Philippines felt the pressure of competitive devaluation, they have far less skeletons to hide in their closets. Fidel Ramos, even more than Lee Teng-hui, has consistently criticized the Asian values and neo-authoritarianism of his ASEAN neighbours. Through a combination of openness to the West, of past efforts and the sheer luck of not having had the time for a full-size bubble economy, the former sick man of Asia seems poised for an early recovery after the region's crash.

'Curing a hunchback with a hammer' – Indonesia, Korea and Japan

For the second group of governments and leaders in the region, a thorough prescription of structural reforms is tantamount to political suicide. First there is the question of the special interests within the ruling circle and families, as well as the institutional use of public financing to bolster political support and allies. Beyond this first layer of obvious obstacles on the path to reform, there lie even stronger problems. Throughout the Malay world in Southeast Asia, government policies and public sector funds have consistently been used to redress the imbalance between the large Malay and Islamic community and the small but entrepreneurial Chinese minority. A level playing field for all would mean that communities whose customs run against individual and competitive behaviour will sink. True, the large Chinese business families of Southeast Asia have as much allied themselves with political rulers as the *pribumi*[15] firms who owe their very existence to political connections; they have also been caught in the financial down draft. In Indonesia, for example, 220 out of 228 firms quoted on the Jakarta stock exchange were in a state of technical bankruptcy by February 1998. The crisis, and the debate over solutions, in particular the hard choices over who would be allowed to sink and who would be rescued, threatened to reopen the ethnic divide. This is not just a case of the poor man on the street protesting against the prices at his neighbourhood Chinese store. In early February 1998, Aburizal Bakrie, the president of the Indonesian Chamber of Commerce, who runs the twelfth-largest group in the country, issued a call for 'redistributing the property of Indonesian companies and firms on a wider basis and giving priority, and a larger share, to natives' over Chinese businessmen. He claimed support from the Golkar ruling party for that move.[16]

Clearly, thorough economic reform and cleansing, with the building up of neutral rules and the simultaneous opening up to international competition that investors now require, remains a tall order. From one end of the region to another, this agenda threatens the political and hierarchical system of Asian societies. Even an Asian-style democracy, where free information and open electoral competition often work side by side with widespread clientele and customary relationships, is not equal to the task. In early 1998, Asians witnessed with their own eyes the slow and painful demise of Japan's top decision-making establishment. High officials at the Ministry of Finance and the Bank of Japan were toppled for having maintained special-interest relationships with the country's financial firms. The confidence of the Japanese public in their civil service and political system was at its lowest point since the defeat of 1945. What the seemingly neutral requirements of the financial big bang for Japan, or of the IMF for emerging Asia imply, if they were to be literally put in practice, is nothing short of a political and social revolution. Kazuo Nukazawa, a leading reformist at Japan's Keidanren, notes that 'Japan's problem lies in that the market was only secondary to its egalitarian political economy. The preponderance overstayed, especially so in the financial system and agricultural policy. But, at that cost, Japan has bought national solidarity and political stability.'[17] And a Korean executive more bluntly cites one of his country's proverbs to Lawrence Summers, the US Deputy Treasury Secretary: 'If you try to cure a hunchback with a hammer, you cure the hunchback but you kill the man'.[18]

The balancers: Singapore, Hong Kong and Australia

The gap between market-oriented reforms, the need for which is universally recognized, and politically related changes that bode ill for stability, is a difficult one to straddle. Yet very few governments can pretend to achieve the former without undergoing the latter. Among those few are the two city-states of Singapore and Hong Kong. Singapore's leaders are clearly aware of the dilemma facing the region around them, a region they often defend on the international scene and for which they are never short of advice. Very early in the crisis, Prime Minister Goh Chok Tong and his colleagues became the region's most outspoken advocates of further economic liberalization and structural reforms for their neighbours. It is essential for Singapore's well-being to exclude any regional move back from the budding free trade system and free capital markets.[19] More discreetly, Hong Kong's chief executive Tung Cheehwa, who kept a defensive posture during the early months of the crisis, began in 1998 to express sympathy for the hardest-hit economies, on the grounds that their fate will inevitably affect Hong Kong's own prosperity. Towards Indonesia, where the stakes are highest, Singapore is by far the single most committed country among the participants of the IMF's rescue package, underwriting nearly 5 billion dollars. And the Singapore government was also ready to play hardball with President Suharto, delaying the delivery of their contribution when Suharto procrastinated on the closure of 16 bankrupt banks and finance establishments. Lee Kuan-yew himself explained that the IMF and the global financial community it stands for have more authority with recalcitrant debtors, and that he would rather not deliver the bad news himself. Having thus set an example, Singapore tries hard to prod Western countries into more action. After an equivocal statement by European Union President Jacques Santer, Singapore's government-controlled media have lashed out at an inactive and indifferent Europe. In a more controlled fashion, Lee Kuan-yew and his son B.G. Lee have rationalized the need for Europe's active participation in 'quelling this panic and reassuring investors' at an Asia-Europe Forum, and expressed the region's feeling that 'Europe had been passive in this crisis'.[20] In February 1998, Singapore proposed to set up a multinational fund of 8 billion dollars for emergency import-export financing to countries and firms where even the short-term credit for ordinary commercial operations was vanishing. This gesture was aimed first and foremost at Indonesia, a significant supplier of the Singaporean trading economy.

But even apart from their own political instinct, Singaporeans and their leaders can only be frightened by the threat of region-wide political instability that results from the crisis. They have companions, too – Australia for example, which is as much a part of Asia as of the West. Australia's Foreign Affairs Minister Alexander Downer initiated in March 1998 a campaign to persuade the IMF and his Western counterparts to adopt softer terms and attitudes towards Indonesia. This is a far cry from the protests of Australia's powerful farm and mining lobbies of only a few weeks previously, which lamented the fact that IMF credit to Indonesia was helping Indonesian exporters to undercut their own prices.

Singapore's Lee Kuan-yew, in his familiar role as philosopher-king reflects prudently on the political lesson from the crisis. According to him, the financial crisis had nothing to do with the superiority of democracy, or with forms of government in general. It has 'to do with integrity, with rigorous systems of governance', says Lee, who places the blame on the 'bribe-givers' as much as the 'bribe-takers'.[21] The crisis has not proven democracies right over other regimes, but only that countries which take a consistent and stern attitude against corruption could sail through unscathed. Uncharacteristically, he conceded that

> There are certain weaknesses in Confucianism . . . You owe a duty to your family and loyalty to your friends, to help and support them. That's Confucianism. But this value is degraded when you use public resources through your official position to do your duty to your family and be loyal to your friends.[22]

The message to neighbours is clear. They are urged to reform themselves, while the West is discreetly encouraged to play a more helpful role.

West wind prevails over East wind . . .

Should we then assume that the Crash of 1997 will, perhaps involuntarily, speed up the convergence between East and West? The loss of steam apparent in all regional cooperation schemes certainly suggests that outcome. The sudden downgrading of Asian firms and sovereign risks by international rating agencies such as Moodys' or Standards and Poors, where Asian firms had previously been judged in a league of their own, also implies that trust in Asian methods has evaporated. At the political and financial level, it is clear that, if only by default, Western models have won the day.

The outcome for Asian societies is much less clear. Both the Westernized rising middle classes of Asia and the *ersatz* Asian values system took a hit. The middle classes have been impoverished by the crisis: in fact, those who survived often brought their savings to foreign banks operating locally, while the losers joined the rank-and-file poor again. For most, this is the end of the trips abroad, of the overseas education for children, and of the taste for luxury brand names that made the fortunes of Western firms and importers alike. Vuitton Asia and the era of trust fund children educated in Western universities are fading, while savers move in hordes to the perceived safety of big-name Western banks.

. . . but it does not win over hearts and minds

Does this signify that globalism and a universal value system have won over Asia and buried Asianism? Certainly not. Although most, if not all, governments chose to paper over this debate in the interests of their market, frustration was building up. Asian middle classes suffering from sudden asset deflation and entrepreneurs groaning under the weight of spiralling debt, the educated young who suddenly see an end to the automatic escalator that has raised their parents' economic and social prospects, all are torn between conflicting perceptions and emotions. This contradiction is revealed in the contrast between public manifestations and some opinion polls. In the same week when students demonstrations and protests against 'King Suharto' and his family escalated to new levels in Indonesia, the *Far Eastern Economic Review*'s poll of Asian executives revealed that around 70 per cent of Indonesian executives believed in the usefulness and practicability of a currency board for the rupiah.[23] This issue was the bone of contention between Suharto and the IMF. In nearly every Asian country, the reaction of those affected by the crisis hovers between anger at political leaders' corruption, and nationalist frustration brought about by helplessness in the face of escalating market forces. While influential and comparatively independent media often side with the former, they also occasionally help to express the latter. In Bangkok, both the *Bangkok Post* and the *Nation* have run violent and extensive opinions and letters against the indifferent or imperialist West. A Japanese researcher based at Chulalongkorn University called the IMF agreements 'new unequal treaties', reminding readers of the humiliations suffered by Asia in the middle of the nineteenth century:

> In the 1830s and 40s, China's addiction to opium . . . contributed to a destabilized currency and an internal fiscal crisis. . . . Thailand and its neighbors are not addicted to opium, but something far more potent and corrupting: money, in the form of foreign direct (and indirect) investment.

Drawing another parallel with Asia's security ties to the United States, he concluded, 'if the old treaties fulfilled US aspirations to be a Transpacific power, the new ones firmly maintain that embedded power structure'.[24] Another writer explains that:

> Having lived the past colonial period that ended in the early Sixties, many Asean leaders hate to see a return of Western imperialism which allows for the domination of their economies, politics and culture.[25]

Many denounced the IMF as a tool for Western economic interests:

> The IMF practices double standards in favour of international banks and creditors, and against local financial institutions, companies, depositors and shareholders . . . No wonder the IMF's main role in Asia is increasingly seen as chief debt collector for international banks.[26]

Security concerns to the rescue

This, however, is a far cry from the triumphant advocacy of Asianism of a few years ago. Nationalist frustration at the IMF or the United

States, xenophobic or integrist community responses and attempts at salvaging independent, if irrational, economic policies are only defensive responses. The proponents of a cultural Asianism have often seen it in terms of a pluralistic renaissance, where 'the renewal of faith and the assertion of multiculturality'[27] matter much more than an imaginary denial of the inspiration from the West. The frustrated expression of 1998 is in reality much closer to 'the strident anti-Western rhetoric' of early nationalist movements, whose 'slogans of liberation rang hollow because the people were made to suffer at the hands of incompetent and corrupt regimes'.[28] As such, they may end up equally ineffective. Were nationalist or xenophobic sentiments to be amplified as the result of the Crash, this trend would increase the political disruption that economic suffering is already bringing about. That disruption, however, would hurt Asian countries much more than the West itself.

Ironically, a much more cogent case against the risk of destabilization brought about by heavy-handed Western interventions and requirements is made by one of its most emblematic spokesmen. Henry Kissinger writes:

> Asian paranoia has encountered American triumphalism. The erstwhile claim of the Asian 'tigers' that they had found the key to rapid growth in a mixture of market economics and authoritarianism is challenged by the American message that remedies for their current ills can only be found in the nearly immediate adoption of our models of globalism and pluralistic democracy.[29]

But, as Kissinger warns, the potential destabilization of Indonesia could reverberate around Southeast Asia for decades. Indeed, after Suharto's fall, ASEAN is going through an even more severe phase of withdrawal, the political condition of its largest member being in an unpredictable state of flux.

The political or security arguments for a rescue of Asia are no help to an Asian or Asianist perspective. On the contrary, far from the claim of an Asian miracle, or from the assertion of a newborn identity, the defence of the region now rests on a bare-bone and neo-realist argument about the need for political stability above all other goals. From a political or strategic point of view, this defence has many historical arguments going for it. But it is a minimalist view of Asia, rather than the imagined Asianism of yesterday.

What remains of Asian core values?

Asianism and Asian values have been built up in the recent past as an *ersatz* set of beliefs meant to bolster one of the following three tenets. The first tenet is the unity of a region, and sometimes of a single country, through a language and ideology that project the communities of the past into an integrated nation. The second tenet is the avoidance of international conflict among states whose relationships were not steadied by history, after the colonial era, or which wanted to balance the power relationships of the Cold War with a regional anchorage. And the third tenet is a collective, conformist and paternalistic approach of civil society that serves to ward off political dissent and to maintain social discipline. These multiple layers are likely to be confusing to observers. The following three ideas have almost no common ground: the logic of community or regional empowerment that borrows as much from the Western politically correct language of equal rights[30] as from the nationalism of yesteryear; the practice of regional consensus in diplomatic endeavours, which takes its deeper cultural justification from the Malayo-Oceanic practices of gifts, tributary systems and council meetings; and the cult of efficiency, social engineering and elite leadership which is a trademark of neo-Confucianism.

From national construction to regional tolerance

The first function remains the most important, at least for the nations of Southeast Asia. Their ethnic and cultural diversity is bewildering, and the potential for conflict was huge in the post-independence era. This is the function of the 'imagined community' that Benedict Anderson[31] first identified for Indonesia, but which fits as well other Southeast Asian post-colonial nations. Elements of globalist Buddhist philosophy had once been grafted on a call for region-wide nationalism by the Japanese military. The rise of overseas Chinese capitalism and the regional ascent of at least three regional Chinese centres (Taiwan, Singapore and Hong Kong) made it possible and even useful to substitute Confucianism for Buddhism. Devoid of all of Confucius's actual teaching about the individual, this ultimate vagary of neo-Confucianism borrowed much from Max Weber's ode to the rise of Protestantism, from Victorian hygienism and from Bentham's utilitarianism. Contemporary Singapore has become the best illustration of this synthetic social philosophy, with remarkable practical success. Singapore's puritanism and culture of over-achievment, however, remain the trademark of an avowedly austere merchant and civic elite, and can hardly translate into either a creative edge or a popular mass culture. After all, the ruling families of Geneva in the eighteenth century were no fun either, even though they created the first capitalist democracy amidst absolutist Europe. In a new twist, Malaysian political figures and thinkers have rewritten the book of Asian values in a far less demanding garb. Anwar Ibrahim, leaving behind his more militant Islamic youth, seeks to discover 'the metaphilosophy of Oriental philosophers' that lies behind so much religious diversity. Another official but astute thinker, Noordin Sopiee, praises a 'feast of civilizations' between East and West that would rest on mutual respect.[32] Again, the secret of Asian values is to be found first and foremost in their syncretism, rather than in a distinct identity. A strong point of the advocacy of Asian values remains indeed that they tend to be more tolerant and even open to new points of view than a more fundamentalist Western mind, as Noordin Sopiee duly notes.

The limits of cooperation through conflict avoidance

The second function of Asianism is a power balancing act and a method for conflict avoidance among nations. What has become the 'ASEAN way' or the 'Asian way' as a theory of international cooperation for the region has distinctive roots in post-war diplomacy. Pandit Nehru's Five Principles of Pacific Coexistence[33] were first coined as a guide to relations with People's China. Chinese diplomacy would make it one of its own dogmas. The so-called 'third way' between capitalism and communism, once practised by Burma's U Nu and Cambodia's Sihanouk, was tinged with Buddhism but gave birth to the neutralist and non-aligned movement: at the 1955 Bandung Conference of Afro-Asian nations, even the Japanese were present in numbers. In prewar days, Japan had propagandized regional harmony under the 'eight pillars of the sky', as well as the 'flying geese' pattern of economic development under Japan's leadership.[34]

Japan's own postwar policy of relying on the US military alliance but avoiding all direct military involvement led to the formulation of two key principles. These were the separation of politics from economics, which allowed Japan to supersede the barrier of the Cold War towards China; and the theme of 'comprehensive security', which emphasized demography, the economy, energy and environment at the expense of hard power relationships. Japan wanted to rebuild an Asian community without the negative implications of political and military leadership.

The formation of ASEAN in 1967 led to appeals and diplomatic treaties for neutralization or neutrality, equidistance or regional reliance, as yet unrealized drawings of a zone of peace, freedom and neutrality

(ZOPFAN) for the region, and the formation of the 'ASEAN way' of conflict avoidance and resolution. In practice, conflicts were forgotten or swept under the carpet more often than they were formally resolved. Actual international cooperation remains confined to a thin strata of top government figures, policy scholars and media writers.

The small nations' club that is ASEAN has effectively limited the influence of Asia's large powers, from Japan to China or India. With the advent of the Pacific economy in the prosperous 1980s, the ASEAN way became an 'Asian way', and it is at the heart of institutional efforts to construct a regional economy with APEC.[35] Seeking to fend off Western pressure towards the institution of free trade through World Trade Organization rules and negotiations, with their potential for international quarrels, APEC's 'eminent persons group' devised a process of 'voluntary, unilateral, step by step concessions' where each country delivered 'down-payments' on its commitment to free trade.[36] Above all, these methods have in common with the region's approach to international relations the same caution against 'emphasizing fixed institutions and rigid rule-based procedure'.[37] The soft approach to regional economic cooperation always had its sceptics. These sceptics point out, for example, that Singapore and Malaysia were the first countries to bring a trade dispute in front of the World Trade Organization instead of settling it themselves in the quiet ASEAN way. It is of course this approach which was put to the test by the financial crash of 1997, and which failed. The lack of mutual commitments, formal channels and binding agreements broke the back of regional cooperation in late 1997, when disaster struck. This failure reverberates backwards, eroding the credibility of regional diplomacy.

Born to lead, Asian style

The third function of Asian values is perhaps the most vital. They represent a culturalist as opposed to universalist approach to modernization. The advocacy of a culturalist approach is often an excuse for preserving authoritarian, or semi-authoritarian political systems. These systems have harnessed the security state, originally conceived in the context of resisting communism, towards the goal of fast development. They have unquestionably succeeded. Voluntarily or not, democratic development has remained stunted. This is the case in South Korea, where the top-down approach in every aspect of society has reduced formal political democracy to a thin and largely symbolic layer. It is arguably so in Taiwan, where dissatisfaction at money politics and the huge influence of the underworld have cast a shadow on the first democracy in Chinese history. Even Japan, with the clash between its clientele system based on personal relationships and a formally free and open political contest, shows the strain of a deep-seated conflict between traditional custom and a modern rule of law environment. As to Singapore, the showcase of Asian solutions, in 1992 it was the only country out of 28 which reached an income per capita of over 8,000 dollars, yet it was not a liberal democracy. As such, it is perhaps more of an interesting exception than a model. All ASEAN countries save the Philippines retain authoritarian safeguards and limitations on the political process, even after the huge strides made by their civil society.

In this context, the advocacy of Asian values can take two very different roads. One is the authoritarian shortcut to modernity, with a claim of success against the inefficiency of democracy, or with a view to supplementing it. That view is particularly popular with the Chinese leadership, who seek reform within the confines of Communist Party authority, and now feel a strong kinship with the national security regimes of the Cold War era. Few in Asia, however, will strongly argue against democracy, although they may plead for transition time, or for adaptation to the requirements of special situations.

Asian society, in spite of everything

Asian values are also a defence against a culturally Western modernity. They serve as a plea for the compatibility of Asian customs with modernity, and do not necessarily contradict the rule of law and political democracy. There are obviously exponents of these ideas who fall in the trap of Orientalism and ethnicized knowledge, often from the well-meaning position of being a Western critic of the West. This is the 'ethnography from the native's point of view', that Clifford Geertz[38] famously advocated to rid oneself of the Western curse. Turning the Trobriand islands into a moral example of redemption for an ailing materialist West after Branislaw Malinowski's famous research on exchange of gifts rituals among Oceanic people[39] is a familiar mistake on the part of anthropologists.

My argument instead rests on demographic research and the historical and spiritual roots of several leading Asian cultures. It is *not* a claim of Asian uniqueness as opposed to a universal Western model. This very Western model has had different avenues and features. For instance, Latin European or French culture and institutions remain different from British or American societies. They lay claim at the very least to a specific modernity that was contemporary, but not identical, to the British or American revolutions and that endures beyond the advent of globalism. At the most, this claim for cultural or societal exceptionality does not lessen as European societies homogenize further and become even more influenced by global culture and America's 'soft power'.[40] At the political level again, Yasuhiro Nakasone, the former Prime Minister of Japan, practises a Japanese Gaullism when he declares that:

> We should keep in mind that a blind faith in the virtue of the market place will shrink or even destroy culture. Japan and Europe sometimes reproach Americans their rigid principles concerning free trade and human rights. If it is desirable to act together as much as possible, one should not insist on the differences of approach . . . it is important to recognize that differences can create complementarities in the political process.[41]

De Gaulle used to say in the Second World War that one might disagree with the Anglo-Saxons, about everything save the essential alliance. A staunch partisan of the alliance with the West, Nakasone underlines that there is no need to agree fully with one another in order to cooperate – a global order does not imply converging cultural identities. The current rage to make customs and practices uniform will be self-defeating if it leads to identical societies that harbour deep resentments towards each other. Being different can be an asset in complementary cooperation. Being identical can lead to fratricidal conflict.

The dialogue between East and West, and the models each holds up in the mirror for the other, or believes it sees in that mirror, will continue for a long time, regardless of the more mundane economic reordering brought about by the Crash. Claiming victory in terms of financial or economic efficiency is not the same as laying claim to holistic cultural superiority. Instead, there are societal and cultural facts, which will help Asia bounce back from the brink. These facts are often buried under the indictment of Asian crony capitalism that is the received truth of the day. Yet they are embarrassingly simple.

Demography as the umbilical chord

The main truth of Asian values lies in the connection between culture and demography, family or social behaviour. We wonder today at the social consequences of a massive crisis that is creating millions of unemployed overnight from Thailand to Korea, with the worst case scenario in Indonesia. The spectacle of thousands of young Indonesian workers herded by the police and army to train stations in order to return to their villages after the closure of a factory suggests that widespread despondency and mass violence are distinct possibilities. The Western experience of unemployment has been in two phases. In the 1930s, the Great Depression was sudden, and the unemployed masses became a major vector of political unrest and of fascism. In Europe after the years of high growth, however, the rise of unemployment has been steady but slow. It took 34 years for French unemployment to move from less than 3 per cent of the labour force to more than 13 per cent. That gradual change and the welfare mechanisms brought to bear on the situation have limited electoral discontent at the polls. Asia's sudden crisis evidently bears a resemblance to the European crisis of the 1930s, and not to the decline of the first industrial revolution after 1973. Will Asians riot? Beyond the pictures of bank employees holding a board that says 'I aM Fired' to denounce the IMF, and the tragedy of Sumatra Indonesians fleeing by boat towards neighbouring Malaysia, there is a possibility of far quicker and wider adaptation to the crisis than we suspect in the West.

This hypothesis rests both on the cohesion brought by Asian family culture. Available evidence suggests that there is far more family stability and solidarity in Asia, however modernized, than in the West. A key factor in the present crisis is the degree of intra-familial responsibility, in cities and in native villages that will be displayed to those who have suddenly lost their income. We should look for a precursor of this attitude in the behaviour of Asians of almost all walks of life towards the elderly in their families. It is evident in the West that an individual or cellular family that will not care for the elderly is equally unlikely to help siblings in need. The individual has become the basic unit, marriage itself being, as some sociologists are now finding out in America, a time-sharing commodity based on profit expectations.

The case for family-based cohesion

Field studies in Asia suggest instead that Asians retain a close and caring relationship with the elderly. Throughout East Asia, the elderly mostly reside with one of their children. The rate of co-residence does not change much according to the urban or rural setting, nor according to educational background. In Thailand, 80 per cent of people aged over 60 lived with a child, the actual figure being higher for cities (82 per cent) than for villages (79 per cent). In Taiwan, the same figure for people aged over 65 was 70.7 per cent in 1989, a small decline from 83.7 per cent in 1976. In the Philippines, 72 per cent of people older than 60 resided with one of their children, the figure being substantially higher for Manila (78 per cent). Overall, less than 10 per cent of the elderly had not seen one of their children in the past week. Even in modern Singapore, where public housing and income are much closer to Western welfare state standards, more than 68 per cent of old people resided with one of their children. The rate is actually higher for better-educated people, and the results of this study note that co-residence serves 'as a buffer and a link between the elderly and the wider society'.[42] Hong Kong, with the familiar but true cliché of old people living alone in caged beds within dormitories, is an exception – much of its aged population consists of refugees who have come alone from China, and who have never founded families during their struggle for livelihood. In China itself, another study also shows the prevalence of co-residence for China's elderly (aged 60 plus). Of the rural elderly, 88.9 per cent live in homes which include at least two generations of the same family ('three generations under one roof' being both the customary desirable, and the statistically more prevalent arrangement). In cities, the figure is still 73.1 per cent.[43] Financial dependence on the younger generation is certainly a factor for the rural elderly. However, it is cited as a problem by less than half of elderly women in urban surroundings, and by only 7 per cent of elderly urban males. The situation looks less promising for the future because of the drop in birth rate brought by the 'one-child family' policy, and because of the much improved longevity of the rural elderly. The demographic transition, with a higher life expectancy, allowed the Chinese to afford their cultural preference for co-residence of different generations. The author of this study therefore concludes that 'housing policies could be reformulated to make it easier for the elderly to live with their children', and that co-residence with surviving siblings, already a statistical reality, can make up for part of the gap in size between generations.[44]

A divergent path towards demographic modernization

The corresponding figures for developed Western countries show that in all cases, less than 25 per cent of the elderly live with their children. The interesting conclusion to be drawn from these figures is that the anthropological systems and core values in Asian societies remain different from the West, and that economic modernization does not necessarily lead to a convergence on key issues. These facts are not so surprising, since they reinforce earlier findings on marriage and fertility in various Asian societies. Again, demographic trends which tend, throughout the region, to reproduce historical transition in Western Europe and the United States do not necessarily lead to the same societal consequences, and are perhaps not brought about in the same way.

For example, statistics show that most Asian countries combine t
universal trend of increasingly delayed marriage with the cultural sing
larity of a rare, and very slowly rising, rate of celibacy. Families ne
form later, but they still last longer on average than in the West, a
remain the overwhelmingly prevalent way of living. During the past
years, almost all Asian countries have witnessed a trend towards delay
marriage for women. The exceptions are Japan, China, Myanmar a
Nepal, for very different reasons. Myanmar and Nepal are clearly on
just starting the process of demographic transition and modernizatic
Conversely, Japan underwent this process earlier than any other Asi
nation – the average marriage age rose in Japan over 30 years ag
Finally, China saw a government-enforced policy of late marriage ta
hold *before* any sociological trend tended to achieve the same effect: t
comparative relaxation of marriage rules has merely had the effect
levelling out the average age of marriage.

For all other Asian countries, women tend, on average, to marry
an increasingly greater age, with their actual age at marriage being mu
less uniform than in the past. Male age at marriage moves more slow
and remains more homogeneous.[45] This fairly uniform trend points
a modernizing effect including education, job status and a quest f
lower fertility. A major consequence is that the most negative featu
of Asian marriage and family structures, the relatively inferior positi
of women, is receding throughout Asia.

The trend towards later marriage for women has an obvious correl
tion in analogous declining rates of fertility throughout the regio
Starting with Singapore and Hong Kong in 1958, and ending wi
Vietnam in 1980, all Asian countries have experienced a major fertili
decline. The Four Tigers (Hong Kong, Singapore, Taiwan and Kore
are all down to a total fertility ratio (TFR) under two in 1995, e.g. und
the theoretical replacement rate. But even the Philippines or Vietna
have seen major reductions.[46] Again, China's politically troubled pop
lation policies prevent a period-by-period comparison, but are equivale
in the longer 1955 to 1995 time frame.[47] Further study shows that t
pattern of decline in fertility has followed distinct ethnic and religio
groups: the Japanese move to low fertility came first, followed by Hor
Kong, Singapore, Taiwan and the Chinese overseas communities
Southeast Asia. For these groups, cultural heritage and socio-econom
trends mattered more than the strong family control programm
enforced by governments. Malay and Islamic populations came la
although the views of government towards religion mattered: 'Whe
political leaders are strong and not constrained by religious leaders, fan
ily planning progammes can, if strongly enforced, erode traditional pr

natalist cultural values.'[48] Universalists will find here a carbon copy of the economic development timetable throughout the region. But Confucianists will be more inclined to 'look East' for a demographic modernization that has spread from Japan to the Chinese periphery, and later to Southeast and South Asia through distinct ethnic communities.

The demographic transition differs strongly from that in the West in another important aspect – marriage remains quasi-universal in Asia, with celibacy rates remaining very low, or rising only very slowly over the past decade in a few instances. In 1980, the celibacy rates (measured around age 50) were between 1 and 2 per cent for all Asian countries except Sri Lanka, Myanmar and the Philippines. Temporary deviations occurred in some cases because of single immigrant communities, or after a temporary gender imbalance (war, famine, etc.).[49] In spite of obvious and often publicized trends (such as the threat of the college-educated single women in Singapore, countered by the government with financial rewards for educated parents . . .), the persistence of a very low celibacy rate is similar in urban China, Taiwan or Singapore in the 1980s. It is nearly identical for rural China, Taiwan and South Korea, whose socio-economic levels are strikingly different.[50] In what might be called the Confucianist heartland, there is a stunningly similar social preference for marriage.

Asian customs as a delayed adjustment?

Other Asian societies have begun to change, although slowly, with respect to marriage. Celibacy rates have risen in Japan, Thailand and Indonesia, for different reasons, and there are also signs for Singapore and Hong Kong, albeit from an extremely low starting point. Interestingly, this is often tied neither to divorce or widowhood. Longevity, and an older age at marriage, ensures better compatibility between spouses, actually reducing the divorce rate in some cases (in Indonesia's Java island between 1964 and 1985, the percentage of divorced women actually fell from 7 to 5, the proportion of widows from 6 to 2). In Thailand, celibacy among women is rising somewhat, while in Japan, almost 20 per cent of men remain bachelors today, the highest percentage in Asia.

It is possible that the above trends represent only a cultural time lag. This time lag would delay the adoption of some customs of Western modernization, such as individualism, low childbirth rates and the decline of the extended family. Seen in this light the survival of Asian family ethics and practices is only temporary. Japan shows the way towards adoption of a Westernized and individualistic demography and family pattern, while the Chinese world, with its stubborn belief in cultural superiority, resists change longer than other communities in Southeast Asia. In that case, the above-mentioned trends point only to a slow transition, rather than to a distinct Asian values system.

The problem with sociological arguments based on time lag is that, just as in economic cases of 'catch-up' and 'one-time increases', they can only be verified after the fact. In due course, we will know if the present trends towards adjustment prevail throughout Asia or if distinctive family patterns remain.

Even so, there remains a strikingly distinctive feature. In many cases, Westernization has not simply flowed from the path of economic development, but has been the result of much more deliberate and complex choices by individual communities or by governments trying to engineer demographic outcomes and family structures.

A revival of tradition?

Again, the Chinese example is striking. On the one hand, family planning is an immemorial tradition that by far predates Communism. Even infanticide, abhorrent to the contemporary soul, stems from a choice of group survival over the individual child. China's demography can be said to have been managed by social customs and political philosophy for centuries, avoiding the risk of overpopulation that Malthusian theory predicts.[51] Mao's totalitarian birth control programme was evidently aided by the existence of this tradition, which had proved successful until the late nineteenth century.

On the other hand, instant sociology has instinctively assumed that the group values that went with China's distinct traditions were gone forever. Under Mao's use of collective terror with the Cultural Revolution and its struggle against 'feudal' customs, the family and the individual withered. Then with the advent of a consumer-based individualism and the quest for money in post-Mao China, the traditional family seemed exiled from the stage. China was effectively slated to become a desert of 'only child emperors', as today's pampered babies are indeed called.

Again, a detailed enquiry shows that this is not the case. Young contemporary urban Chinese residents put *more* emphasis on their obligations to the elderly, as opposed to children and careers, than is the case for their own parents. Cynics have noted in the past that co-residence with the elderly was often a function of housing shortage, or that the elderly furnished babysitting and other free services to younger families. Interestingly, there is no correlation between these 'conservative' (as many in the West would put it) family values and other indicators of conservatism, such as working for the military or in officialdom. In many other ways, and particularly regarding sex and marriage, those interviewed display views that are less conservative than their parents'. There are clearly material co-factors, such as the limited geographical mobility that still prevails in the urban job market of China, or the fact that the family was an island of confidence and mutual help during the stormy Maoist years. But it is hard to miss the obvious conclusion. After 30 years of fanatic communism and twenty years of quick-paced economic reform, and 'as urban China enters an era of rapid population ageing, sentiments of filial obligation remain intact'.[52] Try this for size in Paris or in New Jersey.

A disclaimer: Asian core values should only be used as prescribed

The existence of core Asian values has much to do with family relationships and with a religiosity that usually prefers a moral code to holistic beliefs. These Asian values are only what they are: it is perhaps helpful to remember that all of the above arrangements can be said to originate in the defence of closely knit kin groups against a potentially hostile and unpredictable environment. That environment also happens to be Asian. Asian core values are not, as some would have liked to believe, a sure-fire recipe for economic miracles, much less for moral superiority over the West. Filial obligations fulfilled in Baoding do not allow the Chinese leadership to defend negligent and cruel treatment in Shanghai orphanages. The resilience of the family unit in Java does not entitle President Suharto to fight IMF-inspired reforms with claims that Indonesia's Constitution rests on the family as a founding principle.

I am confident that other enquiries can turn up equally valid examples of core Asian values put into practice. The accent on education as a strong goal for the individual and family is one area, all the more striking as most Asian governments have a mixed record on public education policy. They have usually emphasized basic skills and primary school levels, but they consistently neglect the funding and the reforming of the advanced university level. Again, this pattern comes very close to Latin Europe, where higher education is a notorious loser in terms of public financing. Overseas, is it necessary to point out the extraordinary academic success of American-Asian communities in the educational and scientific field? Much of what Paul Krugman has denounced in Asian miracle economies – the lack of educational resources, the underinvestment in science and technology – is true but only a part of the overall picture given the individual family's propensity for educational effort that exists in Asia. Buddhism and seminaries gave countries such as Thailand or even Cambodia very high literacy rates in the past, as did Japanese colonization of Taiwan and to some extent Korea, and the American presence in the Philippines. There is indeed a systemic crisis at work in today's Asia, which is eroding Asian norms and practices in the area of business and government relationships with the private sector. But this erosion of social practices does not imply the downfall of core Asian values, which rest more on the individual, the family, closely-knit social groups and religious or moral beliefs. Asian governments must get their public house in order, and start working on issues they have often taken for granted. When they do, the West will listen again to Asian values. In the meantime, the much-vaunted resilience of Asian societies is an asset to tide them over the crisis. When the Great Hanshin earthquake happened in January 1995, government and administrative disorganization stood in sharp contrast to the quiet and stoicism of Japanese residents, many of whom had never experienced such a disaster in their lifetime. This resilience, not to be confused with passivity or fatalism, is at work today and will repair the damage done by faulty systems and rules.

Asian values remain a slippery notion. They can be addressed at several distinct levels. Asian authoritarian and semi-authoritarian regimes have used them to counter Western pressures on universal rights and rules. The Crash is dealing a mortal blow to the equation between an Asian political and social path and economic success. Yet even at this level, the inference that Asian patterns of behaviour are the root of the crisis is still unfair, as we have seen from our explanation of the Crash and the discussion of rescue policies since the Crash. Attempts to uphold Asian values by Asian political leaders are really efforts to mobilize flagging domestic support. Attempts by the West to deny the existence of Asian values are often a self-serving exercise. While Christopher Patten waved Thomas More and John Hobbes at an amazed Chinese Politburo when he became Governor of Hong Kong in 1992, Kim Dae-Jung, not to mention the Dalai Lama, often resort to the classics of Asian philosophy and religion to legitimize the struggle for democracy. Democracy, indeed, is a universal concept that can be shared between different cultures and values.

Asian values have a strong hold at another level, that of social institutions and practices. The fabric of societies that predate the rule of law in the modern sense none the less included a sense of mutual balance, agreed patterns of social interchange, and economic management models built on the strength of these relationships. The change of rules enforced by international trade liberalization and the opening up of capital markets collides head on with these institutions and practices. At this level, values do not disappear overnight since they perform a function and are deemed to be as legitimate, if not more desirable, than recent laws. It is also somewhat unrealistic to describe Western rules-based systems as if they did not cope with particularism, group solidarity and social practices. Is Victorian hygienism the only option for societies joining the global economy?

Finally, there are core Asian values that are really patterns of anthropological behaviour. Even more than the above-mentioned layers of Asian values, they may differ from one part of Asia to the other. We have chosen several key variables of demography – patterns of marriage and celibacy, attitudes to old age, variations with modernization and urbanization – to emphasize that Asia's societies, however modern, are simply not Western. The fact does not necessarily imply a preference – there may be many advantages to Western societies, starting with a larger degree of personal freedom. This is really a matter of individual choice. But in the aftermath of a disruptive event such as the Crash of 1997, Asian societies on the whole possess more in-built resilience and capacity to bounce back without tremendous institutional and political change than Western-based societies. Time will tell if they are able to build on this cultural asset.

5 The challenge to Asian identity

Beyond the question of moral and cultural values, this chapter explores the heritage and future of Asian social practices and institutions. Can the prevalence of personal relationships over formal law be called a remnant of the past? Is there not a difference between the construction of political democracy and the complete surrender of social practices which are not based on the rule of law? These issues are important because they may help to distinguish between the rule *of* law and the rule *by* law of authoritarian systems, or between formal systems and informal practices and social institutions in Asian democracies. If these distinctions are valid, they justify the claim to a particularistic Asian identity which uniform Western rules cannot completely supersede. The issue is important to economic reformers in the wake of the Crash. For if you can build a new set of economic rules by fighting deviant practices (such as corruption or fraud), it is another thing altogether to replace time-honoured practices and institutional arrangements with laws which are resented as adverse to the social fabric.

The other side of the coin is the issue of a regional Asian identity itself. Above the flow of Hinduism, Buddhism, Confucianism and Islam, beyond the borders of ancient or post-colonial nation-states, in the face of Westernization, is there such a thing as an Asian identity? Was double-digit growth, as former Prime Minister of Japan Ikeda first called it in 1960, the only binding glue for Asia? Will the Crash therefore lead to a return to a natural state of struggle between hostile national or religious groups and states? We will find that there may be little to positively identify a common Asian culture throughout the region. On the other hand, there is a pragmatic aspiration towards building this identity. In the face of the crisis, Asians are not exacerbating their international differences. They are toning them down, at least in the short time span since the beginning of the 1997 Crash.

Asian identity under siege

The Crash of 1997 has brought home a morass of self-doubt, criticism and denigration of Asia's past achievements. This is justified, since the Asian miracle had been hyped with little caution by some of its local exponents, and the rush of money had papered over all the fault lines and cracks that still exist inside and between Asian societies. Today, every one of these real or potential fault lines is exposed to view. For decades since the Second World War, Japan had built a regional diplomacy of accommodation and behind the scene helmsmanship. It is now exposed as a politically weak and policy-wise indecisive country whose international influence is much below its economic achievements. The Indonesian generals and their ancillary relationship to local Chinese businessmen, the Malaysian civil servants with their inherited separate development plan for peninsular ethnic groups, the Thais with their quiet alliance of court business and Chinese financiers and traders, had built an informal road to riches. They gave extremely short shrift to formal democracy, preferring to practise behind the scenes influence or to force consensus on their subjects and fellow citizens. Today, they appear to be fools who cannot fathom, much less practise, what their economies need. Korean firms built their expansion along quasi-military strategies, with extended lines of financing that allowed them to move faster than a Mongol cavalry. They now look like Panzer divisions caught up in winter slush and snow.

Today, in the light of the crisis that lays bare all weaknesses, one sees only the strictures on market interplay and free competition, the potential for racial strife and chaos, the gross social inequality, the limits on liberty imposed in the name of communitarism or religion. One word sums it all up: 'cronyism'.

And now, Asia as the rest of the West

Gone indeed are the days when progressive Western political scientists and anthropologists hailed Asia's traditional society. They had seen in it the traditional clientage or community culture of Asia's countryside, its built-in resistance to naked market economics and the extraordinary accent that tradition placed on group survival.[1] Western social science still makes an exception in the case of the mythical overseas Chinese business groups, whose cosmopolitanism and founders' puritanism the West is forced to recognize as equal to that of its own original capitalists. Otherwise, we simply have no use any more for native business practices and customs. Free trade, incoming foreign investment, the mutual fund revolution and financial liberalization have done away with all this. Just a few years ago, Western businessmen learned how to present business cards with two hands extended, and how to keep quiet in public places. Recent experiences in Tokyo hotel cafeterias lead this author to believe that the West's average sound bite has risen again to a very high level. In November 1997, one of Indonesia's leading person- alities on the Asia-Pacific conference circuit, and a noted critic of president Suharto's family rule, confided his dismay after receiving a group of Wall Street fund managers who had come to assess his country's economy. They were, he said, 25-year-old kids who had learned only moments earlier where Indonesia was on the map, yet they were clearly giving the country's economic future the thumbs down.[2]

It has been at least half a century since Asia got caught in a time warp. The onslaught of colonial and imperialist rivalries began the destruction of traditional societies. Then communist collectivization, and the Cold War-motivated developmental states, began a forced pace modernization (indeed, a much more bloody one for socialist states). The developmental state, with its export priority and its economies of scale, has survived the Cold War and now feeds on a domestic tradi- tion of high savings as well as on emerging country funds. The pace of change for Asians has not slowed down, it has in fact accelerated steadily. Almost no American alive can remember what life was like without cars, let alone piped water or local newspapers. On the other hand, this middle-class and middle-aged Frenchman remembers houses without running water. Many Asians have known days without food, have lived in makeshift houses without sewage (still a major gap in today's Asia) and yet they have discovered fridges, air conditioning, cars and mobile phones, the Internet and satellite TV within the last generation.

The tornado of change has been hugely beneficial to Asians. Social critics who specialize in pointing to remaining pockets of poverty, and avidly chart their expansion during the present economic downturn, often have a distorted perspective of Asian economic growth. Yes, the number of Asia's remaining poor, at 600 to 700 million people according to the Asian Development Bank in 1997, is still the highest in the world. Asia as a whole represents half of the world's population, and the vast majority of this population living below the poverty line is in South Asia or China. In all Northeast Asian states except North Korea poverty has all but disappeared. In many Southeast Asian states it has been vastly reduced over the last two decades.

Yet it is also unfair to expect that immemorial customs, socially binding ties, a sense of belonging to distinct communities, and the hierarchical ties of clienteles or clans, can disappear within the lifetime of a single generation. Certainly, East and even Southeast Asia are notable for the lack of anti-modernist reactions that have engulfed the Middle East and threaten South Asia. Religious integrism is of course present in parts of Southeast Asia's Islamic communities, but it is so far contained within movements that have a gradual and institutional agenda, and are sometimes quite close to their country's political leaders. Even communism, which turns out today to be torn between taking a conservative role and being a political agent of fast modernization, once propelled itself as much against the so-called feudal society as against encroachments from the modern West.

In this sense, Asia has always been the ideal playground of modernizing ideologies and strategies, a putty model in the hands of social engineers, whether they be communist utopianists who turned the peasantry into collective units, or government and business strategists who engineered the economic miracles of the region. When Mao found out that his favourite toy could not properly take a Great Leap Forward, he broke the toy.[3] Some contemporary reactions appear to be to throw the putty model against a wall.

Indeed, the present economic crisis and the advice offered to, or thrown at Asia, can be summed up in a catchall imperative – 'grow up, do as we do'. Open up, convert to market rules, adopt financial transparency, place regulation over preference, give up cronyism (and the relationships that go with it) for equal competition (and the individualism that goes with it). But what the opportunity of the Crash presents as a modest technical proposal to crank up the engine of the economic miracle is in fact tantamount to asking for a political revolution. In the words of one optimistic pre-Crash observer of Southeast Asia, 'Strong ties between leaders and the economic elite in buoyant economic circumstances help explain why crises of legitimacy are rare in Southeast Asia'.[4] The same phrase, word for word, could have been written about Japan's 'one party and a half democracy' with its incestuous relationship between Liberal Democrat Party politicians, high civil servants and business firms and lobbies. Or about Deng and Jiang Zemin's China, where the Party bureaucracy, the State firm network and the private businesses they have spun off or protected also form a triangle. The Chinese regime's recently popularized plan of combining these interests by forming Korean-like *chaebols* speaks volumes about the inescapable relationship between market and officials.

Take away the 'buoyant economic circumstances', and you do have the prospect of a crisis of legitimacy in Asia. But remove the 'strong ties between leaders and the economic elite', and you throw a very large spanner indeed in the works of the savings and investment model that has made Asia's economic performance in the past. Let us remember Asia has not prospered in spite of the Asian model, but thanks to it, and to international willingness to put up additional capital at different stages in post-war history.

Indeed, the other side of the coin has been a stubborn ability of Asian individuals and groups to move back to institutions and practices from the past whenever possible, or a haunting nostalgia for these traditions when such a move is impossible. And in almost all cases, modernization, or more accurately Westernization, has remained partial. After the Maoist storm of communes and mass mobilization, the Chinese peasants by and large went back to their ancestral customs. Generations of instant sociologists have suggested that Japan was 'changing' and becoming 'more like us' through its very economic prowess. To this day, the assertion remains to be proven at the level of social customs, although political views are fast divorcing the post-war party system.

The ideal of piecemeal modernization

Partial modernization has always been the objective of Asian elites, ever since the reform and self-strengthening movements of the late nineteenth century got under way. This preference is self-evident for political and business leaders who equate authority, and discreet personal arrangements far from the public eye, with success. But the consensus may extend beyond the public leaders and private owners of Asia. In 1994, the American political scientist David Hitchcock polled 100 members of what one could call East and Southeast Asia's intellectual power elite – academics and other influential 'speakers, writers, or scholars'.[5] Within the large choice of societal and individual values they were presented with, an orderly society and 'harmony' were by far the first choices of Asian respondents, followed, one must recognize, by 'official accountability'. 'Think for one's self' was cited as an important choice in only 10 per cent of the sample. Looking back on this poll after the 1997 Crash, David Hitchcock commented: 'The IMF and its American and European cohorts would do well to take these Asian assessments seriously. The recovery of the region's economies will require blending financial reforms with ways of life many East Asians want to hold on to. Cleaning up unreliable financial institutions is one thing, but washing away differing behavioural priorities in a tidal wave of globalization is something else.'[6]

Europeans reading these lines, of course, will recognize the familiar feeling of malaise brought on by globalization. Indeed, fast-track Asia has up to now experienced only the positive side of the global economy. Even children working for ten cents an hour in foreign-owned garment factories were better off than in the poverty of their original surroundings, while European textile workers who lost average-paying jobs took a bottom line loss. In the past decade, wage hikes in emerging Asia, from South Korea to Malaysia, have often become huge and changed the way of life of Asia's working classes. Asia is about to experience the other side of the global coin. Asian elites are clearly not prepared for it, and had instead developed a largely consensual view of economic and business policies, a consensus that did not extend, however, to officialdom and political practice. Western liberals reading the above paragraph, not to mention the tenured Marxist academics[7] at many European state universities, will think this Asian elite and middle class societal consensus is another typical case of what the French writer Julien Benda once called 'la trahison des clercs'[8] – intellectuals betraying the people and lapping up their masters' ideology. Indeed, some of China's top political dissidents bemoan the 'running dog' tradition that makes Confucian intellectuals stick with their masters rather than publicize the truth.

This view is only partly justified. There is in fact no elite support in Asia for the most visible abuses of political authority. Corruption constitutes the most frequent target of public criticism and urban demonstrations, from Manila (1986, the overthrow of Marcos), Rangoon (1988, the surge against Burma's junta), Beijing (1989, the Tiananmen Square protest), Bangkok (1992, the middle class against the military regime) and Jakarta (1998, Indonesia's students against *Bapak* (Father) Suharto). Indeed, intellectuals, Asia's newspapers and the middle classes they often represent are torn between two trends – on the one hand, they have democratizing requests that inevitably point to the Western way, its checks and balances and its accent on individual choice. On the other hand, they are prone to a recurrent nostalgia for a lost Asian world where relationships and the sense of belonging to communities mattered more. They are also highly sensitive to the relativism of many Western critics, and to their ignorance of untold past sufferings.

The nostalgia for dependence

It is therefore incorrect to think that only establishment intellectuals hark back to tradition, as a sop for their masters under attack from Western quarters. The most independent intellectuals, and in particular those who do not need the State's hand to feed them, often display an intense unhappiness with the modernization process. Today's most popular art form in Asia is the cinema. It often reveals a self-awareness of the persisting crack between the compelling and haunting force of tradition, even in its most wicked forms, and the self-realizing but emotionally and culturally barren prophecy of modernity.

From 1995 to 1996, three talented East Asian movie directors made films directly related to emotional attachment in the context of gangs. Asian filmmakers are certainly not the first to find that movies about violence spiced with sex make for large audiences. However, two of their three films were definitely not of the blockbuster variety. These are *Cyclo* (1995), by the Vietnamese-French Tran Anh Hung, and *Good Men, Good Women* (1996), by the Taiwanese Hou Hsiao-hsien. The third, admittedly more commercial, is *Shanghai Triad* (1995) by the Chinese Zhang Yimou. All these movies involve women caught in a sentimental relationship with a gangster and the near impossibility of breaking the attachment.

For Hou Hsiao-hsien, Taiwan's leading director, and one whose films all describe a vanishing past, *Good Men, Good Women* is a downbeat sequel to the romantic depiction of his island's history. Attachment to a hoodlum is the only emotion left to his main character after the earlier tragic political history of Taiwan has ended. In a land that is now converted to perpetual fax and cellular communications, fast-food joints and exercise at the gym, it becomes clear that the lead actress's attachment to a petty gangster has nothing to do with self-interest. Oddly, in this modern wasteland of individual materialism, gangster brotherhoods seem to draw towards them remaining sentimental attachment to the past.

Vietnamese-French Tran Anh Hung, earlier known for his emotional *The Scent of the Green Papaya*, starts *Cyclo* with the lure of a secret gang for a poor Hanoi family, where a young woman falls for a gangster and her brother is made to work for them. Modernity is an Antonioni-like absurd scene of Western tourists lounging at the new local Hilton. While the family wrecks itself on the harsh truth of gangland, it is also subtly made clear that there was no other option than to live an interesting, if criminal, life. In the final scene they escape alive, but back to the empty street life of belatedly modernizing Hanoi.

Finally, Zhang Yimou, the founder of China's fifth-generation school of filmmakers and its best-known director in the West, has cast his favourite actress, Gong Li, as the concubine of a Shanghai 1930s Mafia godfather. A 14-year-old boy from the countryside is recruited as her servant on the basis of having the same surname as the godfather. Zhang Yimou, who makes his compromises with State censorship, has explained his purpose as warning his countrymen against materialist greed, not political oppression. But neither the mistress nor the boy is really looking for money. They are simply caught up, until the end, in the partly emotional, partly forced relationship with the gang leader. In the film's final scene, where the boss allows the boy to live on, he is tied and hanged upside down from a rope, while coins rain on him. The lesson is not about money – you do not end up rich or poor, you end up loyal and possibly rich, or disloyal and very much dead. The movie is about traditional authority, not money.

In all three movies, bondage and the importance of subservience and loyalty in personal relationships take precedence over materialistic aspirations, yet none of the filmmakers romantically fantasizes his subjects as an Oriental Bonnie and Clyde couple. One should not jump from this cultural coincidence among three East Asian cultures to the conclusion that Asians prefer binding ties and cronyism to bland democracy and free market opportunities. None of these movies idealizes gangland life, and the stark picture they paint is also an apt metaphor for traditional authoritarian rule. Were we to investigate the theme of broken family or sentimental ties in general, we would indeed find hundreds of Asian movies made along those lines. But movie makers are at their best when they chronicle the pain of transition, and in this respect East Asian films have replaced post-war Italian movies as moving portraits, in both senses of the word, of their societies. The movement forward is indeed at least as important as the pain they record. If we believe movies to be a monitor of their period, then Asia is indeed modernizing, but in pain. The deepest anxiety it feels about this modernization process lies in the loss of personal relationships, even with the dependence and exploitation they often imply.

The culture of personal relationships

When individuals cannot maintain the emotional attachments they crave, or if these links prove ill-suited to a new way of life, they usually form substitute relationships with patrons that bring an acceptably similar form of security and gratification. We should take note of the fact that in several contexts of Asia's modernization, the relationships that are now called cronyism or nepotism or 'going through the back door'[9] have become more, not less, important in recent decades. This is not so much cultural relativism diverging from universal values as a reaction to forced or instant modernization. A modern utilitarian system is created that recycles the old core values of Asian community relations. The system derives its justification from ancient customs, but it has adapted to serve new purposes. In feudal or Meiji days, high officials would indeed be entertained by geishas courtesy of the merchants who needed their good will. In the recent past, some of Japan's finest have apparently exchanged titbits of monetary policy news with private firms over dinner in no-pants hostess clubs. Under the rules of the guided economy that the Meiji created, and that were perfected in various forms until the late 1980s, there was in fact nothing wrong with favouring a particular firm. It was the legitimate purpose of government to choose competent private hands and to 'guide' those hands with authority. Conversely, it was traditional for merchants to express appreciation of officials with gifts. Geishas were merely the frosting on the cake. Today, we can conclude that traditional custom is degenerating (bar hostesses are really not culturally equal to geishas), yet selective public guidance of the economy has remained a shared imperative. Instead of focusing on the minor corruption involved, should we not conclude more significantly that the traditional interrelationships between various orders in society (officials, merchants, entertainers) has never been broken up, and that they have remained an effective management tool of contemporary Japan? Similarly, in the late 1980s Korea, monetary gifts from *chaebols* and more humble private firms were still strictly codified according to occasion, from top to bottom of the administrative hierarchy. It was not just former president Roh Dae-woo who took home several hundred million dollars as a result. Almost *any* official had his envelope according to the prescribed scale and on the ritual occasions of the year.

Social practices, public customs, individual strategies are indeed recycled from a historical and cultural repertoire. They possess a life, and perhaps a legitimacy of their own, which will challenge new laws for a very long time.

Ever since the American occupation era reform of Japan's administered economy, with the new emphasis on fair trade and competition, and even more after 1987, when new financial rules were imported from Wall Street and other leading Western markets,[10] decision-makers have been operating under what they call the change of rules. In the 1950s, major scandals appeared over favours extended to particular industries at a time of tight resources, but this very seldom led to more than token punishment, and the public generally pardoned tainted servants of the people. Since the late 1980s though, the rules of the financial market run against the dictates of relationships – it is not done any more to allocate stock profits to your friends, and losses to the rest of the crowd. This may seem crude. It is both astonishing and revealing that the quintessential Japanese financial scandal over the past decade, the *tobashi* deal, repeats itself in the same fashion. Through sleight of hand, a broker shifts the profits towards insiders (or to a *yakuza*-related figure, or to 'hundreds' of high officials, as one politician under investigation recently claimed). The resulting harm to market confidence, once these feats are revealed, is enormous. But if a society keeps compulsively repeating the same actions, is it not because there is an implicit code of behaviour that is stronger than the new law?[11] This is indeed what Japan's Vice-Minister of Finance Eisuke Sakakibara once called an 'anthropocentric' model of capitalism.[12] A whole area of Japanese white-collar crime has been opened up, not by a change of behaviour in the subjects, but because of a change in laws over custom. Faced with stiff new regulations, the relation-conscious individual will often infringe them to serve his friends and contacts. On the road, however, the same individual rarely exceeds speed limits. On the other hand, the average individualistic Western driver will very often drive above the speed limits (and lobby to have these limits raised . . .), while he gets much more easily used to the impersonal rules of modern finance.

Connections vs bureaucracy: the Chinese case

In China, the need to nurture social contacts may be dictated by Confucius' well-known prescription of five essential relationships, and by the philosophical importance of attending to human sentiments. But *guanxixue*, literally the science of relationships, is an art form which appeared only in the waning days of Maoist China, and has flowered in the modernizing decades after 1977. The aberrations of Maoism and the extreme struggle against the individual during the regime's mass movements until the Cultural Revolution have brought, in reaction, a revival and a reappraisal of these personal relationships. *Guanxi* (relations) have their code, which prescribes that one should not pay too close attention to the repayment of favours. I happen to know of an old man who, because of his landlord family background, was detained in a pig's hovel in 1948 in Shandong province after the area was 'liberated' by the Red Army. Every night, a neighbour covertly deposited some food at the entrance of the pigsty, and thus saved the old man without ever revealing his face to him. The landlord always speculated that his own formerly benevolent attitude had thus been repaid handsomely at a tragic time.[13] This is the quintessential type of story that can be used to legitimize the use of personal relationships for all purposes, because it rests on a compelling emotional basis. In her insightful study on the re-emergence of *guanxi* in post-Mao China, Mayfair Yang explains that this resulted from 'social resistance against total state saturation', with a return of 'personalistic ethics in everyday life'.[14] Recognizing that personal networks serve the powerful above anybody else, she none the less mentions their enduring moral values. Liang Shuming was a Republican era reformist thinker who produced several syntheses of Chinese culture and philosophy. He wrote in 1949 that British and American societies were based on the individual, the Soviet Union on society itself (along with Mao's future China, one might add), but that China's society was based on 'relationships'.[15]

At this point, a striking analogy presents itself between the new tangle of personal relationships and interests that has sprung up throughout fast-growing Asia, and 'parallel systems' of relationships which appeared in other circumstances of modernization. In his classic study of the Sicilian Mafia's historical relation to its environment, Eric Hobsbawm writes: 'It is a mistake to believe that institutions which look archaic are of great antiquity'.[16] He suggests that 'parallel systems' occur in 'the transition to a capitalist economy', or 'in more general situations of "structural duality" which may be due to the coexistence and interaction of two completely different societies (e.g. Western economic penetration or colonial conquest of primitive societies), to the tension between a developing new socio-economic system and an old one . . . or simply . . . to a society so structured as to produce periodic breakdowns of the system of social relationships'.[17] And he insists that these parallel systems, however oppressive they may be for a majority, and profitable to only a minority, serve to maintain a code of conduct among individuals and social classes in periods of great flux. In rural China, custom calls those individuals who do not know how to maintain a personal relationship network 'dead doors'(*si menzi*). The custom of gifts is not confined to traditional events but is now extended to newly created occasions – for example, married women who undergo sterilization now receive gifts from a social circle that extends far beyond their family and close acquaintances.[18]

Relationships, gift giving and the seeking of favours cannot be reduced to cronyism and nepotism. These last two social practices themselves are not in contradiction to traditional teachings, but represent indeed an abusive interpretation. In the ironical words of the Han Feizi Legalist tradition: 'To perform private favours for old friends is called not neglecting friendship. To distribute alms with public funds is called being benevolent . . . To strain the law to shield one's relatives, is called being a 'superior person' . . . To pass out favours and gain a mass following is called winning the people.'[19] Of course, the art of relationship is then stretched to serve all seasons. *Guanxi* can serve to limit bureaucratic authority with a reminder of the gift-giving economy that applies even to officials, in practice at local levels of the bureaucracy. Or it can be an extension and recognition of the network of privilege and special interests that undermines an impartial state.

The reciprocity of *guanxi* often disappears at high levels. In China, this is because it is simply not recognized, and is in fact fought as illegal, by law as well as by some central political and state leaders. During the 1989 events, the only saving grace of Prime Minister Li Peng was the lack of attacks or even allusions to corruption or nepotism against himself and his family (a quality that seemed to be less often emphasized in later years).[20] Prime Minister Zhu Rongji recently inaugurated his mandate with stern calls for the fight against nepotism and corruption, and thus revived the legalist struggle against debased Confucianism. Deng Xiaoping's succession was in fact marked by a sociological defeat of the so-called 'princeling faction' (*daizi dang*), or the close relatives of leaders who had come to colonize the nexus between bureaucracy and private firms.

In Southeast Asian circumstances, it may be hard to cite this tradition to justify the level of privileged business connections, family preference and graft that has accompanied economic growth. Indeed, there is a sharp departure from tradition apparent in Singapore's reinterpretation of the Confucian tradition to exclude graft and favouritism, or the Philippines' Western-like muckraking press that denounces corruption and gangs, in contrast to the complacent attitude of other Southeast Asian cultures. In the melancholic and tell-all tone that is now Dr Mahathir's, 'we are not corrupt because we want to be corrupt. But people . . . talk about crony capitalism as if we go and find cronies. What we do is when people have the capacity to do well, we give them a hand,'[21] 'We are willing to do away with that', added Mahathir in a rare admission of the problem. Others are not so sure. In several Southeast Asian cultures, cronyism and graft are inseparable from the tradition of political power with the age-old apanages[22] that it bestows on kings and aristocracies. It is also hard to distinguish it from the reverse or positive discrimination (to quote a very Western idiom) that has been put in place to protect local, formerly community- and land-based ethnic groups from the tough market competition by Chinese, Indian and other overseas communities. Western firms and expatriates can after all be seen as a latterday example: the conflict between native-born and 'sojourner' Southeast Asians did not start with the advent of foreign direct investment and open capital markets.

The culture of corruption

Examples such as President Suharto's gilded family are misleading. Of course, the Indonesian former first family's wealth was phenomenal, by any standards, and it grew even larger in the last years, as the flow of foreign investment suddenly increased. In true analogy with the former sultans' power over merchant activities, the Suharto clan with their favourite *cukong* (Chinese businessmen like Liem Sioe Liong and the Salim group, who appear constantly in rosters of the world's largest fortunes) had their hand in every profitable activity of the country. To some extent Suharto was a unique case. First because he held power for so long and also because of his mastery of the military establishment. Second because his central Javanese origins and culture pervaded his style of rule impenetrability, unaccountability, and led to manic attention to court etiquette and personal behaviour around him. It would probably be more useful to point out that in spite of the extreme corruption that pervades Indonesia, Suharto was no Mobutu or even Ferdinand Marcos: throughout his long reign, Indonesia's economic development and most Indonesians' income and livelihood demonstrably prospered.

It is indeed more important to understand why the culture of corruption, far from being essentially tied to authoritarian and military-based regimes, is so widespread in Asian-style democracies. Here again, the Italian analogy presents itself: perhaps the only central government in Italian history that stamped out most Mafia activities was Mussolini's fascist movement. Similarly, one can argue that Singapore's successful stamping out of most corruption and organized crime has much to do with its authoritarianism and public developmentalism.

Whereas traditional Asian bureaucracies offered most opportunities for graft in the field of revenue collection, modernizing democracies with rising economies and loose controls offer most of these opportunities in the field of expenditure and outlay for project. There are therefore obvious connections between the comparatively recent system of elected politicians and the resuscitated thugs and godfathers who utilize tradition. Two examples, those of recent Thai and Taiwanese politics, will serve to illustrate this connection. Thailand witnessed throughout the 1980s the rise of local figures who combined legitimate business activities with political clout over the police and elected politicians, and underworld sources of revenue. A revealing study from Bangkok's leading Chulalongkorn University depicts these new *jao pho*, named after the spirits of those who have known a violent death and need to be appeased like a malevolent god.[23] These figures are usually new rich Sino-Thai businessmen, who ensure their longevity not only with armed thugs, but

also by manipulating parliamentary elections in favour of their candidates – they are in fact known also as 'vote banks' for their ability to
channel popular support. One such character, Kamnan Bo of Chonburi,
a former wage hand in fishing boats, extends his business from construction, trade with nearby Cambodia, tourism in high-profile Pattaya Beach,
and electoral politics, where many of his own relatives succeed in various
parties. In typical fashion, Bo is a consummate philanthropist, tirelessly
donating money to temples, erasing slums and generally advertising an
easy-going personality. Similar *jao pho* exist almost everywhere in
Thailand, with few successful attempts to unseat their political mouth-
pieces: in 1990, more than 60 per cent of Thailand's locally elected
politicians listed their occupation as 'businessmen', usually in the building
industry.

Reports about Thai worthies and their notorious connections with the
Golden Triangle-related drug business are of course part of this picture.
The part, in fact, that receives the most attention, because of the high
international interest in thwarting the drug trade. In 1992, Narong
Wongwan, MP from Northern Thailand, was prevented from becoming
Prime Minister in the government formed after a military coup because
he had been denied a US visa on suspicion of drug connections. But
the pattern of corruption is much more pervasive. The authors of the
above-mentioned study, in spite of their democratic leanings,
make no bones in noting, for example, that the advent of Chatichai
Choonhavan as Prime Minister in 1988 – Thailand's first elected MP
to hold the post since 1976 – also coincided with a spectacular rise in
the level of corruption. A former officer turned diplomat, Chatichai was
ousted by the military, who confiscated some of his wealth, in 1992.

Somewhat forlornly, our Thai social scientists end their study with a
tough dilemma. 'There are grounds to conclude that it is more harmful
to have a society being dominated by an honest military than to have
a parliamentary system with corrupt politicians. At least under a democratic framework there is the possibility of developing a civil society with
the will to control corruption.'[24] They cite two comparative perspectives
– the rise of the Italian Mafia, again, but equally the corruption of
municipal politics in early twentieth century America, also a dynamic
economy in transition after its frontier phase. Indeed, the former ghosts
of Tammany Hall,[25] where the honest politicians were categorized
as those who 'stayed bought', float around Asia. Money politics, graft
and clientelism are not traditions that oppose change. They have been
on the rise as change – both political and economical – occurred.
Democratic forces have criticized them, but few have succeeded, even
locally. Chamlong Srimuang did so in Bangkok. The former general

and governor of the Metropolitan Region, an ascetic Buddhist known as Mr Clean, campaigned against the military coup government in 1992 and was elected mayor in 1996. His campaign symbol was a broom. The only successful political hero of Thailand's new middle class is therefore a maverick rather than a stereotype.

Taiwan raises some of the same issues, including that of the relationship between divided communities and organized crime. Behind the former facade of Kuomintang mainlanders and the new aspirations towards a Taiwanese nation, there lies in fact a jigsaw puzzle. It includes groupings of Fujian-originated Taiwanese who still hanker after their original communities, as well as Hakkas and local splinter communities who have a keen sense of their prerogatives.

Gangs tied to gambling, prostitution and the exploitation of minorities are nothing new in Taiwan, and some of them, such as the notorious Bamboo Gang, have always had ties with the upper echelons of the ruling Kuomintang. The Bamboo Union, the Heavenly Way Alliance and the Four Seas, are old-established gangs, joined by smaller ethnic groups. But, along with the rising prosperity of the island, the advent of political freedom, contested elections and administrative decentralization that put many decisions in the hands of local politicians after 1987, have spawned new underground activities. Cases of extortion rose by 75 per cent in 1990, and kidnappings have become a daily threat. In the old days of Gimo Chiang Kai-shek, the iron rule of the security organs partly took as its justification the sense of public and private safety it ensured. Since the mid-1980s, government outlays for public works have quadrupled, and kick-offs from contractors have become a steady source of income for local officials and politicians. Even more controversial is the connection between politicians and gangsters, a connection that is inextricably tied to the pattern of vote buying in Taiwanese politics.

According to some estimates, between a third and half of all elected legislators have ties with the underworld. It does not turn them into full-time criminals either, as filmmaker Hou Hsiao-hsien has again provocatively argued. In his last flick (*Goodbye South, Goodbye*, 1996), a parliamentarian successfully mediates a conflict and kidnapping between two aspiring bad boys and the locally established gang. What the police cannot achieve, old-fashioned personal mediation easily replaces. Former Justice Minister Ma Ying-Jeou, who led a remarkable anti-corruption drive in 1994 to 1995 and was forced out of office when his efforts went too far, speaks of rooting out the *hong bao*[26] culture, and rightly recognizes 'a lot of these people being indicted are my friends or acquaintances. This is really the most difficult part.'[27]

Illegal activities had turned to modern activities by the early 1990s. Taiwan's longstanding stock market restrictions – and in particular the earlier limitation to only four officially recognized security firms – led to a huge rise in 'grey' market transactions, in a nation where one citizen in four owns stocks. When additional players were authorized, this led to a free-for-all lunge into security trading. Security firms frequently collapse, which has led to sudden downturns in the Taipei Share Index. (For example, the index lost 15 per cent in October 1994 as a result of bouncing cheques from an established broker . . .). Eighteen parliamentarians immediately sprung to the defence of the firm, apparently out of fear of losing their own accounts.[28]

In 1996 to 1997, the question of illegal activities came to a head in Taiwan. The murders of several prominent local politicians and candidates showed that there was no longer any limit on the gangs' activities. The chairman of Kaohsiung (Taiwan's second-largest city) council and the chief magistrate of Taoyuan (one of Taipei's wealthiest satellite cities) were killed. In Taoyuan, eight other council members were also assassinated in the same attack. There was the stabbing of several leading opponents including the Democratic Progressive Party's secretary-general, and even more ominously to the general public a wave of kidnappings, which included the daughter of TV personality Pai Ping-ping. Ma Ying-jeou's successor at the Ministry of Justice, Liao Cheng-hao, declared that Taiwan ran the risk of becoming 'a second Sicily'. President Lee Teng-hui's, whose costly electoral politics are often associated with the rise in illegal funding and underworld connections, has seen his popularity plummet as a result, in spite of having stood up against China's military offensive in March 1996.

At nearly five times the per capita income of Thailand, and with a leading role in global high-technology developments, Taiwan's society is a much more critical factor for the future of Asia than Thailand, not to mention China: with a time lag of a generation, China tends to follow the footsteps of Taiwan's economy and society. The lesson from the Taiwan experience should caution Western observers not to resort to snap judgements on Asian politics and social developments. Over less than a decade, Taiwan has gone from dictatorship to the first fully-fledged democracy in Chinese history, with a remarkably unrestrained press and an enormously creative culture. Taiwan's entrepreneurs usually run circles around their foreign competitors, and if 'small is beautiful' had not been invented elsewhere, they would be a living advertisment for the motto. Together with millions of middle-class professionals and yuppies, they are creating an Asian New Age culture, where traditional teahouses, the practice of *qi gong* (Chinese respiratory gymnastics) go hand in hand with an immoderate taste for expensive cars and French claret. Above all, Taiwan is the only economy in Asia that did not suffer directly from the First Crash of 1997 to 1998 – with very little specu-lation directed at the currency or capital market. The strength of its private entrepreneur culture, and resources from its educational and R&D sector seem to make up for financial market practices that are often as opaque and self-serving as in the rest of emerging in Asia.

Yet Taiwan's politics and public economy are riddled with the special relationships, shady dealings and complete opacity now universally ascribed as the main reason for Asia's fall from grace. These issues have become the first theme of domestic politics. One can speculate that the next stage in the island's history will be a cleaning up of the money politics that have spread with the democratic process. One man, the mayor of Taipei, Chen Shui-bian who is a moderate and often autonomous representative of the DPP opposition, may represent this aspiration in the next presidential election scheduled in early 2000. He is so strong that the ruling Kuomintang has felt compelled to push forward none other than former Justice Minister Ma Ying-jeou, his honest and courageous record now coming in handy. Just as the citi-zens of Tokyo or Osaka, fed up with the corruption and immobility of LDP politics, elected two former actors rooting for clean politics in 1996, and just as the voters of Bangkok have plebiscited Chamlong Srimuang, Taipei's electoral politics announce the wave of the future.

The Chinese are still Chinese

Asian politics are still in transition from clientary authoritarianism to citizen democracy. Unlike most of Southeast Asia, the three Northeast Asian political cultures (Japan, Korea and Taiwan) do not satisfy them-selves with 'trimming the *Banyan* tree' (Michael Vatikiotis), leaving most of their citizens under the shadow of their leaders. But even Japan's older democracy, or Korea and Taiwan, which are most advanced among the 'third wave democracies',[29] remain far from upholding the gospel of market democracy, pervasive rule of law and individualism that is being preached as the only way out of the Crash.

Such realities attest to the impossibility of choosing between global-ization and universal values as a tool for renewed modernization and growth, and the preservation of Asian cultural relativism as a goal along-side this modernization. For the past century, East and West have converged but never coincided. The tension of Western values and norms, and their usefulness in the development process, is everywhere apparent in Asia. The Crash of 1997 is certainly a major stage in the acculturation process for most of Asia. Yet a complete changeover of norms that would turn Asia into 'the rest of the West' flies in the face of every anthropological, cultural and political reality.

At the most, the Asian way existed as a set of political and economic recipes that have cooked up the fast growth authoritarianism of yesteryear, under the guise of keeping the Oriental soul intact while harnessing Western knowledge as a tool. The magic pot that brewed this elixir was spilled on the ground after the Crash. But at the least, a cultural interpretation of Asian societies is justified by stubborn resistance to the change of rules that is an essential component of the universalistic prescription. In 1935, the liberal and pro-West philosopher Hu Shi wrote: 'When two different cultures come into contact, the force of competition and comparison can partially destroy the resistance and conservatism of a certain culture. . . . It can never completely wipe out the conservative nature of an indigenous culture. The Chinese are still Chinese'.[30] These words are strikingly modern. Today's market culture is indeed comparative and competitive. Yet, unlike the brutal Qin Shi Huangdi Emperor (or Mao's violence, which took its cue from this historical model), and in spite of the havoc that an economic depression creates, the market economy will still have to come to terms with Asian culture and social fabric.

The adoption of democratic legitimacy and the electoral process, often viewed as Asia's chief stumbling block, proves easier in fact for a majority of Asian societies from Japan and Korea to Thailand, than a thorough and genuine adaptation to the rule of law. Significantly, the most advanced trading and financial posts of Asia, Singapore and Hong Kong, owe their continuing success to a constant emphasis on the latter, while their democratization has remained embryonic (Hong Kong) or tilted towards the party in power (Singapore). Yet both are to a large extent Western colonial creations, with Hong Kong having remained so until July 1997, and Singapore being often described as more Western than Asian. The markets love them indeed, over and above the region's true third-wave democracies (Korea, Taiwan, Thailand, and the Philippines).

Questioning the existence of Asia

But beyond this Asian reluctance to come to terms with the wider implications of modernization, it is much harder to spot a positive Asian identity in the making. The Crash and the breakdown of regional solidarity and cooperation that it has entailed, the country-by-country approach to emergency solutions and structural reforms as a way out of the mess, and ultimately the complete lack of region-wide agreement on the real roots of the crisis, are telltale signs. The goal of ASEAN, and increasingly Asian, unity has been put forward over the last generation by most of the region's political leaders, drawing an ever-wider circle towards this magnet. China's integration into all of the region's institutions and fora, the three Indochinese countries' recognition of a regional kinship, and the world-wide participation of outside powers to regional dialogue are but one side of the coin. In the dilemma well known by the European community as one between 'extending' or 'deepening' unity, Asian states have clearly opted for a process that implies much dilution, rather than interdependence. In the raging storm generated by the financial crisis, many of the Asian ships have come loose from these weak moorings and started drifting. This is a crucial test of Asia's ambitions to become a region rather than a geopolitical and geoeconomic space. But is the region really ready for it?

For most of the twentieth century, the reality of Asia was taken for granted by the West. Whether out of the nostalgic exoticism of Somerset Maugham, the discreet eroticism of Pierre Loti, or from the various colonial and military experiences that this century has produced, the myth of the Orient took hold of Western minds. With key historical events such as the communist victory in China or the so-called people's wars in Indochina, the myth occasionally became a haunting threat. Many French films about Grandpa's Indochina, scores of stories, real and fictional, involving American Vietnam veterans, attest to the power of this myth. Yet this was a time when, beyond the spiritual layers of Hinduism, Buddhism and Confucianism, the only real sense of Asian unity was imported. Marx entered Confucius' temple on a porter's chair, as the Chinese liberal philosopher Hu Shi saw the event. Victor Hugo became the object of a religious cult in Caodaist Vietnam. These were all expressions of a 'cargo cult' phenomenon that encouraged Asians to digest Western and modern culture at one swoop. The only other avenue to modernity was Japan, and many Asians used it too in the years that led up to the great Pacific War. But Japan was also the first Asian country that wished to see itself as a quasi-Western society, creating its own empire in rivalry with the white colonizers. Again, the soft power of the West prevailed not so much against, but also beneath the samurai sword.

Because colonial historians from the turn of the century until the 1930s saw Asian peoples and cultures at the sub-state level of tribes, fiefdoms and archaic societies, they seldom emphasized the potential for clashes among Asians. Surely, there were flashes of fire to be expected from the Malay *kampungs*, great deceptions engineered by stony-faced

Chinese, threats from Korean roving bandits. But apart from the Japanese, who were the only quasi-modern State and a permanent geopolitical factor, most Asians were seen as benign, somewhat inactive, potentially rowdy but unlikely to start major conflicts. This was unity by default. For their part, Orientalists never questioned the unity of Asia because they never took seriously the contemporary Asia that was offered to their colonial eyes. They preferred digging in the ruins for the remains of the vast spiritual empires that had stretched across latter-day colonial borders. And in those digs, they found the overlapping cultures that made the Orient feel real to them.

Then came the decades of independence, Cold War and finally sustained economic growth spreading to almost every remote corner of Asia. Paradoxically, Asia became real when Asians began to build their own states, e.g. to create borders between themselves. Where Orientalists saw a 'Sinicized Asia', a 'Javanese crossroad' or an Indochinese peninsula, Asians mostly dressed in Western suits and ties (the Nehru suits and *batik* shirts usually came as an afterthought) created nations, armies, industries and finally stock exchanges. Europeans should not be surprised that you need to build up borders and sovereign states to begin creating a sense of a region. After all, the Roman or Carolingian empires were not European, but only Roman or Carolingian. You need first the constant interaction that existed between ancient Greek or Italian Renaissance cities to build up a cultural proximity and interchange. To this one must add walls, borders, armies, states and finally diplomats, international relations strategists and political philosophers to turn a cultural community into the construction of a geopolitical region. Indeed, the national and citizen revolutions of the mid-nineteenth century, which led to total war among European states, also launched the political idea of Europe. The foundations of Europe were laid on the cinders of the Second World War. Cooperative security, shared institutions and federalism are not borne out of the state of nature. They emerge from the hard-learned lessons of conflict. Even today, one still finds parochial Europeans for whom the only reality of their continent is the Christian realm, and who see divisions between Danish, German and French, if not Flemish and Walloon Belgians, as insuperable obstacles to European integration. President Milosevic and the latter-day Serbian crusade to exterminate Moslems (whom they call Turks) bear vivid testimony to the remaining echo from the dark age of the Crusades.

Westerners should therefore come to Asia with a realistic awareness that the unity of region and civilization is neither a spontaneous nor a schoolboy undertaking. Yet once they pass Calcutta, they often raise their expectations and demands. The existence of Asia seems to require a geopolitical version of *All Men Are Brothers* to be played out as a merry tune over the region. Surely, the bamboo curtain separating People's China as well as the North Korean or North Vietnamese states from their neighbours prevented the emergence of a larger sense of Asia. This was the case in Europe too, where 'Europe from Brest to Vladivostok', in General de Gaulle's own words, was an even less credible phrase.

A more recent phenomenon has taken hold among social scientists. From the time that Asia's cityscape began replacing shantytowns with skyscrapers, unspoiled forests were cut down to profit new plantation empires, and pi-pa music was replaced with incomprehensible Asian pop culture, it has become academically fashionable for the West to doubt the existence of Asia. For it is no longer the pristine paradise of archaic communities, except at the edge of the primeval jungle, or in 500-dollar a night coral atolls. Paul Gauguin, the French painter who specialized in wonderful Tahitian scenes, anticipated this trend in the Orientalist tradition when he idolized the Tahitian community but despised the Chinese coolies and shopkeepers who were going to ruin the paradise. Unfortunately, the popularity of Tibetan culture in the West owes as much to nostalgia for an Asian Noah's Ark and to hostility for contemporary China's materialistic culture as to the plight of the Tibetans themselves. A new paradigm has taken hold. When Asian cities become alike, with their smog, coffee shops and overblown financial centres, Westernization is deemed to have destroyed Asia. The Orientalists refuse to recognize this Asia. For the hundredth anniversary of the French School of the Far East, the renowned traditional centre of Orientalist and archeological studies, the celebration card depicted an old Hanoi fort in front of which were parked, side by side, a black Citroen sedan of pre-1954 vintage and a rickshaw. Is this by any chance the Asia they dream of seeing again?

Asia minor, or Asia major?

It has now become fashionable to deride the Asia in front of our eyes – its politics, economic rise, and regional international relations – as a sham Asia, an invention of *ersatz* capitalism and only too real local dictators or bureaucracies. This derision can lead us either to move forward quickly to the politically correct and market compatible code of Western-inspired norms and laws or to move back to the old nativist perspective of Orientalists, when only languages, distinct ethnic or religious identities mattered. A return to the past is not an option for the natives of Asia, of course. But the fast forward route lacks a strong political or social engine to make the trek. The problem, of course, is that Asia, apart from the communist take-over, has not made a revolutionary change from its past to an individualistic society oriented to market capitalism. The revolutions of independence were just short-term outbursts, except when they coincided with the advent of communism. People's power in Manila at the end of the Marcos era, the Tiananmen Square incidents or Bangkok demonstrations, Seoul student outbursts are all telltale signs of the urge to democratize, but none of them has been an organizationally strong and structured movement. Transition has been the key word throughout Asia, and indeed a guided transition in many instances. When Napoleon Bonaparte briefly conquered Europe, he carried the revolutionary Civil Code in his saddlebags. When the Indonesians generals unify an archipelago which is almost the size, and has a much larger population than Napoleonic Europe, they bring a patchwork shibboleth of imported Japanese and Western concepts, together with Malay communitarist wisdom. A student of Indonesian politics notes: 'In the Javanese world of ideas, diverse ideologies . . . are rather fluid liquids which can easily mix together under certain circumstances'.[31] This is the stuff that builds up pride, but it is not enough to create civilizations.

In the search for a major Asian culture, we therefore inevitably turn to the works of the past, whether the philosophical heritage, the stone temples overgrown by the jungle or the wooden buildings that each generation rebuilds according to the original model. Today's Asia may be dotted with remarkable novelists, musicians and indeed the last new wave of filmmakers worldwide. Intellectuals who escape the authoritarian trapdoor are none the less caught in the East meets West dilemma, and therefore form a transitory, minor culture in Asian history. Of course, the difference between major and minor is one of historical or cultural legitimacy, not a judgement of intrinsic value. Minor cultures are often later revealed to be the most fruitful, because they open avenues rather than close them. And there is no self-deprecation to be heard from the other half of Asian culture, with its large scientific and technological contributions in Japan's labs or Taiwan's science parks. Just as in America, Asians are on the front line of applied science, a fact which on its own denotes the cultural improbability of Paul Krugman's prognosis for Asia's economic future. Financiers may mess up financial choices, but such an upsurge in technical learning or R&D cannot fail to spark further productivity advances.

But computer nerds do not create civilizations, dreamers do. Asians mostly work towards their future, but they dream about the past, as their works of creation indicate. The creativity of contemporary Asian cultures is a topic of enormous controversy, depending on the value one grants to recent paintings or other works of fine art. Without going into that controversy, we can agree that no contemporary work of Asian art ever reaches the extraordinary prices fetched by items from the classical tradition, and this in the Asian collectors' own eyes. Yet the sensitivity of modern Asian creators is indisputable, and easily apparent in the novels or films that depict the break with the past. The future seems to belong to a more cosmopolitan or Western art. When I.M. Pei, one of the world's greatest architects, builds the Bank of China skyscraper on the Hong Kong landscape, he makes a statement that is utterly modern. When he is commissioned to construct the new Louvre Museum in Paris, he instinctively recreates the pyramid in a setting that is littered with recollections of antique Egypt. But when he undertakes to build a large hotel in Beijing's Fragrant Hill district, his imagination fails him, and he builds a pastiche of Qing dynasty palace architecture. Unless modern art is itself the continuation of tradition (as is the case in Japanese ceramics), it will not rediscover ancient cultural forms. The failure of Asian cultures to renovate themselves is a criticism addressed to them as far back as the 4 May 1919 iconoclastic movement in China. But that criticism is still valid.

If Asia is not creating a civilization, is it stirring a clash of civilizations? For the sake of practicality, we use here Samuel Huntington's famous characterization of contemporary civilizations in prospective conflict as a starting point (although it dumps together China and the Islamic world, but leaves Japan in a category by itself).[32] While Huntington and other social scientists predict a rise in anti-Western popular struggle and modern 'ethnoreligious' movements,[33] we should be aware that no East Asian culture breeds any such dream today, either as positive a factor of mobilization or as a frustrated antidote to the West's modernizating influence. Indeed, the days of the 1900 Chinese Boxers are long past. The politics of Southeast Asia have been based, at least since 1969 and the Malay-Chinese riots of Kuala Lumpur, on containment of these ethnic or religious outbursts. The state has been entrusted with a balancing act between communities, economic rewards being the name of the game. Enrichment is the only *lingua franca* of Asian societies, but again the golden eggs laid by the proverbial developmental goose hardly qualify as the stuff of dreams. Europeans invented the pursuit of happiness in revolutionary times. Although the tortuous process of European unification has brought as much frustration as enthusiasm, the European idea now feels like a dream that might become palpable in the near future. Needless to say, the American dream is still strong enough to draw the world's huddled masses towards its beacon. The utopia of communism lured millions towards the stark reality of Maoism or Stalinism. Far from the feast of civilization that pro-Asianist ideologues such as Anwar Ibrahim dream about, radical Islam has often turned its dream of purified brotherhood into a nightmare for it's own people.

Instead, and mostly to their credit, Singaporeans, Hong Kongers after the hand-over, Japanese Tokyo University graduates and many others map out a pragmatic path for Asia. In the midst of the financial crisis, Dr Mahathir has moved his official residence to Jaya Putra, Malaysia's new Brazilia-like capital that is unfinished: an engineer's drawing board fantasy. There is no messianism in these plans. But dreams do not catch only the people's attention. They also enthuse high-level policy makers beyond the daily grind of modern international relations. Japan's politicians, Southeast Asian technocrats or autocrats, amorphous overseas Chinese entrepreneurs do not evoke these dreams. Only China, with its pursuit of wealth and power, its undertow of nationalist resentment, has in fact more collective, if somewhat old-fashioned, dreams than the rest of Asia put together. Perhaps this is why the West, against most rational arguments, dreams in turn of a privileged relationship with an immensely capable, and immensely friendly Middle Kingdom. In today's East Asia, the Dream of the Red Chamber still holds a fatal attraction for many Western diplomats and politicians.

Is there peril in the divided house?

For years, there have existed schools of thought that did not believe in the possibility of Asian integration, much less unity.[34] The historical lessons from the past pointed to Japanese enmity with Korea and the Chinese world, to ubiquitous conflict between native Southeast Asians and 'sojourners', more often than not ethnic Chinese brought in by the colonizing powers. State unity was not a given, and Indonesia or to a lesser degree the Philippines still have to contend with centrifugal or separatist trends within their archipelagos. The rise of Islam throughout the region, from Indonesia or Malaysia's mosques to Chinese Central Asia, is another familiar fault line which leads to predictions of conflict. Ethnic and local community divisions abound in Southeast Asia, and even South Korean politics are deeply marked by the strong provincial division that echoes past independent rule. Regionalism in Chinese politics is once again a phenomenon on the rise, and one which is rooted in historical tradition.

Had Asia's fast growth securely pasted together the pieces of this jigsaw puzzle, or had it merely placed a rosy wallpaper over the divisions? Whatever the reality of centralized power, held by Javanese military in Indonesia, by the alliance of aristocracy and Bangkok Chinese merchants in Thailand, by former Malay militants and the civil service in Malaysia, by the Party elite in China, by native Seoulites in Korea, the soothing effects of trickle-down economics combined with high growth rates have at least served to dampen political infighting.

The Crash of 1997, with its sudden economic reversal, was the first, and wholly unexpected test, of the post-Cold War world for the comparatively new nations or regimes that have held post-war Asia in their grip. Political liberalization, improved access to information thanks to new global communications, and marketization and economic opening up to competition are long-term trends that continue to apply today. Yet the cushion of increased revenue for all has suddenly been taken away. Virtually all Asian economies experienced negative growth in 1998, along with a large rise in unemployment and social distress. In traditional Leninist parlance, the ground would seem ripe for political scapegoats, communitarian struggle and a flight into international conflicts.

A quasi-instantaneous conclusion should be the prediction of catastrophic divisions between Asia's new nations, or between the ethnic, religious and community groupings with which most Asians spontaneously identify. The instant international media panic in January–February 1998, when Indonesia seemed ready to return to its historical path of anti-Chinese and Muslim-based riots, was a case in point.

Instead, the aftermath of the Crash appears remarkably calm, and the political climate for international relations remarkably improved. The Crash and the IMF's requirements of public austerity have taken their toll. Throughout Asia, arms purchases and military spending are in sharp decline, some countries pleading with their Western providers for the cancellations of orders they had earlier solicited. The year that has gone by since the Crash began is the first one in recent history when almost no military incident (save a minor Chinese–Vietnamese skirmish in May 1998) has happened over the Paracels and Spratley islands in the South China Sea, or in the East China Sea. Nor has the South China Sea dispute seen any significant proposal or initiative by any participants to avoid the recurrence of incidents in the future. In typically Asian fashion, these high-profile gestures have been toned down, while more pressing issues preoccupy the region's leaders. So much for the modern-day version of Lenin's thesis on the inevitability of war at times of economic crises.

Similarly, several known bad boys in Asia's neighbourhood could have seized the opportunity of new weaknesses appearing on the free market front to launch opportunistic conflict. North Korea, for one, should gloat over the totally unexpected demise of South Korea's *chaebol* capitalism.

Indeed, the North Korean leaders struggling for their survival appear to have taken notice of their brothers' new fragility. But instead of stepping up tension, they offered to open talks with the South, an event that last occurred only in 1990 under grave international circumstances. Kim Dae-jung's victory in South Korean politics signals a new deepening in the country's *Nordpolitik* – its first sign is the willingness to 'separate politics from economics' in dealing with Pyongyang, e.g. to relent on the conditionality of aid and other economic relations with the troubled North. Far from being an escalation of tension, this amounts to practical acceptance of a transitory coexistence between the two halves of Korea.

Other examples of *détente* politics can be found easily. In December 1997, Japan and Russia agreed to find a solution to their own territorial feud over the Northern Territories (Southern Kuriles) before the end of 2000. This may not be the last time a settlement of the issue gets under way, but at least it does not suggest the inevitability of rising tensions in difficult economic times. Over the reunification issue, China and Taiwan renewed their official contacts, interrupted since 1995 in April 1998. Even the traditionally ebullient relationship between Malaysia and Singapore, which had erupted again in local polemics in 1995 to 1996, is being turned on its head by a 'prosper thy neighbour' rhetoric since the Crash began. Finally, Cambodia's Hun Sen, a secretive and violence-prone leader who ousted his co-premier and rival Ranarridh in July 1996, and suffered ASEAN's criticism for this rupture of the 1991 Paris Agreement, could have gained some more respite during these months of regional financial frenzy. He has preferred instead to follow the international script that was required of him and to accept a royal pardon of Ranarridh by King Sihanouk after a farcical trial. Even the Khmer Rouge, operating in Indochina's black hole, have picked the moment with Thailand's assistance to spit out from the depths of the jungle the dead body of former genocide figure Pol Pot.

We all know the old musical that intones: 'There's no business like show business'. In today's Asia, no show is as important or vital as business itself. The Crash does not raise the potential for international or ethnoreligious conflict. On the contrary, it incites the region's states to tone down their immediate geopolitical conflicts in order to avoid compounding the present lack of effective cooperation in the economic and financial arena.

This short-term answer leaves unanswered questions. Were the Crash to lead to prolonged and large-scale disturbance of the region's economy, the virtuous circle of mutual trade and economic prosperity might fall apart. In spite of interrogations regarding Japan's financial seaworthiness, we are far from this perspective. More to the point, the Crash poses a serious challenge to each country's internal stability and regime legitimacy. There is a remarkable absence of international political turmoil in the aftermath of Asia's financial meltdown. But many governments are struggling to ride out the crisis or are fighting for their survival in the face of rising anger. The echo of the Crash reverberates within the narrow confines of each modern nation-state of Asia rather than in the supposedly dangerous open spaces between them.

Conclusion: balancing globalization with Asian identity

Unquestionably, the Crash is a watershed for Asian identity. While Westerners usually have a holistic view of modernization, Asians, ever since the nineteenth century, have taken a piecemeal approach. You could modernize the mind and preserve the spirit. You could import technologies and favour in-house management recipes. Most important of all, personal relationships were the ultimate safety net, and states could dissociate the political status quo from economic change. Asians are pragmatists, and they know that the Crash calls into question these separate and neat boxes. The onset of globalization for Asia, symbolized by the largely deregulated financial market's long arm into the economy, represents a second wave of disruption for Asia, one that can perhaps be compared with the rising flow of foreign goods during the 1930s. A fragile Asian sense of identity is upset, although the commotion is infinitely smaller in Japan, where introspection and debate about Western cultures is a long tradition, than in weaker societies. Yet there is every sign that Asians retain a strong attachment to the roots of their cultural past. They may sometimes confuse this attachment with the wrong practices, such as a debased use of personal relationships. A so-called modern society that highlights only individualism may have little appeal to them, or they will seek to recreate within its confines the old protective shell of Asian social practices.

Part of the conflict will be translated into political action. The questions that Asians cannot solve for themselves are addressed to their governments. What the Crash inaugurates is a new political stage. Stability itself will never be lost from any Asian perspective, for the trauma of Asian revolutions is not far behind. But popular demands will balance two contradictory goals: successful adaptation to change, and preservation of satisfactory institutions and social practices. It will not be easy for Asian governments to walk that tightrope.

6 Challenging Asian politics

The Crash poses an enormous challenge to East Asian governments and established political structures. For half a century, the terms of the agreement between rulers and people have usually been based on the benefits of economic growth. This has been the case even for democratically based political systems. Electoral politics and a conservative bias for the incumbent political forces have fostered stability – Japan's LDP, Taiwan's Kuomintang, and up until recently the politically conservative majority in South Korea could count on the voters' gratitude for prosperity. But even the semi-authoritarian regimes of Asia, and some of the more outright dictatorships, have fostered successful developmental states that depoliticized most expressions of public opinion.

This chapter explores the challenge to political stability throughout the region, or, as some might see it, the chance for political renewal. The advocacy of the Asian way was in better days an informal method of gathering together an Asian front of governments and ruling forces. In the aftermath of the Crash, most governments and their prevailing establishments are having to fight it out within the confines of their respective national political systems. Although the example or contagion of political upheaval may spread beyond, for example, Indonesia's borders, it makes sense to look at regional stability as the addition of discrete and widely different national situations. In this light, only Indonesia, China and Japan's course exercise an immediate influence on the rest of East Asia. That influence, of course, is of a very different nature in each case.

Increasingly, the views of the Asian polity had been in contrast with the West's school of doom and gloom. Gradual industrial decline threatened in the United States, and economic stagnation in Europe. Archaic corporative rivalries were rampant in what French sociologist Michel Crozier aptly termed 'the stalled society'.[1] The inefficiencies of multiparty and multilevel electoral systems tended to shorten any government's time horizon. This made the Asian systems, partly democratic, partly authoritarian or bureaucratic, look more efficient by comparison. Finally, fast economic growth was the best shock absorber of the social tensions from old agricultural societies turned upside down by modernization.

The Asian Crash reverses these perspectives, at least in the immediate future. The monetary and financial meltdown of three Asian economies (Indonesia, Thailand and Korea), the sudden economic stagnation of almost all except Taiwan, and Japan's increasingly worrisome financial slide have consequences extending far beyond the financial sphere. A social crisis throughout Asia is a certainty. Public resentment, although, as we have seen, it involves a degree of nationalist frustration, is now directed against governments that did not predict the event, and cannot shield their population. For many Asians, and especially those who have remained in traditional agricultural or manpower sectors, there is no possible understanding of the Crash. They have never held dollars, much less shares, in their hands. How could they see the sudden prospect of price inflation for foodstuffs and daily necessities as a simple consequence of international financial trends? As for the middle classes of Asia, their life savings were suddenly downsized by the Crash, and in many cases simply vanished overnight.

Asians are on the treadmill of downsizing during a major recession. How their governments and political systems will emerge from this experience is an open question. Of course, both the social and political turmoil, as well as government responses to these difficulties, vary markedly from country to country. Between the simmering cauldron of post-Suharto Indonesia, and the uneasy sniping at Dr Mahathir's rhetorics in nearby Malaysia, there exists a widening gulf, of which the recent onslaught of boat people from Sumatra gives an indication. The tough relationship that persists between South Korea's unofficially organized labour movement and successive governments, including the new Kim Dae-jung administration, bears little resemblance to dispersed and amorphous social outcry in Thailand. Between the new reality of unemployment appearing in Japan in 1998, which in itself is a sea change for Japanese social psychology, and the gigantic problem of structural unemployment inside the Chinese economy's agricultural and state enterprise sectors, lies more than a mere question of proportion.

The initial shock from the Crash of 1997 is now behind us. Asia's economic health, its hidden time bombs as well as the positive actions that could engineer a rebound from perennially strong fundamentals, are some of the most closely watched topics in the global marketplace. So is the potential disruption from political and social explosions. Trends in the first half of 1998 showed that Asian currencies and stock markets can fluctuate wildly at short notice. Three countries have become pivotal to an understanding of Asia's future: China, Japan and Indonesia.

Smaller fish swimming against the tide

The three pivotal countries do not include South Korea, the world's former eleventh-largest economy, which could in fact exert a strong influence on the region. Korea is now a prime example of the type of publicly planned and executed reform that the IMF and Western creditors have been demanding from Asians. But Kim Dae-jung's administration also faces the weight of ingrained traditions and the sheer reluctance of yesterday's mighty economic groups to surrender themselves to the market.

The battle of Seoul that Kim Dae-jung won immediately after his election is a fragile victory. Foreign investment was down by 73 per cent in the first quarter of 1998, as foreign firms mostly disagreed with the high book value that Korean sellers – and, more often than not, the families that own them – were still insisting on. The *chaebols* retain political influence, especially within the National Assembly, which does not support President Kim. Yet the ever-mounting bad debts, now widely estimated to top 100 billion dollars, will force decisions. Widespread bankruptcy of Korea's major firms would put millions of workers on the streets, with the prospect of widespread unrest. As much as the international financial community wants to be paid back for its past loans, this cannot be the best way to achieve it. Certainly, Korea's failure would indicate that there is simply no regional solution that can be successfully applied from the global rescue manual. The future of the country, after Kim Dae-jung's election, and his initially successful tactics for dealing with the country's international debt,[2] is now largely in other hands. As of June 1998, it is predictable that another major international bailout, consisting either of debt postponement, or debt cancellation, will be the key factor in getting the country back on its feet.

The impact of Japan's own credit crunch, and the slide of the yen that is a distinct possibility, will be far more important than the delaying tactics of Korea's economic establishment in determining the final outcome. Perhaps because the Korean peninsula remains one of the world's prime hot spots, it is unlikely that the main guarantor of its security, the United States, would risk political and social chaos. For this reason at least, Korea's increasing private debts in 1998 are likely to be met by matching resources from the international financial community.

Other Asian economies are now much more predictable, or the impact of their policies is less important to neighbours. Taiwan, indeed, is a remarkable exception to Asia's crisis. Its conventional economy and trade obviously suffer from the regional recession. Its financial management has avoided most risks, in part due to the 'Small is beautiful' axiom that could sum up the thinking of locally born executives. The stellar perform-ance of its high-technology industry (more than 10 per cent of Taiwan's GNP, and almost 30 per cent of its exports are generated by the computer industry) links Taiwan to the American New economy. Yet, given Taiwan's diplomatic estrangement, it will be a notable but quiet agent of recovery, certainly not a leader. Singapore is another example of limited slippage during the region's worst economic times. An example of its incredibly quick adaptation and resilience in the face of the regional crisis can be found in the 9.8 per cent reduction in Singapore's average wages for the first quarter of 1998.[3] Its role as a haven will be watched even more closely as the tremors from Indonesian's fall shake the entire region. But for that very reason, Singaporean leaders must tread care-fully. When an upward trend happens, Singapore will indeed fuel it. But it will not be able to engineer that trend by itself.

Thailand and Malaysia are muddling through in their own distinct ways. Thailand's restructuring of the financial sector, with many accepted takeovers from abroad, is an impressive example of creative adaptation. Earlier and better than any of their regional neighbours, Thailand has adopted a policy of facilitating foreign acquisition of Thai firms. In late June 1997, the ceiling for foreign ownership of corporate firms was raised from 25 per cent to 100 per cent. In October 1997, foreigners were authorized to hold a majority stake for 10 years in all of the 58 finan-cial institutions that had been shut down by the Crash. That rule has been applied liberally, and many other firms have undergone a change of nationality in ownership. In late March, Thailand's central bank announced new rules forcing Thai banks to write off bad debts from their books, rather than carrying them forward into an uncertain future. The implication is that these banks, whose non-performing loans might total 35 per cent of all bank credit, will have to look for new capital.[4]

Thailand's two largest banks, Bangkok Bank and Thai Farmers Bank, are therefore already 50 per cent foreign owned, a figure which is likely to rise. Singapore's public Investment Corporation, several leading Taiwanese companies, and above all Japanese banks such as Sanwa and Dai-Ichi Kangyo are thus raising their stakes, while most Western estab-lishments hold back.[5] But Thailand depends heavily on the availability of Japanese capital to move forward, and therefore on the state of Japan's own financial crisis. Meanwhile, a huge rise in unemployment, reaching

8.5 per cent of the working population in May 1998, reveals the depth of the domestic crisis.

Malaysia, the 'do-it-yourself' IMF country, is paying the price for its resistance to international intervention and takeover of its troubled sectors. Its recovery is still threatened by the impact of business failures and an unconvincingly transparent financial sector. However, by refusing the full prescription of an IMF slimming cure for their public budget, the Malaysians hope to deflect some of the social crisis that is ripping Indonesia apart. The Chinese are for the first time being allowed to buy significant amounts of *bumiputra* (native Malay) businesses and by tapping into ethnic Chinese capital, the Malaysians hope to refinance private debts. Reducing the exclusive benefits for Malays may also cure some of the more notorious inefficiencies in Malaysian firms. This strategy will succeed if the rest of the region stops down-sliding. Malaysia's debt does not include a large amount of short-term credit, and creates therefore less of an emergency than Thailand's, Korea's or Indonesia's. It is also more domestic than international, and should not drag on the country's exchange rate. But Malaysia is being passed over by would-be investors because of the overall regional climate. The crisis has finally ended all pretence of cooperation between Dr Mahathir and his lieutenant, Anwar Ibrahim. Where Anwar has steadily endorsed reform efforts, Mahathir is more and more inward-looking and melancholic. Part of his efforts are directed at rescuing friends in trouble – including his son, Mirzan, whose shipping business received a bail-out from Petronas, Malaysia's state oil firm,[6] and Tan Sri Ting, the Sino-Malay businessman who led the giant Bakun dam project until circumstances forced its cancellation. Further international turmoil could very well derail Malaysia's own independent efforts. For years, observers had speculated on a clash between Mahathir and Anwar Ibrahim. During the Umno congress in August 1997, the air was heavy with unsubstantiated allegations, including anonymous letters denouncing Anwar's private life – a serious problem in a Muslim country. Anwar and Mahathir have always complemented each other, and disappointed those who hoped to drive them apart. Lately, however, their declarations became more and more divergent. While Mahathir fumed about another Western invasion, Anwar actually praised the 'creative destruction'[7] which is taking place thanks to the Asian Crash. He also came out strongly in favour of B.J. Habibie, while Dr Mahathir publicly supported Suharto to the end. In June 1998, the conflict moved on to more concrete ground, with Anwar visibly supporting central bank autonomy and higher interest rates, while Dr Mahathir preferred to support demand with lower rates.[8] Finally, Mahathir sacked Anwar and reversed course. Malaysia has become the first Asian economy to stop exchange and capital controls, with some success, at least in the short term.

To some extent, the Philippines remains the odd man out in the Crash. The former 'sick man of Asia', as it was called at the end of the Marcos era, has undergone a slow revival under Cory Aquino and particularly Fidel Ramos. In 1997 to 1998, it is leaving the IMF ward as other ASEAN economies are entering its emergency section. For this reason, the Philippines' budgetary and financial situation has been closely supervised, and there appeared only recently any incentive for a property and financial bubble. It is another sign of the region-wide perception and action of market operators that the peso was hit by devaluation just like the other currencies. An economic slow-down and reduced foreign investment are part of the Philippines' worries in 1998. But the relatively smaller size of its domestic and foreign debt has saved it from the worst turmoil, and leaves room for Philippino firms to increase their global exports while its regional neighbours are paralyzed. With this ambiguous situation, the holding of a presidential election in May 1998 meant bad news. Fidel Ramos has retired to general acclamation – and much regret that he did not seek to circumvent the one-term limitation on the presidential mandate of the Aquino Constitution. A spate of politicians competed for the post, with former actor Joseph Estrada winning the draw after much social demagogy. But it is highly unlikely, under the present regional conditions, that he can fulfil his promises. Indeed, Estrada has immediately adopted an orthodox budgetary policy.

Three key countries – Indonesia, China and Japan

Indonesia, China and Japan present the economic uncertainties and political options that will make or break the region. Each country reveals a very different type of problem.

Indonesia's convulsions after the fall of President Suharto are the greatest immediate source of regional instability. Not only has Indonesia seen its economy implode, losing 75 per cent in dollar GNP terms, but the lid has been lifted on powerful religious and ethnic forces, in an atmosphere of economic and social doom. How the Indonesian crisis is resolved will shape Southeast Asia for years to come.

China has not been a major factor in the making of the Asian crisis. Neither is it a substantial part of the solution, in spite of all the hype about China's newfound sense of regional leadership. The Chinese, in fact, have been content with sitting on the sideline of any issue regarding the crisis. Although they have made some political mileage out of their well-advertised resolve not to devalue the yuan, their attention is transfixed on domestic problems. And there is indeed cause to worry in that area. China combines a strong reformist will with some of the worst problems usually associated with the region's woes. The mere hint of a Chinese devaluation as a reaction to a domestic recession is enough to send the region's markets reeling. China is therefore important in the sense that a backlash from the Crash hitting its economy may prompt it to devalue. Alternatively, social trouble is also brewing, and may derail the government's reform agenda.

Last but not least, Japan's financial system is steadily deteriorating, and only a strong political will can solve the huge overhanging debt that cripples the country's growth and prevents it from playing its full role as a regional economic leader. The deflation that is happening as a result of a loss of confidence on the part of the Japanese public is making the resolution of every problem even harder. Whether this leads to a second Asian Crash, or Japan's political leaders decide at some point in the near future to slap capital control measures on their markets, effectively ending an era of capital deregulation, the results may be momentous for the global financial system.

It is these three countries, and only these, which hold the key to Asia's recovery. They will determine whether a turn-around is possible in the coming two years, whether Asia's financial Crash of 1997 turns into a long-term recession, or if a further collapse endangers the global economy. Furthermore, there is simply no purely economic predictor for these three countries, since political systems and long-term social forces are now at stake. Whether Suharto's former associates endure or chaos leads instead to a new power shift between Indonesia's military, the Islamic parties and the democrats, is a major imponderable. Whether Japan and Korea's post-war trinity associating government, big business and politicians is genuinely dissolved cannot be decided by market forces alone. Whether fear of the Crash syndrome pushes China to finally dismantle its state enterprise system and face the social consequences, is a political choice with momentous implications.

Downsizing firms within a shrinking economy

During the first phase of the Crash, the tension was not completely apparent between the demands of an open financial system and the pull of the escalating social crisis. Only in Indonesia was the problem starkly outlined by the huge gap between the IMF's contempt for an appalling level of financial wrongdoing, and the government's historical experience of riding the tiger and their sense of caution in ruling a politically divided country – to wit, a 210 million-people composite nation with customary ways and many trade-offs. Today, the political and social crisis that has resulted from the Crash is glaringly present throughout Asia. It has become a key factor alongside the cold financial requirements of a return to health. Until 1997, most Asian governments confidently chose the path to fast growth with the belief that it also fostered stability: even closed communist systems, one by one, opted for opening up and economic integration. The fast growth also papered over the inequities of a guided economy system where public policy favoured friends and directed household savings towards the goal of financing the economy. Whether they put their money in postal savings accounts, as in Japan, or in notoriously rigged security markets elsewhere, Asians simply financed their economies without drawing the corresponding dividends. The rise in wage earnings, and the windfall profit from real estate, were enough to satisfy them. Today, for the first time, the requirements of a return to this fast growth under-mine short-term political and social stability, and the prevailing modes of governance.

Several Asian governments are therefore faced with a dilemma that is familiar to all political leaders who have sat in the IMF's waiting room to have a tooth pulled. They are torn between two objectives. On the one hand, there is the international prescription for reform, cut-back of public expenses and restructuring of the domestic economy at a time when the Crash has already stirred up a recession. On the other hand, they are also faced with social difficulties of a magnitude unseen in recent Asian history. There is simply no comparison between the disguised unemployment of involuted agrarian economies or even communist collective work units, and the sudden destruction of millions of jobs in comparatively modernized sectors that is happening today. The first was a continuing situation often compensated for by family or social solidarity, in a context of 'shared poverty' (Benedict Anderson). The second is a fallback after decades of incremental improvement. If Indonesia's unemployed or partly unemployed population fell from 60 per cent to 10 per cent of the labour force between 1970 and 1996, a leap back to 20 per cent does not invalidate the past record of growth. Yet it will still be resented as a brutal event. In March 1998, Indonesia's official unemployment statistic indeed doubled to 8.7 million people, and it is officially estimated to double again during the rest of 1998, reaching 17 per cent of the labour force. This does not take into account underemployment in the important informal economy. Indonesia was proud to become a self-sufficient grain producer, and Suharto received the FAO's gold medal for this achievement. Within one year, weather disruption from El Niño and huge forest fires have turned Indonesia into a rice-importing country, needing at least 5 million tons of rice for 1998. Famine was already gripping part of the countryside in the spring of 1998 with food riots speading during the summer.

Although less dramatic, Korea's social crisis has also been swift and brutal. Unemployment rose from 2.1 per cent in October 1997 to 6.5 per cent of the working population in March 1998, and 8.5 per cent by August. The figure will obviously continue to increase, as the *chaebols* shed more employees, and the wave of smaller firm bankruptcies continues. Only a quarter of Korea's unemployed draw any compensation, the rest being dependent on family solidarity. After riots broke out on 1 May 1998, Minister of Finance Lee Kyu-sung promised to include 6 billion dollars of new unemployment compensation in the public budget. Soon after his inauguration, President Kim Dae-jung had struck a deal with the unions and the firms, exchanging the end of life-long jobs for unemployment compensation. But the *chaebols*, strapped for cash, are reluctant to deliver their own part of that deal.

The other side of the picture, for Korea as well as for other hard-hit economies, is the reality of inflation. The sudden shortage and price rise of essential commodities, which is as much a consequence of hoarding for export as of the monetary devaluation, threatens the livelihood of average wage-earners. While the overall price index only registered a 9.5 per cent year-on-year increase in March 1998, the actual price of most essential products has risen much faster. Wheat flour is up by 330 per cent, sugar by 50 per cent, propane gas by 50 per cent, cabbages by 22 per cent and instant noodles by 17.4 per cent. Hefty cuts in luxury good pricing or big consumer items cannot compensate for these hikes.

By comparison, the climb of Singapore's unemployed to 2.2 per cent for the first quarter of 1998 is trifling, and Taiwan's stability at 2.3 per cent of the work-force is another sign of strength. Japan's steadily rising unemployment figure, at 4.1 per cent in May 1998, may also seem benign. Given the bias in official statistics, it is equivalent to a 7 per cent rate according to US or British criteria. The trend fits with the popular perspective of gloom that describes a greying country in the twenty-first century that will lack the resources to finance its retirees. Japan's widespread psychological despair will probably matter less in the long term, as there are huge pockets of strength in the economy. In the short-term perspective, however, this pessimism becomes a self-fulfilling prophecy that threatens the country's financial balance, and therefore the region.

Twilight in Jakarta

In 1965, President Sukarno's long reign ended in confusion, with the three elemental forces in Indonesian politics (Islam, the military and progressivism) shadow boxing against one another. Finally, a relatively junior general who headed the special forces unit based in Jakarta, General Suharto, pulled the chestnuts out of the fire. To this day, nobody is really sure of what took place in 1965, although there is agreement on the fact that Sukarno, through his combination of romanticism and tactical plays, had lost touch with reality.[9]

What happens after Suharto was already a favourite topic on the diplomatic circuit and in Jakarta households alike, before the Crash. For the last two occasions before he sought formal re-election, Suharto had been clever enough to defuse pressures against him by alluding to possible retirement. Yet the man who seized power in impossible circumstances, then held on to it for more than 32 years, was neither a wimp nor a megalomaniac who had lost touch with the reality around him. Tommy, Bambang, Tutut and other relatives of his large extended family may have disgraced him by their greed and empty headedness. But Suharto himself was far above them. As the reincarnation of traditional monarchs, he had taken nothing – it all belonged to him, and Suharto was always present, smiling and congenial, to receive expressions of gratitude. He had never let down close friends from the distant past, when he was an up and coming colonel based in Central Java. Muhamad 'Bob' Hasan, the ethnic Chinese businessman who became a government minister and a close confidant from that era, is living proof of this. B.J. Habibie, Suharto's ebullient Vice-President and successor, owes his later career to the fact that Captain Suharto once upon a time lodged at his mother's place, in the Outer Isles. However, he had never let any power holder – in Indonesian terms, it means a general – come even remotely close to a near equal position.[10] Several succeeding army chiefs and aspiring successors, such as generals Nasution and Yusuf, and more recently Ali Moertopo, Benny Murdani and Try Sutrisno demonstrate this. The first was retired and died in suspicious circumstances, the second was side-lined, then retired and the third was 'promoted' to the vice-presidency – which involved giving up control of the military. Probably the most tense situation in recent Indonesian politics happened in 1983, when mysterious death squads began 'cleaning' the Javanese countryside and cities of criminals and political opponents alike. Ali Moertopo, former head of the army's Special Operations unit, was said to have started the enterprise with Suharto's implicit backing, but was later left with the bill for this action.

In 1996 to 1998, secret squads were again kidnapping opponents in Jakarta. This time around, they released them more often than not, usually after psychological or physical intimidation. Meanwhile, Jakarta's feared military security service, Bakostranas, pulled in for questioning Indonesia's most outspoken Chinese businessman, Sofyan Wanandi, on the pretext that he was somehow involved in giving 'aid to underground terrorist organizations'. As it happens, the Wanandi family had been very close to the above-mentioned three generals, and had been quite vocal in recent years over the need to scale back the authoritarianism and corruption of the regime. It is also a leading Christian family. The accusations against Sofyan Wanandi were first leaked by a weekly belonging to 'Bob' Hasan. And Lt. General Prabowo Subianto, the new head of Kostrad[11], is married to Suharto's second daughter. He is also on the record for his strong Islamic and anti-Chinese convictions. It's a small world. Has anything changed in Indonesian power politics?

Pulling strings

Meanwhile, Suharto put General Wiranto in overall charge of the Army – a no-nonsense crew-cut modernizer who had the nerve, in recent years, to discipline officers engaging in such violations of human rights as the Dili cemetery incident in Timor, and who condoned Indonesia's new human rights commission. Wiranto, at 51, belongs to the mainstream tradition of the Indonesian military, suspicious of Islamic groups and refusing to turn against the Chinese. On the other hand he was now directly responsible for law and order, daily challenged with demonstrations and riots – he would be remembered as the hand that pulled the trigger, if that course became inevitable. In any action by Suharto, we should look for the balance. In this case, the son-in-law general and the chief of staff balanced each other nicely. Not only did the two officers reportedly hate each other, they also stood for opposed political solutions to the present mess.

When the IMF threw its requirements at Suharto, he reacted in the same characteristically dual fashion.[12] He called in respected technocrats from the former 'Berkeley Mafia' on the one hand, people who had been shunted aside when they became a hindrance to Indonesia's first family's enrichment. Then he designated B.J. Habibie for the vice-presidency, in an openly defiant gesture. Not only was Habibie a high flyer with a huge track record of public spending, but the German-trained engineer had chosen to tread the Islamic path to power. Founding several Muslim associations and centres of research, openly advocating discrimination against the Chinese, positioning himself as a trusted yes man to the family clan, the man had everything the international community was *not* looking for. As a native Bugis on his father's side from the Outer Islands, whatever thick Islamic layer he may don, Habibie cannot have gone down well with Javanese generals looking for one of their own.[13] The Habibie family's own economic ascension mirrors Suharto's, a fact which probably inspired trust of the former president, but which will not help when the time for a clean-up starts.

Habibie had therefore mostly been a pawn in the presidential strategy of blowing sand in the IMF's eyes. In early February, an Indonesian researcher with ties to the military took pains to explain, for the benefit of the *Far Eastern Economic Review*'s readers, how ceremonial the office of Vice-President really was, and why the Army 'ultimately plays the decisive role in determining who manages Indonesia and how'.[14] When Suharto installed a new government after his re-election by the rump Parliament, he surprised his crowd again. While he got rid of Minister of Finance Mari'e Muhammad, who for years has resisted B.J. Habibie's spending requests, he essentially installed a set of family faithful around Bob Hasan and his first daughter Tutut[15] as Minister of Social Affairs, including her own gynaecologist as Minister for Health. The Habibie party seemed already over.

Suharto's crafty games were again evident in the follow-up to the second agreement with the IMF. Suharto had explicitly warned against the disastrous measures of some IMF requests, such as huge price rises for petrol. On 5 May, before flying off to Cairo for a summit of leaders of emerging economies that ironically looked like a remake of Sukarno era 'Conefor' (Conference of Emerging Forces), his government suddenly applied in one sweep the price increases scheduled for a whole year. Within a fortnight, Jakarta's Chinatown and several shopping centres were burning, set aflame by the city's underprivileged, perhaps with a helping hand from unknown quarters. While the armed forces used surprisingly little violence on what were Jakarta's gravest incidents since 1966, hundreds of looters died in these building fires.[16] When Suharto returned from Cairo, armoured vehicles and crack troops restored order to a city where millions of middle-class Indonesians fear chaos more than anything. Once more, the wily peasant, Suharto, had graphically 'proven' that he was indispensable. While the Western media played the situation as another version of Ferdinand Marcos' ousting from power by a democratic coalition, Suharto courted chaos to keep his position, as the only game in town for the international community. On 17 May, Suharto claimed special emergency powers from Parliament.

Is there life after Suharto?

Thirty-two years of a successful, if corrupt, dictatorship have completely transformed Indonesia's political situation. The West, always out for a heroic (and preferably quick, because our attention span is short) struggle with a happy ending, was looking for a 1965 in reverse. Even Megawati Sukarnoputri, Sukarno's daughter (whose first name was chosen in recognition of the forces of electricity in the modern world), would like to play a Cory Aquino or Aung San Suu Kyi lookalike. The tides are turning, and on 9 February 1998, when Megawati gave a speech at the end of the Ramadan from her own home, US ambassador Roy Stapleton sat beside her. Suharto's days were evidently numbered and his family could hardly hope to keep its stranglehold on the economy after his departure. By May 18, House Speaker Harmoko, head of a parliament that had 're-elected' Suharto two months earlier, was calling for his resignation after receiving a visit from student demonstrators.[17] On the same day, ICMI[18], an association with close ties to B.J. Habibie, itself began demanding that Suharto turn his job over to the Vice-President, his lifelong friend. When Madeleine Albright called for Suharto's departure, the stage was set. General Wiranto was reluctant to shed blood in the streets. B.J. Habibie, formerly the president's closest associate, thus confronted Suharto with a call for resignation that some Habibie cronies uttered publicly. In a remarkable turnaround, Habibie's first acts were geared towards the IMF and the US treasury. He separated the Bank of Indonesia's governor from the government, thus granting an autonomy that was a key IMF request. By nominating the former Bank of Indonesia's head, sacked by Suharto only months before, to a ministerial position he clearly disavowed the old President's evasive tactics – of which he had been an essential part. By sacking Tutut and 'Bob' Hasan, he downgraded the Family's political influence, while he nominated a group of close advisers from the associations he controlled.

In the end, the IMF did not overthrow Suharto – his closest associates did so. The situation is strikingly similar to 1966, when Suharto himself brought to Sukarno the news that he must resign. B.J. Habibie took pains to emphasize that he had no part in the final outcome, yet the former president refused to speak to him after his resignation. Habibie commented: 'It's a natural process, aging, you know'.[19] If true, that leaves only the military as the real agent of change in those critical hours. The action was presumably made easier with the unspoken promise that the system would endure. The promise will inevitably be broken, as kicking out the former royal family becomes politically expedient. Little will come from this, however. Expropriation is a fruitless exercise within the present international financial system. It has taken a decade for the Philippines to recover a very modest fraction of the Marcos family's immense wealth abroad. The Marcoses could almost pass as simple folks compared with the combined wealth of the Suharto's clan. So the downfall of some of the top cronies, especially those who take the wrong side at the crucial moment, will be merely a bonfire offered to the IMF – and to Indonesia's poor, who might otherwise turn their rage on the Chinese neighbourhood store.

Once again, Indonesian politics in flux

Beyond the ritual fall from grace of the old dictator, are Indonesia's politics likely to fall back into the black era of 1966? Major peaceful factions are calling for political changes, while many former Suharto stalwarts have deserted. Again, Indonesian politics are in flux. This is also a consequence of the institutional system set up under the New Order. Only three parties, nominally representing Suharto's New Order, Islam and democracy were allowed to compete for elections, and their campaign period was restricted to a one-month interval every five years. Their heads were effectively nominated by Sukarno (as evidenced by Megawati's ousting from the Democratic Party's leadership in 1996). The two historically dominant Islamic leagues in the country are not represented in Parliament, while four of Suharto's six children sit on the wider People's Consultative Assembly. A majority of MPs are in fact nominated from 'functional constituencies', a system that goes back to the Sukarno era, and they include 75 military officers.

At the same time, political debate in the Indonesian press, the role of universities and academics (especially inside Islamic groups) and the action of non-governmental organizations are extremely widespread. Major dailies such as *Kompas*,[20] respected weeklies such as *Tempo*[21] (now *Editor* after being banned in 1994) and scores of others provide important inside information about the fights among government factions. *Republika* emerged in 1993 from the ranks of ICMI, to counter them and to support the Habibie faction. Only Chinese-language newspapers are strictly banned. *Tempo*'s ban in 1994 (it had openly criticized Tommy Suharto for his role in the bankruptcy of the Bapindo bank) became a *cause célèbre*, with many retired high military officers, and some in active duty, criticizing the ban. For more than a decade indeed, Indonesia's army, which is still tainted with the blood of the 1965 massacres, has turned increasingly liberal. The Group of Fifty in 1979, another officer faction that supported the Democratic Party of Indonesia (PDI) in the 1991 election, and retired Benny Murdani's continued patronage of democratic and liberal forces are cases in point. One reason is that its successive chiefs, as we have seen, have been frustrated by Suharto who instead advantaged the first family and the Habibie faction, playing with Islamic sentiment in the process. Censorship, more often than not, takes the form of telephone calls and 'appeals'.[22] The New Order culture does reveal itself in the complete banning of topics having to do with separatism (the Dili incident was cathartic in this respect, because the press broke ranks for the first time). Criticism is expressed through euphemism and the business of inside news. Of *Tempo*, the anthropologist Benedict Anderson once wrote: 'Is *Tempo's* mannered knowingness exactly what's required of a non-oppositional opposition?'[23]

The remark goes further than the press. Alliances, and even attitudes to Suharto, varied according to circumstances. Suharto himself enjoyed shuffling the cards – for instance, nominating in December 1995 noted critics of Habibie to ICMI's council.[24] A host of new parties or quasi-parties have appeared in the last three years, but their membership and influence are minimal – this is Jakarta politics at best. On the other hand, the two main Islamic leagues claim a huge following. The cleavage between them reflects a historical division among Islamism. Until December 1997, Nahdlatul Ulama,[25] Indonesia's largest Islamic organization (claiming 30 million followers), would have been deemed an essential actor. Its path has twisted in a strange way during the past decade. NU was always a *santri* (devout) organization, whose youth league was involved in the massacres of 1965. Yet it is also a conservative group which has separated religiosity from secular activities. Its astute head, Abdurrahman Wahid, has remade it into an effective opposition force. In effect, Wahid has also pledged protection for the Chinese and the democrats, initiating the first post-Suharto alliance. After years of playing hide-and-seek with Suharto's entourage,[26] Wahid suffered a stroke in December 1997, and his organization immediately felt his absence. Largely for this reason, Muhammadiyah,[27] the second league (claiming 28 million members) has emerged with Amien Rais. Muhammadiah is the other branch of Islamism, with a modernistic – and sectarian – goal of remaking civil society. Yet the youthful-looking Amien Rais, with degrees from Notre-Dame University and Chicago, is an unlikely *taleban*[28] for Indonesia. He has also often supported both Suharto and Habibie, and he was a member of ICMI, until 1996. After Wahid's stroke, Rais rose to the occasion and has been preaching a political alliance of progressive forces, promising tolerance to other ethnic groups – essentially Wahid's old line, but perhaps less credible in view of his lack of credentials.

As the Suharto era winds down in the agony of the Crash, we are witnessing conflicting trends that have always existed in New Order politics and even earlier, but which the economic collapse of Indonesia is bringing to the fore. A large officer corps, almost entirely trained in the United States even after Congress suspended official training programmes,[29] falls silent as the risk of a power struggle increases. The worst is not to be assumed, and it seems likely that the Fidel Ramos example will be followed. Ramos, a West Point graduate and a Marcos era general, defended democracy under Cory Aquino and practised it himself as a one-term president, retiring on course in May 1998. In spite of the army's strong financial interests, there is plenty of room for secular, modernistic officers to steer Indonesia. They will need to find able politicians out in front, however, and they will be handicapped by the predictable demise of Golkar, Suharto's historical party.

The other modernistic group is clearly represented by Habibie's mixed Islamic and chauvinistic high-tech clan. The call against the Chinese community, and Habibie's enmeshed relationship with the Suharto family, have harmed it considerably. While middle-class democrats are better represented in Jakarta than anywhere else, they lack the relays in rural Indonesia that are needed for electoral politics. The support of the grassroots Islamic leagues is going to be crucial to hold together the provinces. The arrival of *tchador*-clad women at the student-occupied parliament in May 1998 is an ominous sign of possible pressure from below. Ever the chameleon, however, Habibie started his new reign with concessions to the democratic centre. Indonesia's largest union, headed by Muchtar Pakpahan, a freed political prisoner, has been legalized. While holding on to his constitutional rights to serve his term, Habibie has conceded general elections for 1999, a move clearly aimed at defusing tension while putting off major political changes at the top. Even more recently, he has hinted that his own term may be limited by these national elections. Evidently, the army and General Wiranto have the upper hand in power politics at the centre.

The greatest uncertainty, as always in Indonesia, lies not in Jakarta but in the outreaches of a huge and diverse archipelago. Suharto's combination of the iron hand and flowing clientelism held it together. Democracy or even partial democracy will place a limit on the army's authority, while it is doubtful anyone can cast the net of patron–client relationships as wide as Suharto did. To quote the prophetic conclusion of a historical work on the post-1965 explosion of political violence:

> Old conflicts dating from the Revolution and from the postcoup massacre continue to simmer between the placid surface, while new ones, stimulated by aggressive government development projects and perhaps also by increased awareness of basic human rights, are

growing apace. The implications for Indonesian politics are worth considering. To the extent that Indonesia's military-bureaucratic state has been successful in undermining local state structures, in Bali as elsewhere, turmoil or collapse at the centre may well imply widespread political violence in the hinterland.[30]

One of the most obvious flashpoints is the status of Timor. It is perhaps encouraging that Jose Ramos Horta, the leader of Timor's independence movement, has saluted Amien Rais's conversion from militant Islam to the advocacy of tolerance, including on the Timor issue.[31] Amien Rais's sudden acceptance of self-determination for Timor, however, may be too much for the military to swallow.[32] While Indonesian democrats are likely to be sensitive to the risk of separatism and national dislocation, Islamic movements will use the autonomy issue as a lever to contain a predominantly Javanese army. Again, Habibie has not gone along with his own followers, sticking instead to military control of Timor. He will be very hard put, however, to resist the pressures for decentralization of authority from Jakarta to the provinces. Even more generally, the electoral process will generate more of the kind of radical opposition that was seen in the first months after Suharto's downfall. As R. William Liddle has aptly predicted, 'During election campaigns there is bound to develop a process of outbidding for the *santri*[33] vote between Islamic and non-religious parties and among competing Islamic parties in which the rhetoric can easily become inflammatory'.[34]

The Asian Crash has set the wheels of history moving in Indonesia. Yet the absence of obvious political successors once Suharto's personal network is disbanded is a disquieting aspect. An equivocal stand-in for that role, Habibie will either end up as a pawn of the more liberal-minded military or will reveal his true colours as a player of the Islamic tune in order to create his own electoral base.

China: a choice between devaluation and recession

A growing unemployment problem is certainly the most important consequence of the Crash for China. It builds, of course, on an existing structural labour force surplus, partly coming from improved productivity in the agricultural sector, partly from the demographic wave of new entrants into the labour force. The first factor is extremely hard to gauge accurately, but several studies have put the size of the excess agricultural labour force at 150–200 million people. Redundant farm workers and others attracted to the cities have become the major force reshaping the country's demography and feeding the so-called 'floating' population. Luckily, new entrants into the labour force are already reduced in numbers from only 10 years ago: after more than a decade of huge growth that reflected the post-Great Leap and early 1970s equally high birth rates, the average yearly number of entrants into the labour force has fallen from 24 to 17 million. It will still take more than a decade to see this figure fall to 13 million, or roughly 1 per cent of the overall population.

Urban unemployment in China is undoubtedly on the rise, spotty and contradictory figures notwithstanding. At the beginning of 1997, there were possibly 12 to 15 million unemployed in Chinese cities, while 20 to 30 million workers hold superfluous jobs that might be suppressed in the near future. China's reform agenda of streamlining the bureaucracy and public firms is likely to hit traditional workers' strongholds, such as the railway system and state textile plants. Harsh decisions are still being made, as when Jia Qingling, Party secretary for Beijing, announced the sacking of 300,000 workers over the next three years. It is highly unlikely that China's very diverse and mostly experimental social security and unemployment compensation programmes can deflect the shock from so much job destruction.

These figures have been well-known to Chinese leaders. It is on this basis that Deng Xiaoping chose fast growth over the stability of the state economic system in 1991. At the time, a 10 per cent annual rate of GNP increase was thought to be the minimal level at which unemployment could be contained. China's current plan has a target of 6 per cent yearly increase for the labour force, not counting the transfer of jobs from agriculture to industry and the services. Prime Minister Zhu Rongji has estimated, soon after his nomination in April 1998, that a growth rate of 8 per cent for the GNP was the minimal level necessary to keep social problems in check.

Month after month, and for reasons that are largely outside its power, China is now falling behind this objective. The official growth figure for the first half of 1998 fell to 7 per cent. Other indicators, such as a strikingly low rate of energy production (under one per cent for the same period), suggest that this is only a partial view of the true slow-down. Industrial production itself is also slowing down significantly, and inventories are up by 14 per cent. By April 1998, China's leading consumer price index had declined for five months in a row, demonstrating a fall into deflation. In recognition of these problems, China's government has launched a huge programme of public investment in capital projects, often hailed abroad as a Chinese Keynesian programme to jump-start the economy. At 750 billion US dollars for the next three years, the programme requires the government to double its public bond offerings in 1998 compared to 1997, and to expand its overall investment by an annually compounded rate of 24 per cent over those three years. Such a goal is both untenable and probably useless, except as a measure to protect public employment.

First, the true public deficit in China has always been vastly under-estimated by the published figures from the central state budget. Not only do these figures still suffer from such gimmicks as counting foreign from abroad as a receipt *before* the deficit figure is computed, but this budget does not take into account China's huge local administration finances. Neither does it tally the losses by more than half of the firms in the state enterprise sector. In the first quarter of 1998, state enter-prise profit fell by an overall rate of 83 per cent from the previous year, suggesting that the entire sector is plunging in the red. Second, a major public investment programme will out of necessity be managed in China's so-called 'second budget', equivalent to Japan's FILP.[35] The data in this second budget are a statistical abstraction, the central government having very little actual control over the expenses that flow out of largely uncon-nected departments and firms. Third, another laudable objective of the Zhu Rongji administration also interferes with the goal of a controlled support for the economy. In April 1998, the government simultaneously adopted a target of immediate payroll cut of 50 per cent for central administrations, including the People's Bank of China which is simul-taneously entrusted with important new tasks. Downsizing the bureaucracy is a lofty goal. But either it is delayed, or disorganizing the tools of central control at a time when there is an all-out call to increase public investment will lead to loss of control by China's central govern-ment.

Such a prospect is not necessarily the worst outcome in real economic terms. Unleashed local energies, if not mammoth projects that end up as capital losses, have allowed the Chinese economy to leap forward in the past. But there is simply no way to achieve this without a high level of money creation, loans, and deficit spending. The social treatment of growing unemployment, the losses of most state firms, and the require-ments of reflating the economy, imply huge spending. At the same time, it is impossible to maintain China's former intake of foreign capital – Hong Kong's economy is not in good enough shape to provide it,[36] and international investors are not coming in at the same rate as previously. A dip in foreign direct investment of only 10 per cent during the first quarter of 1998 is attributable to the presence of an exceptionally large oil refinery deal with British Petroleum, unlikely to be repeated. Unitary receipts for exports are of course falling. The reduced export prices that many Chinese firms are already practising are a portent of this trend. It is true that China is not forced to choose devaluation as a solution to the Asian Crash. It can choose, in fact, between devaluation and a deep and dangerous domestic recession. China did not cause the Crash, and is currently refraining from a voluntary devaluation that would throw the region into renewed havoc. But the pressure is steadily building up behind the dam and the *de facto* drop of the Chinese currency on informal exchange markets reflects this trend.

The issue of trust in Japan

Japan itself faces another type of social and political issue. As public trust in the domestic financial system evaporates, the Japanese debt problem, both public and private, becomes unsustainable. A spending plan of 125 billion dollars, unveiled in May 1998 and representing 7 per cent of Japan's GNP, is a high-stake gamble. It has in fact been demanded in very strong terms by the G7 countries, and particularly by the United States. If the markets do not believe the money will be effectively spent, it will have little effect. But if the public concludes, on the other hand, that Japan's public debt is reaching threatening proportions with these outlays, the crisis of confidence will grow into another financial débâcle. This is precisely what may happen, as the economic downturn bankrupts enterprises and projects that might otherwise have been viable.

Fundamentally, the issue is trust in the government's ability to manage the debt problem while stimulating the economy. The many ties that bind politicians with special interests once served to bolster confidence in Japan, Inc. Today, they are a major liability for the Hashimoto government and his eventual successors of the same colour. A second financial emergency or Crash, what seasoned market analysts call a 'double dip', would produce a new shockwave throughout Asia. New evidence is coming to light that exposes an even deeper crisis than previously thought possible.

Japan's admittedly high level of private bad debt, estimated at 580 billion dollars by the Hashimoto government, is thought to be compensated by the world's number one stock of currency foreign reserves – more than 230 billion dollars at the beginning of 1998. The book value of Japan's overseas financial assets, helped by the current account surplus and by the rise in the dollar, kept increasing, reaching 125 trillion yen (923 billion dollars at 135 yen per dollar) at the end of 1997, or 12 times Germany's net assets. In the long term, of course, the preservation of these assets may be essential to offset the retirement needs of Japan's ageing population. Household savings are thought to top

10 trillion dollars, an unmatchable figure. In theory, the industrial competitiveness of Japan's top multinational firms – the Sony, Toyota, Kyocera paradigms of contemporary business success – are also an indefinite source of trade and current account surplus. Who, in fact, would dare to bet against their future?

Snowballing debt

Yet the Asian Crash, and the financial crunch and demand recession that result from it, create a rising challenge to this theory. First of all, Japan is perhaps the prime example of an economy caught in the middle of capital liberalization by the Crash. The first phase of Japan's 'big bang', put into practice in April 1998, allows Japanese citizens to entrust their financial assets to foreign banks, brokers and mutual funds plying the Japanese market. In a last act of outright public intervention on the stock market, the government committed 8 billion dollars of postal savings deposits to prop up the Nikkei index in late March 1998. The move was derisively dubbed PKO (Price Keeping Operation), after the Peace Keeping Operation law to allow participation in UN operations. Its timing could not have been worse, as it served notice on the average Japanese saver that his money was effectively used to fix share prices. Most predictions envisioned a gradual turn of individual Japanese savers to the new foreign competition, but they moved with a vengeance in April 1998, reversing the tide of the current account balance for the first time in recent history.

At the same time, the pressure against the yen depleted the Bank of Japan's central reserves by 18 billion dollars in a single month. There is no telling, of course, how a speculative bout against the yen may end: the Bank of Japan has deep pockets indeed, and US longer-term interest may dictate a return to closer cooperation in managing the dollar–yen relationship. In May 1998, in fact, there were signs of this trend in the favourable public declarations of some Clinton administration figures regarding Japan's new spending package. Yet the longer-term implication is that Japan can no longer rely on its closed-doors financial system, with the limitless resources available to the postal savings network and the secure cross-holding relationship among players, to finance itself.

Perhaps a more positive factor can be found in the decision, forced by events, of Japan's foremost private banks to admit and write-off huge amounts of losses for the fiscal year ending in March 1998. Bank of Tokyo-Mitsubishi, Japan's first bank, wrote off nearly 10 billion dollars, while Fuji Bank, Japan's second financial establishment, followed suit with 7.5 billion dollars. 'Probably more will come this year', warned

Toru Hashimoto, Fuji's President.[37] Most other banks have followed suit. Certainly, these provisions and losses prevent Japanese banks from expanding credit in the coming years. The credit crunch, and Japan's stagnation or recession, will continue as long as the debt write-off process is incomplete. Yet, for the first time since 1991, Japan's private financial establishment is bowing to reality.

Meanwhile, familiar ghosts of Japanese public finance are turning into a nightmare. Japan's public deficit, already momentous at 7 per cent of the GNP, is compounded by the huge loans due in the depths of Japan's public corporations, local administrations and by the subsidies or favourable contract terms these bodies spread around the country. Japan's Fiscal and Loan Investment Program (FILP), has long been known as the bogeyman of Japanese public finance. Far from the official orthodox rules of the 'first' government budget, this is where politicians find the treasure trove for their pet projects: from Japan's huge public works or its manicured rural environment to barely disguised subsidies for key constituencies, such as the restaurant industry, it is the true heart of Japan's political economy.[38]

In normal times, the pay back of FILP loans is always an issue, since many of them are political in nature. After seven years of stagnation, and a deeper recession started in late 1997, the public debt problem could escalate. Officially, Japan's public debt is equivalent to one year of its GNP (4.5 trillion dollars), a dangerous level that some Western countries (e.g. Australia, Belgium and Canada) match. Pessimistic assessments put the real amount, with the inclusion of FILP, at two and a half years of GNP, or more than 11 trillion dollars. Other hidden timebombs include the underfunded retirement programmes of many Japanese firms, the 700 billion dollars of overseas liabilities by Japanese firms (including Asia bubble loans) about which accounting remains sketchy. Many real estate values are still overestimated, once again presenting house owners with the dilemma of mortgages that are worth more than the actual resale value of their houses. Lastly, in line with the Japanese tradition of 'overloaning' and *keiretsu* partnership with banks, many Japanese firms are highly leveraged[39] – a four to one ratio of debts to assets is frequently cited as an average, which is not so different from the Korean situation. Of course, the value of shares and real estate has a huge bearing on this ratio, and any improvement in this respect would immediately turn the situation around.

In real economic terms, not everything that *can* go wrong *does* go wrong. Lending and borrowing are acts of faith in the future. The US economy is the world's prime case of international borrowing and huge consumer indebtedness.[40] Yet the last seven years have seen its performance soar as a result of industrial performance and investor trust. In the past, Japan was a master in the art of overextending its financial means, with the Ministry of Finance occasionally reining in public debt and restoring financial balance until another burst of activity followed.

And now, a Japan that does not know what to say?

These times are now long gone. The prestigious Ministry of Finance, long held to be the ultimate locus of economic power in Japan, is falling victim, together with the central bank, to a strong anti-corruption drive that is also a political consequence of its failure to prevent the crisis.[41] The list of 117 ministry officials disciplined for improper ties with private firms allegedly includes Mr Sakakibara, Japan's 'Mr Yen' whose past was also probed for other cases of possible wrong-doing. In the string of suicides which resulted from the inquiry, the most telling case is that of Takayuki Kamoshida, the Bank of Japan official who was himself in charge of the investigation. He had earlier announced the bank would punish 98 employees for accepting 'excessive' entertainment.[42] Within the bank, there was great pressure to forgive what was, after all, fairly usual conduct. Outside it, the clamour for more severe action mounted. Much more than the successive scandals in the private financial sector, this story reveals the agony of uncertainty that grips Japan's officialdom. For months, Japan's press has been trying to outguess the Tokyo Public Prosecutor's special investigative squad, speculating in great detail on the fate of individual officials who are almost always named, and therefore thrown to the wolves before a case is even built up against them.[43] Japanese social norms have always combined respect for officials with extremely high-handed treatment, including ostracism, of criminal suspects. In one swoop, Ministry of Finance officials fell from the first category into the second.

The case further illustrates the fractures that are opening between the traditionally united actors of Japan's political system. Some Liberal Democratic Party (LDP) officials are thought to have encouraged the prosecution effort, since a weakening of the Ministry of Finance's power base would enable the Hashimoto administration to adopt more easily its special spending plans and the 'big-bang' liberalization agenda of finance. The Bank of Japan's governor Matsushita has been the target of a resignation campaign, with some politicians calling for the dissolution of the Ministry of Finance. That call itself echoes the 1945 to 1946 era, the only moment in contemporary Japanese history when the book of bureaucratic power was rewritten with new rules.

The Ministry of Finance thus draws all attacks. Yet the lack of political initiative is even more troubling. The LDP has never been so secure in its hold on power in recent years. In 1993, a revolt against its faction leaders led to the formation of an opposition coalition that won the elections, with Horimuri Hosokawa becoming Prime Minister (and lasting only eight months). New political forces were formed, with the LDP fearing especially the ascent of Ichiro Ozawa, its former secretary general who left the LDP after being denied the mayorship of Tokyo. One of the key factors that boosted Ryutaro Hashimoto into the Prime Minister's office in 1996 was that, as a reputed nationalist and exponent of Japan as a 'normal state', he could compete with Ozawa on the same footing. Few observers noted at the time that almost all new political forces were really created by former LDP members, and that the actual number of Socialist Diet members was already down in the 1993 elections.[44] Five years later, the chickens have come home to roost. Japan's opposition dissolved in late 1997. In spite of electoral reform instituting single seat constituencies and party lists for 200 MPs, the new parties were totally unable to unseat the established LDP politicians: Ichiro Ozawa's electoral base was reduced to a few percentage points. In times of economic crisis, the Japanese voters are turning even more conservative than is customary, out of fear for the unknown. Japan's political system now combines widespread rejection of party politics, admiration for lone reformers and an overall fatalistic preference for the usual suspects on election day.

Whereas a fundamental, if unwritten, law of electoral democracy dictates that incumbent politicians suffer the consequences of an economic downturn, Japan's deep economic crisis has actually put the LDP back in the driver's seat since 1996. And in line with this trend, LDP factions actually preferred to see Hashimoto stay in power, since this spared them the agony of difficult policy choices.

Japan's political scene has again become one where indecision prevails. There are a few signs of alternative choices. Naoto Kan, himself a former LDP member, is busy reforming an alliance of the opposition under the new label of a Democratic Party, which immediately became the Diet's second party at 131 seats, relegating the Socialists to obscurity. Naoto Kan is unusually popular and in fact consistently figures as the public's first choice for Prime Minister – were it given a choice, one might add. The reason is simple enough. As Minister of Health during the Murayama LDP–Socialist coalition government, he unfailingly punished the officials from his ministry who bore a responsibility in the HIV-tainted blood scandal.

The July 1998 elections for the Upper House seemed to prove that Naoto Kan's move was the right one. His party came in second, while the LDP failed to retain a majority of seats. Keizo Obuchi, a former minister of Foreign Affairs with middle-of-the-road views on solutions to the financial crisis, replaced Hashimoto. Political trends since that date are disquieting. The opposition is using its lock over the Upper House to filibuster the debate on economic reform measures. The political gambit of early general elections is therefore put before the struggle to prevent a looming financial crash. Even weakened, the LDP remains the only government party, while it is unlikely that an opposition coalition would have even more trouble putting together a coherent economic programme.

Challenging the Asian way

China's problems are brewing, the winds from the Crash bringing a cold rain on its economy. Not only is Japan's capacity to act regionally as a financial and economic power impaired, but the stability of its financial market is in doubt. Indonesia is both the prime victim of the Crash and a serious danger for Southeast Asia. Here, the Cold War era political system is unravelling, and an unknown chapter is being written at the worst possible time for the region's economy.

The spectacle of Indonesia, the largest of Southeast Asian economies, suffering an economic meltdown that is likely to lower its GNP by as much as 25 per cent in 1998,[45] with an IMF strong arm intervention that probably increases the trouble more than it contains it, will remain in the memory of the region. Yet the political establishment of Indonesia is surviving the demise of Bapak Suharto, whose talent for inscrutability always duped his political opponents but who could not outrun an unleashed pack of international creditors. For Indonesia to avoid the explosion of latent tensions and secessionist temptations will be a feat. Of course, the army, with its massive economic stake and political participation, especially at the local level, has not said its last word yet. At this point, however, it simply lacks any legitimacy for ostensible intervention at the national level.

The endgame of Suharto's three decades plus of paternalistic power with development was always hard to predict. Avoiding intervention into another country's political affairs was first and foremost an ASEAN motto, because it fitted the requirement to tame the Indonesian giant – China came in a belated second under the same policy of see no evil, hear no evil, speak no evil. While the Asian way was best argued for by Asian graduates of Oxbridge and Harvard, its real purpose was to keep the region in one piece, despite the tremendous differences and opacity of most of the Asian regimes. The Philippines' People's Power episode never challenged this policy, because neo-colonial history had made that country different, and more Western in its formal political system. But the fall of Indonesia's New Order is a different matter.

Will it lead to an outburst of democratic protest throughout the region? A prosperous era of fast economic growth has not brought about political democracy. A fatal financial crisis, followed by sharp recession in the real economy, could unstick the glue that held together the region's semi-authoritarian states. The market could usher in political accountability of governments to their people. This perspective is one of democracy based on the triumph of the international equity market – after the bankruptcy of at least one, and possibly several borrower nation, a new management takes over and brings in the political system that best fits market economies.

A no-win situation

This is, unfortunately perhaps, a rosy scenario. The international financial community, whether one considers the IMF as its proxy or G7 as its backer of last resort, has very contradictory attitudes to the region's problems. Some of its requirements for reform and structural change may amount to a death sentence for the old political system of tutelage and cronyism. But a new regime, unencumbered by the legacy of past authoritarian systems, would still be accountable for debts incurred previously. For the pre-eminent goal of Asia's main partners is not so much to foster democracy, but to force a change in the way Asians play the international economic game. The pressure is just as strong on Japan or Korea as on Malaysia or Indonesia, even if the first two countries, because of their might and influence, do not get the same treatment.

Meanwhile, Asian governments risk being hanged with a different rope. They have all enjoyed unusual stability due to the long-term economic growth that they fostered, or at least allowed for. Whether they participate in a democratic or in a more authoritarian regime, Asians have had no practice in what is a favourite sport among Western democracies – kicking out incumbent political forces whenever the discomfort index increases. Indeed, Asian governments have traditionally built pockets of subsidies and projects that amount to a cushion for leaner times. Under the sudden international systemic requirements that the Crash of 1997 dictates, these politically based attitudes are impossible to maintain. It is therefore predictable that the first wave of governments brought to power after the Crash will soon be accused by their populations of violating the customary compact of Asian political systems. A rift is already appearing between Kim Dae-jung's reform policies and the basic requirements of Asia's only militant and powerful unions. After some initial hopes of turning the corner, Chuan Leekpai's government in Thailand is heading into deeper political problems with the forces of malcontent. In China, Jiang Zemin and Zhu Rongji's reform agenda is much harder to execute under conditions of increased economic difficulty. And there is simply no amount of reform that can save Indonesia from its huge debt burden.

Asian political stability on the international agenda

Immediate political reactions have focused on anger at the web of cronyism and interest groups that have engineered the Crash. Longer-term reactions will again be based on expectations about economic performance and what most Asians think is an equitable distribution of that performance – protection of basic subsistence and full employment, anything else being a matter of industriousness and the right connections. This is precisely what the reformed Asian governments are not able to deliver under the new international market conditions. On the contrary, they are expected to take the floor away from established subsistence levels, and seek to install a more individual and entrepreneurial approach to enrichment that contradicts social custom and political protection. The full agenda of globalized economics is about to hit Asian societies, and it will be as much or more of a shock as the reactions it has provoked in the European context. Again, this will be in a situation where electoral outlets to sentiments of frustration are either almost non-existent, or may provoke an institutional crisis at every turn. No Asian-wide sentiment of a regional community will be enough to help individual governments ride this storm of malcontent. At times of crisis, Asian countries have simply no collective bargaining power with the other key elements in the triad, America and the European Union. In fact, for a perhaps temporary but unpredictable time the triad's Asian component does not exist anymore. In its place we find a disparate assortment of Asian states directly exposed to global forces.

Paradoxically, those governments who have stuck to their guns since the Crash began may stand a better chance of later being exonerated by their people. Whether they believe it or not, they can at least pursue a political agenda that includes nationalist feelings, and also consistently defend egalitarian (in Sun Yat-sen's old sense of the 'people's livelihood' for the Chinese world) or community-based policies in ethnically-divided nations. China and Malaysia spring to mind in this category.

For this scenario to unfold, does the Crash of 1997 need to repeat itself with a second meltdown? Since no rise in exports from Asia of any magnitude can really counter in the short term the devastating financial damage from the first Crash, a second Crash was already underway in 1998. Purse tightening and a lasting recession are the only solutions to avoid another breakdown. In this case, there is simply no benefit to be had from reform and adaptation of international market requirements. In the short term, as has happened in Indonesia, they simply bring more misery than any Western country has accepted since the Depression of the 1930s.

If this hypothesis came true, the political systems of Asia would start to unravel, with democratic regimes just as vulnerable as locked-in authoritarian states. After the first wave of political shock that has unseated the three governments of the countries that have asked for IMF assistance (Thailand, Korea and Indonesia), this is the development to watch.

The only major alternative for this hypothesis does not lie solely, or even importantly, with decisions made in Asia. It requires a new international deal on the debt and capital problem in Asia, and a strict application by Western economies of free trade rules to themselves. Cancelling increasing amounts of emerging Asia's debt, and letting the flow of goods produced at devalued prices enter the huge consumer markets of America and Europe, are the only global answer possible if the free and open international system that we call the global economy is to be maintained. The consequences are painful: because of a drop in Asian imports, Asia's trade surplus with the West is likely to grow from 90 to 250 billion dollars in 1998. This answer also runs against the trend of the previous decade. It witnessed more and more informal, and sometimes self-avowed arrangements towards managed trade. It also saw the opening up of financial service trade and capital markets become the key issue of international economic relations between Asia and the West. Today's breakup of Asia's economics is forcing a reconsideration of those trends.

This will indeed be the tall order facing Western nations in 1999, as it becomes clear that Asia's crisis is long-lasting and more than likely to draw other economies into its vortex.

7　A Faustian deal for Asia?

Over a year after the first Crash, we understand much better the scope and the nature of the crisis. While initial predictions of a fast rebound were the product of wishful thinking, several educated guesses can be made on Asia's mid-term prospects. They all hinge on the courses of action that are going to be taken both by Asian and Western governments. No one believes any more that the first Crash was a cyclical adjustment crisis of Asia's financial system. The tidy econometric models that predicted a slowdown of regional growth, conceding perhaps economic stagnation for Thailand, have been swept away by the regional recession which now points to the possibility of a second Crash. In June 1998, almost all East Asian economies are in full recession or on its threshold. Taiwan, the Philippines and China are the only exceptions, although most economic indicators in China point to a very fast decline of growth, and perhaps the clearest indicator of this is the fall of China's imports (by 3.8 per cent on a year to year basis) and exports (by 1.5 per cent) in May 1998. For the second quarter of 1998, Hong Kong's GDP drops by 5 per cent, Korea's by 6.6 per cent, Malaysia's by 6.8 per cent. Japan itself has experienced negative growth since October 1997. Even Singapore, whose GDP still grew by 5.6 per cent in the first quarter of 1998, entered recession in the second quarter according to a Merril Lynch estimate.[1] Indonesia's economy is the hardest hit, with a shrinkage of its currency and gross domestic product in dollar terms (−12.8 per cent for the 1998 GDP). The same projections forecast in 1998 −5.3 per cent for Thailand and −2.2 per cent for Malaysia. More importantly, a major social and political crisis has occurred in Indonesia, and to a lesser degree in South Korea, which will further compound economic problems. Throughout the region, many banks are either bankrupt, or kept alive by public subsidies. This leads to unavoidable nationalization or to a takeover by foreigners. Governments have been replaced (Thailand, Korea, Indonesia) or they suffer from a widespread loss of confidence (Japan, Malaysia).

There is, however, simply no indication that a democratic system of leadership constitutes a policy insurance against the crisis. When the Australian dollar falls to its lowest level in the past 15 years compared to the US dollar, as it did in June 1998, nobody points at the Australian democratic process as the root cause of the problem. The Philippines' apparent exception among ASEAN nations is simply due to its less advanced stage of growth in the first place, and to the stricter regimen its IMF mentors had imposed on the government. IMF prescriptions are excellent at helping an economy to stay lean, but they seem to over-reach their target when they are applied to economies in need of a slimming cure.

There is no guarantee of safety to be gained in the short term by creating or joining an open economic space such as the Asia-Pacific free trade zone envisioned by APEC. The economies that crashed first are precisely those that had pursued an ambitious programme of economic liberalization without fully grasping the need for adequate oversight and regulation. Had it remained in place, the old-fashioned Asian economic model might not have achieved as much economic growth in the first place. But it would have done a better job of containing the damage from a downturn in demand or investment.

Today, Asian mutual competition for foreign capital, whether it be direct investment or financial credit, is obviously much more intense and difficult than only a year ago. Political ill will surrounds the issue of any additional IMF or IMF-related package. The US Congress is balking at any additional contribution. Japan, the country that is reputedly not living up to its role as an economic dynamo in Asia, has actually put up as much as 42 billion dollars of contributions to crisis-affected Asian countries. Granted, a Japanese economic upturn would have more effect than any aid package. Meanwhile, the United States, which is still perceived as the potential saviour of Asia, has only contributed 11.8 billion dollars, or a mere fraction of the capital that has been flowing from Asia to the US capital markets in recent months.[2]

The region is therefore left with few options. In principle, an awakening of Asian monetary and financial cooperation, a more united voice in front of international financial institutions and a region-wide effort to regulate competition in capital and investment markets are needed. Japan, at least in the first half of 1997, and Singapore more recently are willing to guide this movement and work towards an orderly exit from the crisis.

For political reasons, however, the so-called Asian solution remains a fiction. First, Japan does not have the requisite financial manpower to put into practice the rules-based and more transparent financial system that is required. Japan has never been a champion of these virtues within its own financial system. Both countries know only too well the penalty for stepping on their neighbours' sensitivities in this respect. Early on in the course of the Crash, Lee Kuan-yew, who has often come under criticism for his strong advice to fellow ASEAN leaders, explained that international institutions such as the IMF were useful in avoiding neighbourly lectures. Japan much prefers to exercise indirect commercial and banking influence, rather than stand accused of reconstituting the Asian Co-prosperity Sphere. To become real, regional cooperation must overcome these political and historical obstacles.

Second, China, whose cooperation, or at least neutrality, is indispensable, pursues an entirely different strategy. It is based on the United States in the key role of favourite enemy, arbiter and occasionally ally on almost all international issues. The extremely high consideration that China's official think tanks and media display for the US economy is every day more striking. One can thus find in recent publications a full-size exposition about the New Economy and the advent of a cycle of global prosperity led by the United States. In advance of President Clinton's June visit, one could also read rather plaintive pleas for the United States' financial cooperation:

> Only preventing the crisis from spreading can truly benefit the United States. And, enabling China to more effectively prevent the crisis from spreading is the key to this strategy. Helping China maintain the exchange rate of its *renminbi* is also a key strategy for making China a larger market for the United States, thereby enabling the United States to maintain its economic growth for a longer amount of time.[3]

The times are gone when the slogan 'China Can Say No'[4] was the fashionable statement in Beijing. China has perceived the basic ambivalence in the United State's financial and monetary policy towards Japan. It is also worried by the Asian crisis and seeks political means to distance itself from it. Together with the United States, it is therefore forming a new quasi-alliance. It may be used by both nations to avoid a form of regional organization that would be detrimental to their national interests. For the United States would like nothing less than to see Japan break away from the Cold War era system of lopsided international relations, and China would like nothing less than seeing Japan exercise effective leadership of any nature over East Asia.

But in spite of appeals to the United States and also to Europe, there is no saviour appearing in the battlefield. Following the IMF's bitter prescriptions, swallowing the medicine as Michel Camdessus advised Indonesians, is not enough, since it fuels a recession and bankrupts scores of otherwise healthy firms in the process. The IMF in fact insists that it is there not to promote economic growth or save private firms from themselves, but to balance the books and avoid a threat to the global financial system. Restructuring the economy and proceeding through the final stages of opening up national economies to competition is equally lethal under those circumstances, since it leads to cut-throat competition among similar economic systems.

In practice, therefore, most of the region's economies find themselves facing a Faustian deal. They have only one way out if they want to avoid a long and crippling recession, with a second Crash looming over them. They must accept the takeover of firms and capital market shares by foreigners. Financial mergers and acquisitions foster the hope that debt burdens will either be assumed by new owners, or greatly reduced by the banking institutions that have trust in these new owners. Capital market shares may be ceded with the hope that the resulting capital influx will provide the fuel to start Asia's economic engines again. Stalling without any tailwind is not a realistic option to avoid a crash.

How Asians behave towards this Faustian offer is the essential political story of Asia's future. At present, the offer is one they cannot refuse. The already open nature of their capital markets allows local investors and savers to try and escape from the region, compounding the capital shortage issue. The only other route is for Asian governments to nationalize each country's private debt problem, spreading the burden across the entire society. The task is equally daunting. The public entities collecting the assets of failed banks and companies will in any case be faced with the issue of foreign buyers.

The implosion of regional trade

With a year of hindsight in observing trade statistics, we can see that none of the hard hit countries are jumpstarting their economies with increased exports. Changes in monetary parities, even from a massive devaluation, only result in trade balance shifts after a delay known to economists as the J-curve. It is therefore not surprising that East Asian trade did not move much in the first months after the Crash. But figures from the first quarter of 1998 or from the month of April are revealing. Overall, intra-regional trade has receded considerably. Japan, East Asia's most significant trading nation, saw its year-to-year imports from the rest of the region fall by 15 per cent in April 1998 (and even −21.4 per cent from Malaysia, −24 per cent from Taiwan and −28 per cent from

Indonesia), and its exports to the same region fall by 18 per cent. The percentages apply to yen-denominated figures, and would be even more marked if expressed in dollar terms.

South Korea's exports to the region fell by 10 per cent between January and April 1998; Chinese exports to East Asia fell by 9.5 per cent over the first quarter of 1998. Singapore's exports to most East Asian countries, still buoyant in February 1998, were in sharp retreat by April. Taiwan's exports during the first quarter to Japan fell by 24 per cent, and to ASEAN economies by an average 27 per cent. There is no mistaking the sense of regional and mutually reinforcing recession. In some cases, the drying up of even short-term export credits, the unavailability of container ships (since imports from the rest of the world are crashing even further) and the wide currency fluctuations are simply interrupting trade.

Even if receipts from regional exports had been booming, they could not compensate for the mounting financial losses that both public and private institutions are experiencing. Some Asian countries' exports to the rest of the world are in fact picking up speed, as predicted since the monetary devaluations. This is true of China and even of Japan. Chinese exports to the US went up by 21 per cent in the first four months of 1998, and by 30 per cent to Europe in the first three months of 1998. In April, Japanese exports to the US on a year-by-year basis went up by 29 per cent, and they increased by a whopping 61 per cent towards the European Union. The trend is much less obvious for Korea or the Southeast Asian economies, which do not have the financing available to take advantage of their lower costs.

It is interesting to observe that only Japan and Singapore have granted significant trade financing or credit guarantees to the region. They are the only partners to have recognized the specific problem arising from a trade credit shortage, and to have addressed it. Singapore in fact has tried for several months to get an international trade credit operation under way, and has earmarked 60 per cent of its bilateral relief grant to Indonesia for that purpose. Obviously, self-interest is also involved, since Japan and Singapore's foreign trade are hardest hit by the regional recession. Singapore's money will go first to its own exports to Indonesia, and in a second stage should help Indonesian companies restart their exports to third countries through Singapore.[5] Instead, sales to Asia amount to a much more modest amount for Europe and the United States, while the cost of keeping the door open to exports from Asia could run much higher.

The United States appears to be least involved in this aspect. If there is indeed a market of the last resort for Asia, this market today lies in

Europe more than in the United States. America is riding a long economic boom, while Europe's upward cycle has just started. The figures also suggest that an American market which has been fully open for two decades is also much more competitive and perhaps saturated with the type of core consumer goods produced in Asia. In Europe, where many prices were traditionally set higher, and where the penetration of Asian goods was more limited, there seems to exist a wider margin for immediate expansion. European economies are therefore seeing their trade deficits with Asia, only recently wiped out, expand again much more quickly than those of the United States. Since Asian capital flight to the United States is also stronger than to Europe, one can see there is not much disadvantage to Americans in leaving the door open to Asia's exports. Europeans will be feeling the pinch sooner, and expressing their dissatisfaction.

In short, regional trade is crumbling. Global export figures, together with shrinking imports, may attenuate the present recession for Japan, or slow its arrival in China. No other Asian economy is getting any lift from exports. In any case, they do not even begin to address the magnitude of the financial sector's problems throughout the region.

Bankruptcy in the financial sector

The actual cost of dealing with a systemic financial failure is often underestimated. The bail-out of Argentina's financial sector in 1980 to 1982 cost 55 per cent of its GDP,[6] and years of economic stagnation imposed by a currency board with stringent internal requirements. Besides, there is no previous experience in the emerging economies concerning stock market crashes of this magnitude, since capital markets never had the importance that they had acquired in Asia over the last decade. Malaysia, Hong Kong, Korea and Singapore had reached a market capitalization that was above a year of their respective GDP, reaching almost three years for Malaysia.

The crisis of Asian banks and financial institutions has therefore increased in intensity between 1997 and 1998. Singapore's large banks are the only ones that can endure the sting of heavy provisions to cover bad loans without losing their capacity to enforce a financial strategy. Singapore's first establishment, DBS,[7] has set aside 320 million dollars in provisions, yet, like its Japanese counterparts, it is also busy acquiring assets in the region. The recapitalization of Japan's banks themselves, whose bad loans are still not fully appreciated, may cost upwards of 20 per cent of the country's annual GDP. Yet they are still buying up assets.

Restoring a balance between the state and the market

The prospects are more grim for others. South Korea and Thailand may have to contribute one-third of their annual GDP to the rescue of their banks and financial companies, Indonesia and Malaysia one-fifth, with pockets that are of course much less deep than Japan's. Thailand, the first hit financial system of the Asian Crash, is furthest along on this road. The country's central bank has taken over seven banks and in effect, nationalized them. The list includes some with military ties and institutions belonging to Thailand's first banking family, the owners of Bangkok Bank.[8] This step is in addition to the eight financial establishments that were taken over in the first months of the Crash (from a total of 56 firms that were closed) and in addition also to four banks nationalized in early 1998. Only three of Thailand's major banks really remain untouched: the Thai Military Bank, which is really a private arm of Thailand's military establishment, Thai Farmers Bank and Bangkok Bank. These last two have been able to float large bond issues in order to recapitalize. Even these leading establishments were compelled to sell subsidiaries to foreign buyers in order to achieve this result.

In South Korea, the big corporations' debt to equity ratio reached 5.5 in May 1998. The pressure on lending institutions is therefore increasing. The government has already nationalized two banks (Korea First Bank and Seoulbank) in the first quarter of 1998, earmarking 35 billion dollars to buy up bad loans, recapitalize banks and provide insurance to depositors. On 20 May, it announced a further increase in both the size of the fund and its nationalization programme. As banks stand insolvent, the government will become their principal equity owner for what is viewed as a temporary and emergency period. The funds for these operations either come from the IMF rescue package, or have to be raised from the domestic market. In either case, this will severely hamper Korea's public spending capacity in other areas.

Malaysia's private debt problem is almost as important as Korea's. Credit reached 165 per cent of its GDP as a result of competition after capital market liberalization. Malaysia's Bank Negara has already been assigned the task of sheltering failing finance companies, in what amounts to a public takeover of much of the nation's credit institutions. Ironically, these financial firms sprouted up during Malaysia's capital liberalization policy in the period leading to the Crash. They are now folding and therefore putting financial credit decisions back in quasi-governmental hands. Like China, Malaysia is explicitly following the American example in setting up a public relief institution for its private financial sector. The Asset Management Corporation, formed in May 1998, advertises its transparent accounting to counter claims of favouritism, and has in fact taken J.P. Morgan and Arthur Andersen as advisers. Yet the new public corporation has the ambitious goal of taking over non-performing loans and assets in the hope of turning them around and reselling them. There remain doubts on the country's ability to raise the necessary financing in a context of economic recession.

None of these three countries has been delinquent in addressing the crisis of its financial sector. While Chuan Leekpai's government took the lead in forcing the closure of bankrupt institutions, Korea is also announcing stern measures to force the *chaebols* and other Korean firms to acknowledge failure when it is there. And Malaysia's government is fighting against its reputation of favouring political friends of the ruling party.

It is not only the Asian model, or its ideological platform, which is falling apart as a result of the Crash. Neo-liberal sentiment and blind market logic are also challenged. Several Asian governments are still following textbook prescriptions on the move to market economy by privatizing state enterprises. Yet in the same breath they are being forced to nationalize financial firms, taking back unto their own hands decisions that they had been persuaded to release from the neo-liberal market perspective. One can always call this move an emergency or temporary decision. Still, this shows the extent to which capital liberalization programmes have been incautious during the previous era.

The involuntary nationalization of credit which is happening in all three cases – not to mention Indonesia, where almost all banks are now insolvent – will test their political will to an unusual degree. In a context of recession and liquidity crunch, these governments will have to choose and decide who fails and who is allowed to pull through. In essence, all credit decisions previously made by the banking sector will now be made by an arm of the government, however autonomous this arm may appear.

This is precisely the dilemma that has constantly befallen Japan's ruling LDP politicians since 1991, and which they have not been able to solve. They could either be responsible for a large number of fore-closures and massive political and social discontent, with the near certainty of losing the next elections; or alternatively they might buy time into the future, trying to carry forward the backlog of debts and insolvent companies, in the blind hope that the ship can be set afloat again by a new economic tide. Finally, LDP secretary-general Koichi Kato announced on 20 June 1998 that Japan would introduce a so-called 'bridge-bank' patterned after the Resolution Trust Co. of US savings and loans fame. Belatedly, Japan initiated the process of public takeover of a failed financial system. Because the scale of its bad debts dwarfs any previous experience, it is predictable that Japan's public involvement will not be a brief experience.

Asia's governments are currently helped in making unpopular decisions by the obvious gravity of the situation, which in several cases amounts to an issue of national salvation. But the retrenchment and restructuring decisions are not an instant cure – the agenda is there to stay for the long haul. Ethnic and community interests built into existing political systems, factional politics allied resting on economic special interests, and above all the anger of laid-off workers will soon become major political obstacles.

For this reason, a victory of neo-liberal prescriptions is unlikely to happen in Asia beyond the first aftershock of the Crash. Foreign direct investment, equity purchases, loans and bail-outs from the global economy are simply not forthcoming at a rate that would make a market solution feasible. Politically, the best economic policies can go wrong if they fly in the face of citizens' interest – even more so, one might add, if Asia's political systems undergo further democratization. The former Asian model of mixed economy, with its recognition of community and special interests, its degree of job protection and its preference for social safety over free market play, is far more likely to attract voters. This is particularly true of Korea, where the shock from globalization is extreme.

The political dilemma of Asian governments is therefore acute. On the one hand, they must court international creditors and potential lenders of last resort, and therefore show quick results in their books. Today, even if the IMF has relented on its public budget-cutting requirements, this mostly means wielding an axe in the middle of Asia's worst recession. On the other hand, the demand for protection or relief from the crisis is bound to grow more acute. Governments can only combine these two demands by building a political and social consensus. Some may choose to forget the balance of welfare with market that is a requirement handed down from Asian cultures and social models. They will perhaps be hailed by international financial institutions and advocates of neo-liberal policies. And then they will be overthrown in the next elections, or by an outburst of social unrest and xenophobia.

On the other hand, no Asian government today can hope to ride out the crisis by either going it alone, or combining an overall IMF relief package with a closed shop policy to solve the credit and solvency problems within the domestic economy. All have to appeal, as they have already started to do with variable enthusiasm, to foreign capital.

This will not only ease the liquidity crunch that is trapping Asian economies. It will help to adopt unpalatable decisions when the responsibility is split with foreign investors. Indeed, the Mahathir–Anwar debate in Malaysia, beyond the political game that caused Anwar's fall in August 1998, perfectly symbolizes the issue. While Anwar expresses market responses (letting firms fail), orthodox monetary policies (raising interest rates) and global cooperation, Mahathir symbolizes state resistance (protecting firms in the national interest), traditional welfare concern (lowering interest rates to avoid a socially crippling recession) and the preference for a regional solution that incorporates an element of political resistance, or at least bargaining, in the face of the demands of global financial market forces.

A regional response to the crisis?

It is precisely at a regional level that the lesson from the painful rescue operation of 1997 to 1998 will be drawn. The painful months from July 1997 to March 1998 have witnessed the breakdown or the irrelevance of intra-Asian, and even intra-ASEAN cooperation.

Many factors have led to this situation. They include competitive devaluations and 'beggar thy neighbour' speeches, a failure of many of the region's political leaders to comprehend the nature of the crisis, which they insisted was a short-term speculative outburst, the complete lack of a regional leadership that is torn between a shy and involuted Japan, a swaggering but fragile China, and an ineffective ASEAN.

These factors have devastated the region's integrative process. By early January 1998, Asian economies appeared to be 'rudderless, like a fleet caught in a raging storm'.[9] In February 1998, Lee Kuan-yew went so far as to employ the past tense in mentioning Japan's leading role in regional affairs.[10] As we have seen, an American-led reluctance to join a Japanese initiative in 1997 for Asian emergency cooperation had also contributed to this breakdown. As for China's often vaunted cooperation with its neighbours, this has been vastly exaggerated. In the words of Gerald Segal, 'China has merely demonstrated the power of the passive – a promise not to fail or to foul-up the plans of others is not active leadership that shapes, let alone re-shapes the region'.[11]

There was therefore no solution for any of the ailing Asian economies but to take their case to the IMF, or to implement quasi-IMF moves in the case of Malaysia. Japan's increasing crisis of financial confidence in 1997 to 1998, with a domestic recession and deflation, has precluded in any case a strong role by what remains, by sheer numbers, the world's second economy.

Yet Asians have not remained inactive among themselves, and have often searched for bilateral or regional arrangements that would ease the pain. In so doing they have had to change their language altogether. One hears no more of the celebrated consensual, unilateral, voluntary and informal agreements that were used to define the ASEAN way. In fact, when ASEAN's new secretary-general Rodolfo Severino first tried to pick up the pieces of regional cooperation, he was no longer dismissive of the institutionally focused process of European integration, and recognized that there were changes to be made in the way ASEAN worked.[12]

It is important to identify the buds of regional cooperation that are appearing out of the storm. They point out to much more concrete advances than the often grandiose but abstract plans drawn up in the heyday of the miracle economies. As early as December 1997, the new Chuan Leekpai government in Thailand was touring the G7 governments to plead for a quicker and larger rescue operation. In Washington, they received a nod and a wink that the Thai leaders gobbled up hungrily, after having gone through the experience of a complete let-down by their Cold War ally. Facetiously, a Thai newspaper commented: 'It is a waste of time to delude yourself that you received a positive signal from Washington. The people who could demand repayment of our debts are in New York, and they do not send out signals before they make that demand.'[13] But after a trip by Finance Minister Tharin Nimmanhemin to Tokyo, Japan accepted the principle of converting debt repayments from US dollars to yen. Both countries' self-interest was at stake, since Japan had much to fear from a Thai default on its private or public loans. The step was quickly described by the Thai press as an acceptance of the yen zone. This was also in essence the first example of a true Mexican-type solution to the bad debt problem, with Japan in the shoes of the United States, of course. Japan would similarly try its way with bilateral agreements for Indonesia.

A second example is Singapore's effort to launch an international mechanism of export financing in order to relieve Indonesia's industrial and primary material firms. Originating with Singapore's Monetary Authority, the plan involved the backing of Indonesia's central bank, together with well established foreign banks. The plan had a cool reception from the West. Although no public stance has ever been made against these proposals, it seems clear that Western political leaders are loath to present to their voters an Asian rescue package that would result first and foremost in the promotion of Asian exports. Either these leaders have completely failed to predict the scale of the recession hitting Asia, or they have felt that explaining to their voters the need for export packages would be a self-defeating task. A G7 finance ministers' meeting in London in March 1998 was preceded by the rumour that it might adopt a large trade finance package, but to no avail.[14] This situation continued up to and including the second ASEM meeting in London in April 1998, where a much smaller-scale fund for teaching financial market techniques to Asians was established in conjunction with the World Bank (and was exactly like an earlier Japanese fund). Yet both Japan, Singapore, Taiwan and China have established such export facilities with Indonesia.

Let us draw a partial conclusion. In the future, it will become clear that the West, in the mistaken belief that the Crash would remain regional and perhaps limited in its effects, preferred to exploit its advantage and refused to extend a hand to countries and companies which now lack any financial credit for exports. In contrast, East Asian governments have acted pragmatically to salvage what they could in intra-Asian trade. These bilateral financial arrangements may grow into future regional ties of a very concrete nature.

The third example is the recurrent talk about using regional currencies for trade, or moving to regionally pegged currencies that would displace the dollar anchor. Although the first half of this idea is usually associated with Dr Mahathir, and therefore tainted with an anti-Western hue, it did not originate publicly with him. In early January 1998, the Philippines' Minister of Trade and Industry said that 'the time has come to trade in our own regional currencies, without using a third currency that has nothing to do with the trade'.[15] In February, Mahathir took the idea to Indonesia, Thailand, Singapore and back to the Philippines. His plan was set up for 'study' after the Thirty-third Conference of Governors of Southeast Asian Banks in Bali. Clearly, the idea is loose as yet, and is often linked with the alternative use of the yen in intra-Asian transactions. Japan's Vice-Minister of Finance for International Affairs Eisuke Sakakibara promised to increase the use of the yen in Japan–ASEAN trade. These ideas have received official approval in Singapore, the only monetary authority that really counts in Southeast Asia. A *Singapore Business Times* editorial argued that 'the moment was opportune for a yen bloc'. In actual terms, though, it pressed more widely 'for central banks to begin building more yen and euro reserves – and for Japanese banks to make a psychological switch from US dollar to yen lending in ASEAN. Of course, the US will not like the idea of losing some of its currency hegemony but Asia must not let that stand in the way of reform'.[16]

By April 1998, the supplementary facility to the IMF, to which a November meeting of the region's finance ministers and Central Bank representatives had paid lip service a few months earlier, had still not materialized. Another idea gained currency: a monetary and financial early warning and surveillance agreement, whose conception is now entrusted to the Asian Development Bank (ADB), and praised by the ASEAN secretariat as an example of regional financial cooperation. Indeed, the project involves a new level of financial and monetary transparency among participants. ADB officials emphasize their cooperation with the IMF,[17] yet there are some aspects which testify to the resurgence of an Asian regional solution. The Japanese and ASEAN backers of the idea named it the East Asian Financial Caucus, a clear and symbolic reference to Dr Mahathir's earlier proposal of an Asians-only economic alliance. The new institution will be entrusted to ASEAN itself after two years, which would ironically put it in Jakarta, where ASEAN's secretariat is located. Hong Kong's monetary authority chief executive Joseph Yam Chi-Kwong has called for an extension of the ADB's role in becoming a regional lender of the last resort, and has even emphasized Hong Kong's readiness, as one of the non-borrower members of the bank, to contribute heavily to this new guarantee.[18] The Asian Development Bank, traditionally under Japanese influence, is now prominent in giving financial advice to several Asian governments, including China, on the management of their financial sector. There is also a separate debate shaping up in the United States regarding the applicability of an Asian solution based on an evolution of existing international financial institutions. The Asia Society in New York has compiled a policy report under the leadership of former assistant secretary of state for East Asia Winston Lord which emphasizes the reform of international finance agencies.[19] Here and there, voices are raising the concern that the IMF is not up to the job.

By the time the present crisis is over, Asian leaders will remember a few facts. First, that outside intervention took months to shape up during the Crash of 1997. Second, that the talk about market rule and financial orthodoxy slowly relented. After some time, much more consideration was given by the IMF itself to the need for subsidies or social spending. The IMF has begun condoning practical arrangements to share the onus of the debt between private lenders and debtors – after the South American and Mexican pattern. However, during the crucial nine months (from August 1997 to April 1998) when the IMF's policies rode roughshod over Asia's economies, a wholesale recession flared up.

Third, Asians will realize the symbolism of the small vessel fleet with regard to their situation. In February 1998, the World Bank's Joseph Stiglitz seized on the image and concluded that 'even with the best economic management, small open economies remain vulnerable. They are like small rowboats on a wild and open sea. Although we may not be able to predict it, the chances of being eventually broadsided by a large wave are significant no matter how well the boat is steered'.[20] In other words, the fact that some of Asia's most dynamic economies, under guidance from APEC, the IMF standard prescriptions for liberalization, and pressure from international finance firms, chose to free capital movements in and out of their economies, without teaming up regionally or setting up adequate regulations and safeguards, has turned into a disaster. This, and not only real or imaginary sins in managing development, has capsized their boats. As the specialist on emerging economies Jagdish Bhagwati noted, 'these meltdowns could have occurred if Alan Greenspan were managing these economies'.[21] Asians will also take notice that transparency is not in itself a guarantee against future crises. Europe's Northern economies, among the world's most transparent, went through some very rough episodes in the early 1980s. Germany, whose firms largely ignore international requirements for financial disclosure, and often eschew any introduction on Wall Street for that reason, has remained immune from financial breakdown.

Asians will therefore undertake to mix the financial market reforms, regulations and transparency enhancements that international investors are demanding with hard-nosed regional developments that should give them a stronger hand the next time around. They will almost certainly seek to subdue some of the short-term or future speculation that has ripped apart the region's economy. Particularly telling is the present attempt by Taiwan's central bank to ban non-deliverable forward currency contracts. This is the instrument of choice for brokers seeking to protect themselves from a currency devaluation – and who have ended up speeding up that devaluation through their moves. Taiwan's monetary and financial authorities are the best example in Asia of mixing tight supervision and a dose of nationalism with financial opening. Their better judgement today is to retreat from complete capital market freedom.

Asian repo[22]

Asian governments will also try and consolidate regional cross-holdings of firms, as a compromise on the road to foreign takeover of their economies' key sectors. There is evidence that several regional alliances may be forming up in this respect. The two best examples concern countries that have combined varying degrees of political acrimony in the past with effective economic ties and mutual dependence. A case in point is the increasing activity that Singapore interests display in nearby Malaysia. Singapore Investment Corporation, the state's investment vehicle, which has also acquired recently Thailand's 12th bank and taken a share in Thai Farmers Bank, is negotiating to acquire a large stake in AMMB, one of Malaysia's largest banks. Singapore's business press has been extremely protective of Malaysia's economic policies, while it did not hesitate to criticize the actions of President Suharto and his government. If Malaysia relaxes, as it has announced, its pro-Malay legislation, there is a clear possibility of seeing a form of Singapore–Malay union revived in the economic field.

Even more striking is the deal to swap equity that is under consideration by the world's two largest steel companies, Nippon Steel and Korea's Pohang Steel Company (Posco). There has been no deeper rivalry in the past than that between these two national flagships. Posco's losses and the government policy of allowing for foreign ownership are forcing a change. Nippon Steel itself is worried by the undoing of equity cross-ownership ties in Japan, and is being forced into an expensive buy-back programme of its own shares. By teaming up, the two companies will avoid another round of fratricidal price competition, and will become an even more powerful force in the global steel industry.

This deal is likely to remain isolated, however. Like many other international investors, Japan's firms will not match the high price that Korean sellers still demand for their firms, and the possibility of violent labour clashes is also a deterrent. Even more significantly, Korean nationalism is likely to balk at Japanese ownership of firms. For the time being, most would-be buyers from Japan are still standing on the sidelines.[23] Certainly, the important role that Japanese banks play in taking over Thailand's financial institutions is a more classic case of an Asian buyout between two partners which entertain few reservations.

We can see quite clearly why these examples will not go a long way towards easing the financial solvency problems of firms throughout Asia. Japan itself should be the main engine for a regional solution. The odds are that it cannot deliver this solution, for three main reasons. First, Japan itself is groaning under the twin burden of bad debt and a domestic recession. The bail-out efforts it has already contributed, and the cost of meeting provisions from the Asian bad loans of its banks and trading companies, is already very large. The level of debts within its own domestic economy simply prevents Japan from becoming a lender or a buyer of the last resort for the region. Japan no longer has the financial oxygen available to replace some of the air that is being sucked out by the regional depression.

Second, the steady decline of the yen is by itself a disincentive for Japan's firms to go regional. Their best hope is to cut costs and regain competitiveness by centralizing their operations at home.

Third, Japan does not today have the political clout to engineer an Asian-inspired rescue for the region. The same Western countries that opposed an Asian Fund in the initial phase of the Crash now press the Japanese government for action. Minor spokesmen for the European Union now parrot US Treasury Secretary Robert Rubin, repeating that only Japan can save itself and Asia. This is a self-exonerating exercise, which will prove futile when the Crash expands still further. By putting the blame on Japan, they further isolate it in the Asian region. It becomes politically even harder for other Asian countries to engage a cooperative process, and even easier for them to blame Japan in the face of their own public opinions. China is especially adept at this ploy.

Regional solutions are therefore of an even more limited breadth and likelihood than national solutions at the present time. It is only when the urgency of the crisis recedes that they will come again to the fore.

Asia learns a lesson

Good lessons never come cheap. Western countries can point to the combined financial contribution they are making through the IMF to restoring the integrity of Asia's financial systems. They can also cite the debt deferments provided by private banks. Yet the inadvertent Western gains from the situation are stunning. These include a fall in oil prices by 40 per cent, in other primary materials by 30 per cent, lower inflation and interest rates for the economy. In terms of business psychology, there was in 1997–1998 a detectable atmosphere of restored consumer confidence in the strength of Western economies. 'Spend and grow rich – it's the American way', concluded one commentator.[24] Above all, no short-term economic, political or social challenge is coming from Asia. Even China's economic rise leaves it 'a fragile and flawed power',[25] which America will occasionally use to lean on its recalcitrant Japanese partner.

In the psychological dimension, what is a gain for the West translates as a loss for Asians. Certainly, Asians have understood the harsh lesson taught by investor behaviour on immature financial markets. They know that they should blame themselves for the lack of regulation or overseeing, the combination of naive opening up of capital markets, remaining opacity, and blind search for quick returns that combined to engineer the Crash of 1997.

Yet another lesson can be drawn from this episode. After all, the above-mentioned defects belong to a failed transition towards free capital markets, not to the Asian model. Greed and the pursuit of short-term financial results have been essential factors moving markets and the cult for short-term profit became universal under the neo-liberal era of the 1980s, while the Asian model was commonly praised for its focus on long-term investment. This perspective is now reversed.

The lesson is therefore double-edged. Yes, Asia's thirst for foreign capital forces a surrender of its social practices in favour of universal and transparent rules. But is the sudden transformation of developmental economic models into wide open financial constructions not also to blame? And has the West not relentlessly pushed for the adoption of this new financial economy, using the leverage of trade surpluses as a bargaining tool? If, as may be the case, Asians have to get to work to reconstruct, and in the first place to simply reflate their domestic economy, why should they pursue a complete change over to international financial rules that often play against their customary instincts and into the hands of better trained operators?

Asia has moved incredibly fast since the mid-1980s on the path of economic and financial deregulation and liberalization. Contrary to many sarcastic comments made since the Crash began, these policies have become the binding glue of Asia's renewed relationship with the West. Even today, whatever the grumbling about international speculation, and despite obvious doubts on the best strategy for them, no Asian nation has pointedly retreated from major commitments towards financial liberalization. Most have in fact taken steps forward in order to try and lure back investors. The scramble for capital is the most pressing concern. It also involves a fear of being undercut by other neighbours' own moves.

It is therefore fascinating that in spite of the Crash, there have not yet appeared articulate political or theoretical exponents in Asia for restrictive or protectionist policies. Those in the West who have launched a rearguard fight against the devils of globalization do not really have counterparts in Asia, even as it is hit by the backlash from ill-executed financial deregulation and globalization. Asia certainly has its hard-core nationalists and conservatives, who argue, like Shintaro Ishihara in Japan or Deng Liqun in China, for the defence of the old nation-state against every form of foreign inroad and influence. But that is merely opinion stirring, not a coherent economic or political doctrine. Ironically, it is the West which is both the source of the revolution in market capitalism and of a fairly coherent and doctrinaire opposition to it. Patrick Buchanan[26] for America's radical right, Emmanuel Todd[27] for France's 'brown and red'[28] rejection of Europe's move towards federation via the market, present interesting arguments against globalization. Even

Kenichi Ohmae, who often passes as the closest example of an econo-mist turning against globalization, is actually much more accepting of the international marketplace and its laws than these Western critics. He essentially advocates a 'swing of the pendulum' for the region's coun-tries 'by redefining their role from that of central provider to that of region state catalyst'.[29]

Only Dr Mahathir, in fact, has expressed forceful political opposition to the huge step forward of globalization that results from the 1997 Crash. 'Asian countries will prosper again, but not as Asian countries. Their economies would be dominated and run by the huge foreign corporations, practically all owned and managed by non-Asians.' And he envisaged the possibility of a 'guerilla war' by Asians 'seeking to re-gain control over their economies'.[30] Mahathir cuts a lonely figure these days. What is more, he laces his speeches with denunciations of the international media and intimations of conspiracy theories that ruin most of his efforts. Yet on his central topic of economic sovereignty, he is the only major figure in Asia voicing openly what many Asians think. Lest my judgement be seen as an unlikely support for Mahathir's often blatant anti-Americanism, may I cite the New York-based Asia Society eminent persons group's recent report on the Asian crisis:

> If the United States is viewed as using the IMF as a front to pursue a narrow nationalistic agenda, or if American firms are seen to be simply taking short-term advantage of current difficulties to buy up local firms at bargain prices, anti-Americanism – always latent and lately rekindled – could grow and undermine the moral basis of US leadership.'[31]

There may be other defects in Dr Mahathir's effective leadership, not the least of which is an occasional pursuit of policies that, albeit pragmatic, contradict his pet theories. Yet he is fundamentally right in his political diagnosis about the future. The combination of a liquidity crunch, rendering insolvent otherwise viable businesses, with massive capital flight from the region under the new market freedoms, leads to expropriation of Asia's capital. Since the politics of Asia after independence have been based on nation-states and economic sover-eignty, it is unlikely that this process will proceed without major political conflict.

The fire sale is on

There are clear signs that the scramble for capital in Asia is leading to an acceleration of purchases by foreign investors, which is sometimes akin to repossession, since the terms can be extremely unfavourable to sellers. For the first half of 1998, mergers and acquisitions in Asia have reached 45 cases with 10.6 billion dollars involved, twice as much as the year before.

One of these signs is the lifting of direct investment restrictions or ceiling on foreign ownership by several countries. These moves are not just undertaken to satisfy hungry market requirements, since neither investors nor buyers are falling over themselves to enter Asia. In part, they may have been designed to give international financial organizations such as the IMF token concessions. More generally, they demonstrate an anxiety to attract whatever foreign investment is left. For example, South Korea announced a complete deregulation of such key economic sectors as retail oil, property and water supply, all effective before 1 August 1998. The caps on foreign ownership are being eliminated. Almost all companies will be fully acquirable, except key firms such as electricity utilities and Pohang Steel (restricted to 30 per cent). Thailand has repeatedly lifted upwards its cap on foreign ownership, while Malaysia is considering a case-by-case review of its 50 per cent ceiling. China itself, which only two years earlier had restricted the sectors in which foreign direct investment was desirable, is again widening the scope in order to chase investors. And of course, Japan's Big Bang, itself much more the result of pressure for structural change from the West than of any Japanese design, is resulting in easier access to Japan's capital markets. Above all, it allows foreign finance firms to compete equally for the savings of the individual Japanese, who had hitherto been boxed into their own system.

The result, in spite of the worsening crisis, is a tangible wave of acquisition throughout Asia. American multinational firms were the first, with their immense cash flow from financial profits on Wall Street, to take the advantage and either take over partly owned subsidiaries or competitors. Brand distributor companies, such as Coca-Cola, Eastman Kodak, Procter & Gamble or Gillette were particularly quick on their feet, snapping up in Korea for example the ailing subsidiaries of *chaebols* which were forced to retrench. Financial institutions have come next, scavenging the ruins of Asian capital markets for choice items. AIG,[32] which already has a strong foothold in China, has applied to buy from the Life Insurance Association of Japan – in effect, the industry coordinator – a group of forty-three collapsed Japanese companies. AIG has also been able to acquire a majority stake in a Malaysian insurance company, benefiting from the kind of special authorization which it also received in Shanghai from Chinese authorities a few years ago – apparently, the level playing field is still tilted towards some. Merril Lynch took over the marketing offices of Yamaichi Securities, Japan's fourth-largest stockbroker, after it went bust in November 1997. It is also considering acquisitions in Korea and Thailand. Travelers Group also bought a quarter of Nikko Securities, Japan's third brokerage. Citibank would have acquired First Bangkok City Banks in November 1997, if hidden bad debts had not scared it away. Perhaps one of the most strategic takeovers envisioned is that of Daewoo's automotive business by General Motors. Daewoo was always a part supplier to, and a buyer of technology from GM, but their ability to draw on Korea's extremely low production costs thanks to this acquisition will reverberate through the world's car industry.

Europeans are also present, although less aggressive. Among European banks, ABN Amro of the Netherlands has been the most active, taking over Bank of Asia, Thailand's eleventh-largest bank with an innovative approach: the actual selling price will only be settled through independent evaluation after the dust settles, and hidden losses are accounted for. Société Générale has acquired the marketing and research branches of Peregrine in Hong Kong. Most European banks have actually retrenched, though, handicapped by their large loan exposure. Industrial firms are more aggressive. BASF has bought several Korean firms, becoming the country's largest foreign buyer in the midst of the crisis. Volvo has purchased Samsung's construction equipment unit for 572 million dollars – as well as a business skyscraper in downtown Seoul for a mere 7.5 million dollars. A previously barely noticed Belgian brewing company now owns Doosan, a company that sells 40 per cent of Korea's beers.[33]

It is likely that these examples will turn into an even larger flow of acquisitions. For many Western firms are criticizing the level of prices that Asian owners are still asking for their firms. This is particularly true of Korea, where many foreign buyers are waiting in earnest for further trouble among Korea's big names. Daewoo's chairman himself has suggested the formation of a new nation-wide bank that would combine foreign participation with a pooling of financial resources from Korea's large group. It is not certain that this compromise between domestic and foreign capital would succeed. For the time being, Korean firms are busy consolidating their situation by selling subsidiaries to one another. As for Indonesia, foreign firms have not even entered the fray yet, and the political trouble stemming from the changeover from a Suharto family economy to unstable patrons may slow them up for a while.

The issue of ownership

The issue of property has always been more sensitive in Asia than in Europe and the United States. The context of colonization, the mixed-economy tradition, the national nature of most of the region's developed or incipient capitalist systems, mean that actual property is much less multinational than in the United States or especially Europe. Closed property, cross-ownership, the preference for personal relationships over contractual relations, are an essential characteristic of the Asian economic model, on which the high saving and investment pattern was premised. It is this ultimate feature of the Asian model, much more fundamental than trade and industrial policies, that is being dismantled as a result of the 1997 financial crash. In the financial area, most of the region's capital markets had remained restrictive to foreigners.

True, Asia is beginning this change of ownership from a very low starting point. The holding of Japanese securities by foreign investment firms was still only 2 per cent of total equity in 1996. A projected quadrupling to 8 per cent in 1998 does not yet reverse the prevailing structure of management or ownership. But American investment in Japanese properties, for example, has quintupled to 20 billion dollars in a year. This is not surprising, when real estate prices in downtown Tokyo stand at about 20 per cent of their 1980s' peak.

The change is happening with a speed that no other region has known. Major changes of ownership nationality in Europe have spread over several decades. Britain's post-war downslide, and its financial restructuring under Thatcher and Major's stewardship, have internationalized British capital, now the most open in Europe. France's major firms used to have a cross-holding pattern that was very similar to Japan's, with the average Frenchman's savings tied up with either state institutions or public banks. It took the succeeding and contradictory policies of socialist and conservative governments, from 1981 to 1997, to unwillingly unstitch these relationships that suited almost everybody within the mixed economy. Unfavourable tax policies and the prohibition of private pension funds mean that foreign mutual and pension funds now own more than 40 per cent of the Paris Bourse. Germany and the Netherlands, not to mention Switzerland, have kept their cards much closer to their chests. In textbooks on economic models, Asian capitalism was always closer to the so-called Rhine corporate capitalism than to the British-American financial model.

If Asians have been so reluctant over the past decade to surrender some of their national sovereignty in the interests of regional cooperation, one can surmise that a massive influx of foreign, and largely Western ownership will indeed become a large political and economic issue. Certainly, international firms may well prove to be wiser investors than, say, former President Suharto's relatives. Experienced multinationals will know enough to Asianize their operations, appearing as good local citizens. Sophisticated young Japanese, for example, may find some appeal in being rid of some of the constraints of domestic employers.

For the time being, a Faustian deal is being enacted. Promises are being made to remake economic rules and systems. Asian firms will often change hands, and perhaps Asians themselves will Westernize at an even quicker pace than before the Crash. Yet when the tide finally turns and Asia recovers, it is more than likely that Asian national, cultural and social practices will reassert themselves. For short-sighted Western firms now buying into Asia, the feeling of a knife going through butter will prove to have been a temporary experience. The basic conflict between Westerners who require a level playing field and Asians who interpret this request as an obligation to play the games according to Western rules is not over yet.

8 Conclusion

Two scenarios for tomorrow

Asia's downsizing is now a reality. With the burst of bubble economics, it was not only the bloated and overextended firms and markets that took a direct hit. The simultaneity of falling currencies, falling equity markets, receding GDP figures and indifferent export performances is telling. Today's Asian crisis is not a cyclical adjustment or even a correction of the excessive optimism of the past. It is Asia's major economic emergency of the past 50 years, far surpassing, for example, the effects of the 1974 oil shock. In fact, the similarity of today's trend with the pattern of the 1929 to 1939 world Depression is being slowly recognized.

The Crash of 1997 was never a purely regional event, patterned after other crises in emerging economies. The issue of yen–dollar monetary relationships, the role played by Japanese and other international capital in triggering the events, and finally the impact of East Asia's economy on other regions, always made this Crash a threat to the global financial system. We are now discovering that a crisis which remained largely regional in its initial form has global implications indeed. Its very occurrence presses the need for the international financial system to change.

A standard response to the Crash has been for the West to beckon Asia further on the road to being 'more like us', e.g. to speed up economic and financial liberalization. The advice ignores the fact that if the Crash is a systemic disorder that has some roots in the global system, and not just in Asia, there can none the less be Asian responses to this emergency. Asian polities and social practices, the interests of nation-states and the issue of ownership and economic sovereignty may trigger responses that do not belong to the catalogue of all-out market policies. A minimal compromise from the West must be the recognition that our systems, too, mix market economics with regulation from above and public guidance. A further step would be to admit that the historical low point for the value of East Asian assets is perhaps not the ideal moment, from a long-term political point of view, for buying these assets. Some restraint must be exercised.

To map out the future of Asia, one should forget the short-term views of business economists who have failed to forecast a falling house of cards over the past year. Neither can one follow instant predictions based on sunshine views of the Asian model's past fundamentals. There are two key factors at work. First, the collective psychology and political attitudes of Asian citizens and their leaders are now more important than any economic factor. Second, the choices that will be made by the leaders of the West's industrialized countries in the coming months, and therefore the degree of global cooperation in resolving the crisis, is the other deciding factor for the future of Asia. Since Asians, including many of their government and business leaders, are now stunned and reactive rather than proactive, most of them cannot be counted on for forward-looking leadership. The best they can do is to follow adjustment plans at the level of national economics. Only decisions made by the global community can turn Asian economies round, with the cooperation of Japan.

By mid-1998, the latest fashion in solutions for the crisis was to encourage each country to serve as a liquidator of the last resort for its domestic bad debts and failed companies. Weak Asian governments are unrealistically expected to play this role by themselves, when this will clearly fuel major political instability. Why should they strain themselves to ensure that Western creditors are paid? Obviously, it is better for them to wait it out, until these creditors reduce their own expectations. And indeed, the West's recent political history does not set an example for them. The current Western leaders whose slow response may leave open this possibility are in fact riding on a new prosperity often brought about by their predecessors' actions. In the United States, George Bush failed to be re-elected essentially because his sound long-term budgetary and financial policies sowed short-term discontent. John Major paid the political price for awkwardly continuing Maggie Thatcher's economic policies and laying the ground for a phase of renewed economic growth. Even in France, the politically inauspicious budget-cutting and social cost containment policies of 1995 to 1997 put the economy on better ground, yet drowned the government that led those policies.

But we would like politically weak and insecure Asian governments, often presiding over social tinder barrels, to behave like Maggie Thatcher in 1982, or perhaps like the elected Roosevelt in 1933. Roosevelt himself 'frequently confessed to his ignorance' of economics 'but had the virtue of not being doctrinaire'.[1] The set of domestic measures (including the

Tennessee Valley Authority and the National Recovery Act) that he adopted during the famous initial 100 days of his presidency did not constitute an economic programme, but were decisions tailored to restore confidence. Not even Roosevelt gave a priority to international economic relations in 1933. This resulted in the failure of the World Economic Conference in June–July 1933. Could Ryutaro Hashimoto or his immediate successor do better than FDR? Of course not.

Two aspects indeed stand out. First, only the world's leaders of the financial system can undertake responsibilities such as being the lender of the last resort, or can start a global process to share this responsibility. This concerns the United States and the European Union in consideration of its monetary unification. Japan, on the contrary, has weakened considerably over the past decade. In spite of it being the world's first lending country until 1997 and having the world's largest pool of external assets, Japan's failure to establish itself as a monetary power, as defined by the yen becoming an international reserve instrument, leaves it a second-rate nation, unable to take the risk of lender of last resort. Like smaller Asian countries, it is now compelled to take care of its domestic debt situation first.

Second, in spite of these possibilities, the US and Europe are predominantly looking at Asia's crisis through the perspective of their domestic economies. Denying the impending possibility of an international financial breakdown, and piling the blame on various Asian countries for their own sins, is merely a short-term way to exonerate the West's own responsibility in the deterioration of the situation. The West now enjoys a wave of prosperity with abundant liquidity. It wishes to predominate as a universal value and rules-based system. Yet when the time comes to act on the consequences of the Asian Crash, the West suddenly hands over leadership to Japanese and other Asian politicians. In a situation of free-floating financial flows, how could they themselves engineer a reversal over the short term? Containing the damage cannot be achieved by the countries in crisis alone, and this includes Japan.

Tables 8.1 and 8.2 outline two possible outcomes of the Asian Crash.

The first scenario – international inertia leads to the Second Crash

The first scenario is based on the continuation of present international attitudes and policies towards failing Asia, including Japan. In this scenario, IMF-directed or -related rescue packages stay at present level, granting that even the IMF does not insist any more on balanced or positive public budgets when economic activity is in free fall. Beyond

Table 8.1 First scenario for the future: international inertia

Immediate local consequences	Second Crash	International response	
		Plan A	*Plan B*
■ Low local costs	■ Chinese devaluation	■ Global deal	■ Failure to
■ Export-oriented Asian economies	■ Japanese restriction of freedom capital	to share the burden of	respond
■ Yen's value eroded	movements	the debts	■ Regional destabilization
	■ Low foreign investment		
	■ Trade war		

Table 8.2 Second scenario for the future: International Resolution Trust

	Conditions	International action
■ Reconsideration of IMF conditional policies	■ First scenario becoming an imminent possibility	■ Creation of an International Resolution Trust in conjunction with Asian governments
■ Western states initiate a global solution to the Asian liquidity crisis	■ Necessary effort by Japan to overcome its own financial crisis	■ The West adopts a policy of voluntary monetary creation to help overcome the Asian liquidity crunch

the occasional expression of concern or fabricated optimism, the only additional encouragement that major Western economies provide is a commitment to keeping the door open to rising exports from Asia.

This attitude will have lopsided results. Those countries and firms in Asia which still have available credit or self-financing will soon benefit from a situation where local costs are at a historical low point. Instead of moving to a domestically based growth and marketing approach, they will go even more in the direction of being export-oriented. This is already happening for a handful of top firms in Japan's manufacturing sector, whose equity value moves in inverse relation to the yen exchange rate and in complete isolation from other companies.

Meanwhile, from Seoul to Shanghai and Surabaya, the domestic heart of Asia's economy will be suffering from massive deflation and increasing social distress. Since the door to the region's capital markets and to individual saving accounts now swings both ways, Asians will keep exporting their available liquidities, further bringing down the region's currencies. Should Asia's and especially Japan's central banks be adventurous enough to follow the 'friendly' advice occasionally given to them to print currency, this would not stop the money from leaving the country. Instead of concluding that monetary inflation will lead to prosperity, individuals and companies might well think that another wave of currency depreciation is looming. By making this move, monetary authorities would merely convince their citizens that the downward spiral is likely to accelerate further. Asia's liquidity crunch is no longer a lack of local monetary creation – it is the result of a conviction that any deposit, loan or equity purchase is more likely than not to go down the drain. Certainly more savings are being generated by the Japanese than at any other time in recent history. They just do not enter or do not stay in Japanese institutions any more. Trust in the future is now the fundamental issue.

As the reader will have surmised, this scenario is that of the Second Asian Crash. Since June 1998, we have already made headway down this road, with the yen's value steadily eroding, and Japan's regional capacity to act even further impaired. In this case, the Chinese government has few options left. It refrained from devaluation of its own currency in 1997, when that move alone would have brought the region's currencies further down. Although Chinese propagandists have obviously not been averse to making some mileage from this self-control, it is not them, but ignorant foreign commentators, who have suggested that China might lead the region's economy. Chinese leaders know much better, having experienced at first hand the multiple crises of a socialist economy reforming itself. Political instinct will take the helm, with few Chinese leaders ready to explain to their people why they should choose to bankrupt China's export economy in order to maintain a stable exchange rate with the US dollar. After a more or less decent interval, China will devalue, thus compounding the region's problems – although by that time, these problems will have become so self-evident that the Chinese will hardly be blamed for breaking a promise that they simply could not keep.

If such a scenario unfolds, the leaders of the global financial system will go down in history as having complacently seized on the short-term benefits to Western economies of the First Asian Crash, refusing to acknowledge both its systemic nature and its global implications. Capital flows leaving Asia from July 1997 to the Second Crash will have been a one-time bonus, after which a major disruption of the global system is in store.

For the Second Crash will not remain a regional event. Japan's ailing financial sector and threatened firms want a bail-out and the West requires Japan to launch an instant restructuring of Japan's essential business relationships. But up to this point, we have seen Japan's political leadership under Ryutaro Hashimoto behave in a wooden, paralysed way, trying to harmonize these contradictory requests. Japan's own financial officials primarily express the fear of capsizing Japan's economy with one false move. For over a year now, Japan's economy has therefore been slowly sinking. It is this slow motion which has made the sinking politically acceptable. We should not conclude from this slow event that Japan's leaders would easily agree to a quick and painless economic death. We should not conclude either that they are deligitimized in the eyes of their citizens. Of course, Ryutaro Hashimoto's own popularity is at a low point. But even the results of the July 1998 nationwide elections indicate that the LDP has no real competitor, with 29 per cent of voters supporting it. All other political parties received minimal support indeed, with Naoto Kan's new alliance coming in second with 20 per cent of the vote. An even wider alliance of all opposition forces would lack coherence, as recent experience has demonstrated. It is possible, in spite of previous disillusionment over Japan's political system, that the same Japanese who now turns his savings over to local branches of Western financial companies feels that the country is in a state of national emergency, and therefore rallies behind Japan's historical post-war ruling party. The issue of preserving social institutions and national identity will bear increasingly on political choices.

'Viewing hell' (*jigoku miru*) may be a necessary stage for the Japanese establishment to galvanize its energy. Were the first pages of the second Crash scenario to unfold, it is highly likely that even the cooperative and flexible LDP leaders who have inherited the postwar system would break the pattern. The *dirigiste* instinct, long castigated through debates about the restructuring and liberalization of Japan's economy, would return to stop the process.

The second likely outcome of a Second Crash, after the Chinese devaluation, is that Japan would severely restrict the freedom of capital flows from the country, suspending or reversing the course of financial liberalization. The move would have far-reaching consequences throughout the region and the world. It would immediately justify other stops being put in place, especially against short-term capital movements, throughout Asia. Again, the suspension of free capital movements is not a prehistoric action. France used it in 1982, when the advent of a leftist government created a massive capital flight out of the country.

True, this move would have its penalty, since it would dissuade foreign investment from entering the Asian economies where too many capital restrictions are put in place. But the capital drain from Asia would also abate, and exchange parities would be less severely threatened than today. The group of Western developed countries would of course clamour against a rupture of the liberal international economy, again forgetting that in the past this liberalism has actually been achieved piecemeal and with considerable retreats. The West would be hard put, however, to sanction Asian economies with a retaliation that could only take the form of a restricted access to its markets for Asian commercial exports. Interrupting free trade regimes would indeed hurt Western economies much more, initiating a process of trade war escalation that would not spare the industrialized West's internal trading relations. The much more likely outcome is that the leaders of the Western industrialized system would finally sit up and listen, then undertake a major negotiating process to rescind Japan and Asia's policy moves.

The Plan A response to the first scenario – towards a global New Deal

Down the road, the event of a Second Crash leads to a choice by the West of its appropriate response. Let us call this choice the crossroads between a plan A and a plan B.

Plan A is a global deal between the principals of the world's financial system, in which the IMF would merely play the role of an adviser and note-taker. This time, the blame for what would cease to be called an Asian crisis is spread much more evenly, with some of the other culprits sharing the burden of the financial losses. The creditor banks which have fuelled the capital bubble in Asia and in some other places as well would have to face their responsibility in the Crash. They, and ultimately their depositors, or alternatively the public authorities who agree to sharing these losses with taxpayers, or in some cases the buyers of their remaining assets, would finally have to pay for part of the wreckage in Asia's economies, lightening the load burden and ensuring above all that everyone pushes in the same direction. For until the Second Crash, the interests of the world's banking system and those of bankrupt Asian economies have remained thoroughly contradictory, in a classic debtor-to-creditor relationship.

Plan B as a failure to respond to the first scenario – regional destabilization

The alternative to this third consequence of a renewed Crash is plan B. Plan B is really a well known and worn out politician's response: when in doubt, do nothing.[2] Western economies and their political leaders would let Asia drown in its own puddle of debts or undergo a long and painful stage of regional regression to *dirigiste* economies with minimal growth and constant international economic polemics. True, there is a jingoistic element in some sectors of Western opinion which would see this without much displeasure. That is unlikely to happen if the West's leaders remain rational, for two reasons. The first is that such an episode in Asia's economies would carry only disadvantages for the West. Asia would lose its significance as a market and yet it would carry out a mercantilist export policy, in the hope of regaining some economic leverage. The second reason is even more compelling. A prolonged recession or stagnation of Asia's most advanced and emerging economies will destroy the stability of the region, by threatening both its political structures and weakening the model role that Japan and the NIEs have played towards politically less advanced countries. All the benefits of an international cooperative regime would be lost to major regional actors such as China, and possibly Vietnam or North Korea, who would be left to their own instinct in international relations: a not so desirable outcome. The hidden tensions that have resurfaced in Indonesia and elsewhere would explode, political struggle being the natural fashion to divide a dwindling pie. Plan B is therefore a political fiction that only a very pessimistic mind can follow.

The second scenario – liquidating the debts, not Asia

The second scenario is more rosy, and also more difficult to put in place initially. It starts from the opposite premise. The IMF, or more accurately the Western decision makers who govern it, see the past limits of their actions, and undertake to correct them. Most probably the first sign of such a recantation would be a downgrading of the IMF's role itself. For if it is indeed tough to explain to an Indonesian wage worker that his wage is cut in half and the prices he pays are doubled in accordance with an IMF policy, it will be even more difficult to persuade the average Western Congressman, Bundestag or Parliament member that his constituents should fork out more taxes because international financial officials on Washington's 19th Street said so. Western governments must stand out in front.

Politically, the likelihood of the second scenario increases only if the threat from the first scenario becomes real. In other words, it must become evident that the first wave of separate and highly conditional rescue attempts of several Asian economies is going to be drowned out by a tidal wave of insolvency and financial losses, widening the circle of bankrupt countries. Korea's downfall in December 1997, after all, woke up Western decision makers who had not been all that moved by the spectacle of Thailand or possibly Malaysia's economies going to the dogs. What about Hong Kong or Singapore, key conduits for Western capital and nerve points of Asia's economic region? Their threshold of pain, although quite high in itself, is not as high as Japan's, which has immense savings and a large domestic economy. To put it simply, Hong Kong and Singapore are the two world economies most dependent on international trade and capital flow – the two sectors hardest hit since the First Crash.

A monetary and financial failure of one or the other of Asia's Meccas of free trade and free capital markets is certainly a very undesirable and ugly event. The soundness of their public policies, the size of their currency reserves and public holdings in principle prevents an outright failure. In fact, each has succeeded at its own choice – Hong Kong has preserved the local currency's peg to the dollar, paying the price for this with the deepest economic recession since the Cultural Revolution's red scare in 1966. Singapore is the only economy in Southeast Asia which has not yet slid into outright recession, the price for this being a reasonable devaluation of the Singapore dollar. If the regional recession continues and if the monetary storm picks up speed again, these positions will become impossible to maintain. The policies that Hong Kong and Singapore pursue, with considerable wisdom in both cases, and not without some warnings to the international community in the case of Singapore, would become completely irrelevant. Regardless of the captain's ability, these two ships would suffer massive storm damage. In this case they would cease to function as effective sources of regional capital, further impairing the outcome for the region.

The likelihood of such an event would put a stop to all the neo-liberal rhetoric that has generally been used as a tool against Asian economies since the Crash started. The firms based on the continuation of that liberal system would see one of its fortresses endangered. And the unspoken contract between China, or Indonesia, and the West would vanish: Hong Kong and Singapore serve as buffers and intermediaries in all sorts of transactions, shielding more rudimentary economies and societies but also fulfilling the needs of many large foreign firms active throughout the region.

Is such pessimism necessary? It is still remotely conceivable that the West's leaders will change their course before such an outcome unfolds. The mere continuation of trends as of mid-1998, with a large-scale domestic recession, a worsening of the region's debts, a near paralysis of Japan's policy initiatives, and a looming economic storm in China, should be cause enough for alarm.

Our second scenario therefore consists of an earlier unfolding of plan B from the first scenario. Before and not after a Second Crash of any magnitude happens, Western creditor nations reconsider their policies since the First Crash. The first sign of such a turn would lie in a resumption of joint monetary cooperation between Japan and the United States, possibly joined by the European Union which makes up the rest of G7.

Such an action may in fact have started to unfold on 17 June 1998. After an increasingly speedy slide of the yen's value against the dollar, China has delivered thinly veiled threats of the imminent devaluation of its own currency. For the first time in over four years, the Federal Reserve has sold dollars to prop up the yen – punishing forward speculators in the process.

Such a move remains short-term and reversible, however. In a true decision to tackle the Asian crisis head on, the G7 countries should arrive at a number of wider conclusions and policy recommendations.

Policy recommendations for the second scenario

1)   *Forget about the short-term capital tax and other gimmicks*

When Nobel Prize winner James Tobin thinks up a tax on short-term capital movements in the quiet of his study, it is a conceptual breakthrough. When Chile's Pinochet government applies a variant of the idea to short-term dollar deposits, it makes good sense for a developmental state with a need to encourage long-term investment and penalize conspicuous and import-laden consumption.

But when the idea crops up repeatedly as a solution to the Asian crisis, we immediately know it is a non-starter. Like almost all restrictions on capital movements that are thought up to prevent speculation, it is based on universal agreement, the least present commodity at times of severe crisis. At present, the first thing that Asian economies need is credit, however short term it may be. The short-term transaction tax is an excellent idea for consideration by Asian boats, and in fact by the world-wide fleet, when choppy waves will have abated and there is time for negotiation and implementation. Here, as in many Western recommendations for the past year, we are really talking about the next crisis, not the Crash of 1997 or even the Second Crash.

Talk about the short-term capital tax has no influence, therefore, on our plan B in either the first or the second scenario. As far as Asians are concerned today, it is just talk.

2)   Linking private and public debt

Instead the first recommendation should be an officially explicit end to the hypocritical pretence that Asia's private debt overhang and the rescue of public financial systems are not inextricably linked. This head in the sand attitude by self-righteous advocates, one of the IMF's worst mistakes in the first months of the Crash, has enormously aggravated the magnitude of Asia's debt problem. When several Asian economies – including Japan – have a bad debt problem that dwarfs the size of public budgets, public economic policy becomes simply irrelevant to the problem. Again, if the pilot steers his boat brutally over a choppy sea, all he may end up with is a broken rudder.

True, international banks are no angels. One look at the situation, which they have in fact known on a much smaller scale in Latin America, and banks start withdrawing any new credit, while lobbying for their governments to act, e.g. for taxpayers to foot the bill which debtor countries can no longer pay. Left to themselves, a number of banks might also quietly decide to bury the bad debt problem in their books, provided some interest payments are made, meanwhile hoping that an economic upturn puts the principal back in their line of sight. That, after all, is how the real estate bubble of the 1980s was mostly carried over in Japan and parts of Europe, if not America.

The only problem with this scenario is that the scale of Asian debt is simply too large to allow for a sweep of the broom under the rug. The West's decision makers therefore have to solve the debt issue themselves and to tame their banks in the process.

3)   A Western policy of creating excess liquidities

Indeed, the West should start taking in the implications from the financial crisis that has started in Asia but is steadily growing and eroding the global system's operating margins.

The first observation should be that a capital loss that now far exceeds one trillion US dollars will not be made up by the region itself. Neither the smaller economies, whose size most often does not reach that of an American state or a European province, nor Japan with its own peculiar drawbacks can achieve this. Meanwhile, the Asian crisis is effectively reducing the fear of inflation in the West, and lessening the need for restrictive monetary and credit policies. After the flood of financial capital coming in from Asia, these capital flows will inevitably dry out. Domestic recession and monetary implosion are wiping out local savings, and the money that's not being invested today in Asia's economies will not produce outflows tomorrow.

The good advice that some Western officials and economists are giving to Japan, which is to print more money in order to create liquidities that balance the bad debts, should be reversed and addressed to its own authors. Behind the short-term capital abundance that we are witnessing, there lies a drought when the flow from Asia stops, and Western exports flag down, leading again to the capital shortage experienced by the West through the 1980s. Should the Asian recession tip off a downturn in the West's main stock markets, and especially on Wall Street, the drought would instantly become blistering, for it is in those stock markets that the real potential of monetary creation lies, while the Federal Reserve and the new European Central Bank pursue tight monetary policies.

4)   An International Resolution Trust Co.

My second observation is therefore that it is in the Western economic interest to recognize and address this risk before it becomes a reality. The West should ride on its current economic prosperity and help liquidate Asian debts, rather than the debtors themselves. A voluntary policy of monetary creation is inflationary only if the money that is created immediately floods a particular market. In this case, the amounts created would go towards filling in the black hole that is sucking Asian economies in. To achieve this goal, an International Resolution Trust Corporation should be established. It would combine Asian and Western governments' resources, international financial organizations as providers of additional funds, private syndicates that would be encouraged to acquire the new corporation's paper. The corporation would deal with the similar public companies or entities that are appearing in several Asian countries. By serving as a conduit for rescue loans, by brokering debt liquidation and temporarily managing remaining assets in bankrupt firms, it would exercise a strong influence. That influence, however, would not be confused with the role of economic policy adviser or decision maker, which is best left to governments themselves or to direct regional and international cooperation. The resolution corporation would operate on private lines, while economic policy and economic advice are a political matter that involves many considerations.

The other benefit from such a course would be long-term political and economic gain in Asia. Asians today experience the insecurity of a transitory situation from the Asian economic model, or what locally passed as this model, to so-called universal, in fact Western rules which they fear as much as they desire. Bankrolling some of the pain of transition, which for Asians is entirely linked to the change from one system to another, is a wise investment, just as Marshall plans and more recent grants to former communist countries have had extremely positive results. Again, the move would not put unearned money in Asia's hands, but merely help to wipe the slate clean of excessive and unsustainable debts.

Would such a move increase the moral hazard that a bail-out creates? In other words, would it instil in future financial actors the certainty that they would be bailed out in case of a major crisis? Not necessarily. First, taking away some of the credit and liquidation process, e.g. the life or death decisions, from comparatively weak Asian governments to complement and steer them with a responsible international agency would actually decrease the risk of cronyism and protect these governments from much of the flak. Moral hazard is there when everybody is sure to win at every throw of the dice. But having almost everybody lose as a result of a systemic breakdown is not a successful pedagogical experiment either.

Over the first year of the Crash, Asia received virtual promises of funds, but far less actual infusions. The international rescue's magic consists in pulling a white rabbit from a hat and then making it disappear again. In other words, it seeks to recreate confidence with funds it mostly does not spend. Unfortunately, the trick does not go down well with adult and experienced audiences, especially when they feel hungry enough to eat the rabbit alive.

The moral hazard argument should not be heaped solely onto Asian borrowers either. It is high time to ponder the conclusion of the Orange County financial meltdown of 1994. When this affluent county of Southern California lost 1.6 billion dollars as a result of an unexpected hike in interest rates ending its adventurous play in derivatives based on borrowed money, Orange County did not despair. Today, it has recovered almost half of these losses from legal proceedings and out of court settlements involving the financial firms which advised the county at the time: KPMG, Crédit Suisse First Boston, Merril Lynch. South Koreans will be happy to learn that Orange County is suing Standard and Poor's for rating its bonds too highly.[3] We wish Orange County every success with its future finances. But is not this the Western equivalent of the quintessential Japanese *tobashi* deal?

My third observation is that we should stop marvelling childishly at the fact that this or that country is creating a debt resolution institution 'just like in America'. The notion that China, for example, could adopt across the board standards of solvency for public firms, and that the paid presence of a big name in international accounting is further proof of this, flies in the face of evidence. We are also putting too much pressure on excellent political reformers such as Kim Dae-jung or Chuan

Leek-pai, not to mention Anwar Ibrahim. Could they really sentence to death a large number of their countries' firms, thus creating massive unemployment and come out as victors in the next domestic political contest? This would be a supernatural trick indeed.

Just as aid agencies have developed methods and criteria for judging projects and granting or withholding aid, international financial organizations must now create specific vehicles that will solve the debt problem in conjunction with local governments. The temporary loss of sovereignty could be accepted at this point because these new institutions will come with gifts. And the process in conjunction with local financial officials will go a long way towards training a new generation of regulators and overseers for Asia's capital markets.

Funding for this novel form of international financial cooperation must of course be split in different ways. It should find the priority support of Japan whose Asian Fund proposal came close to this type of institution, although it remained public in nature. If bankrolling Asia's comparatively well-heeled debtors helps to avoid massive defaults that would hit Western banks, it is well worth a contribution by Western taxpayers. Contributions (along with reforms) made *before* a major breakdown tend to increase confidence and therefore multiply active economic results. Bailing out Western banks *after* technical bankruptcy, as French taxpayers have learnt through the Crédit Lyonnais case, is hardly an enticing task.

5)   Balancing the need for market reforms with Asian political and social requirements

The market has no friends, and economics does not punish sinners. In the judgements made about East Asia since the Crash, there have been moral overtones indicting Asian societies and politics. Perhaps, as we believe, some Asian states should be castigated for their poor record of enforcing human rights, or for the corruption and favouritism that pervades their actions. The point is that investors and market judges were never overly sensitive to these problems when Asian economies were in full bloom. Some political and moral lectures sound like afterthoughts. We much prefer to stick with the recent Asia Society's observation, which is also our own: 'The crisis struck countries with different political systems – democratic and authoritarian. Similarly, those countries that have escaped the worst effects of the crisis also have diverse political systems.'[4]

Building fair and accountable political institutions should not be equated with turning the management of national economies over to the financial market. In fact, if the West keeps confusing the two issues, it is going to end up with a failed Asian transition on both counts. Asian governments, for their part, are faced with two competing imperatives.

They must adopt and apply financial rules that will restore business confidence after the Crash. It is by no means obligatory that all these changes be predicated on the liberalization agenda. Ending insider deals, breaking apart huge groups which have built up too much influence on economic policy making and ensuring the remuneration of domestic savings according to the market are tasks that belong to the liberal agenda.

Another set of tasks consists of reforming banking systems, improving the regulation and supervision of capital markets, ensuring the basic livelihood of ordinary citizens with subsidies or fixed prices for basic products, creating or extending social protection. They imply a conversion of the Asian state and a redirection of its guiding hand, not its fade-out.

Asian governments will also need to preserve long-term investment on productive projects. Formerly, the high rate of domestic savings and their low remuneration financed the public capital account, allowing governments to back industrial development, public works and large-scale projects. Since the central taxation basis in most Asian countries is rather limited, the opening up of capital markets has meant that the financial resources for long-term projects must often be found internationally. Is it really possible to have private international financing of Asia's future infrastructure programmes? Much domestic and foreign capital over the past few years has preferred the short-term profits of speculative ventures, especially when they did not appear so risky. Asia's financial systems must be rebuilt in part along the lines of the international market. But the Asian state must also recover its essential function of funding infrastructures and other long-term projects, and perhaps of taxing its citizens for that purpose, instead of relying solely on the market.

Restoring this balance between the state and the market, renovating public action rather than abolishing it, is also a political necessity. The basic problem in most Asian societies remains the paucity of intermediate bodies between the state and individuals, as well as the thin legal culture which leaves either bureaucracy or customary practices in charge. Given these shortcomings, purely market based political systems, whether it be democratic or authoritarian, may become unstable. In spite of all the Western talk about the absence of social standards in Asia, most Asian states have an ethical responsibility to their citizens. Food and social safety, public order and in Northeast Asia a limitation of income inequality are part of the Asian deal. Abolishing these traditional goals and practices for the sake of speeding up the move towards a free market economy in the wake of the Crash would unleash a backlash. A historical and cultural compromise must be sought.

The final lines of this book are, written as Asian economies and polities stay on their downward course. My hope is that the scale of possible events outlined above will indeed exert some influence on Asian and Western policy makers.

Notes

1 Introduction: a crash course in history

1 Among them was the IMF, rather than the World Bank. See Shalendra D. Sharma, 'Asia's Economic Crisis and the IMF', *Survival*, vol. 40, no. 2, Summer 1998, pp. 27–8.

2 Paul Krugman has celebrated his victory on his web site with some irony: http://web.mit.edu/krugman/I_told_you_so.html.

3 See Bank for International Settlements, *The Maturity, Sectoral and Nationality Distribution of International Bank Lending, Second Half 1996*, Basle, July 1997. Founded in 1930, the BIS has presided in 1988 over the negotiation of the new international bank ratio of reserves to outstanding loans, known as the Cooke ratio. The BIS was blamed after the Crash by governments for too much delay in issuing its reports: they now appear almost two months sooner. But would the principals have read them in any case?

4 Bill Emmott, *The Sun Also Sets: The Limits to Japan's Economic Power*, 1989, Touchstone Books. His book predated the 1991 Tokyo Kabutocho crash, from which Japan has yet to recover.

5 In his recent history of Korea, Bruce Cumings explains that development coexisted with 'one of the most unstable political systems in the world'. The intense mobilization within the Korean model has had a wrenching effect on society and politics. See Bruce Cumings, *Korea's Place in the Sun: A Modern History*, 1997, W.W. Norton, London and New York, pp. 337–8.

6 Non-governmental organizations.

7 Two economists actually predicted the event. See Ronald McKinnon and How Pill, 'Credible Liberalization and International Capital Flows' in Takatoshi Ito and Anne Krueger (eds), *Financial Deregulation and Integration in East Asia*, University of Chicago Press, 1996. Ronald McKinnon will appear later in this book as the best analyst of the US–Japan struggle via monetary policy which has led to the present brinkmanship in 1998.

8 See for example *Financial Times*, 11 December 1997 for a summary of his criticism directed at the IMF.

9 World Bank, *The East Asian Economic Miracle – Economic Growth and Public Policy*, Oxford, Oxford University Press, 1993, pp. 6–7.

10 One of them, former minister and LDP diet member Arai, confided to the press, however, that he had been chosen as a scapegoat because he was of

Korean descent, and that 'hundreds of others' had benefited like him from padded accounts with security brokers. See *Asian Wall Street Journal*, pp. 20–1.

11 BIBF was established in March 1993 and accounted for a third of Thailand's foreign debt by 1996.

12 François Godement, *La renaissance de l'Asie*, Paris, Odile Jacob, 1993. Published in English as *The New Asian Renaissance*, London and New York, Routledge, 1997.

13 Happiness over somebody else's misfortune.

2 An explanation of the 1997 Asian Crash

1 Paul Krugman, 'The Myth of Asia's Miracle', *Foreign Affairs*, vol. 73, no. 6, November–December 1994, pp. 62–78.

2 Paul Krugman, 'Will Asia Bounce Back?', speech for Crédit Suisse First Boston Conference, Hong Kong, March 1998.

3 Random Access Memories.

4 TFP breaks down economic growth between several components: the accumulation of capital and labour, a residual factor being attributed to the effect of technical change. What was originally called 'factor X' (Harvey J. Leibenstein) now includes not only the impact of technology, but also ideas, e.g. improved management and human efficiency. The notion remains subject to much debate.

5 Alwyn Young, 'The Tyranny of Numbers: Confronting the Statistical Realities of East Asian Growth Experience', *The Quarterly Journal of Economics*, August 1995, pp. 641–80.

6 Ronald I. McKinnon and Kenichi Ohno, *Dollar and Yen: Resolving Economic Conflict between the United States and Japan*, Cambridge, MA and London, The MIT Press, 1997, pp. 22–8.

7 Zuliu Hu and Mohsin S. Khan, 'Why is China Growing so Fast?', IMF Working Paper, Washington DC, 1997.

8 Chang-tai Hsieh, 'What Explains the Industrial Revolution in East Asia? Evidence from Factor Markets', Department of Economics, University of California, Berkeley, 41 pp., January 1998, p. 4. We are thankful to Dr Chang-tai Hsieh for making his unpublished paper available to us.

9 The Ming dynasty reigned AD 1368–1644, and the Qing AD 1645–1911.

10 Mark Elvin, *The Pattern of the Chinese Past*, London, Eyre Methuen, 1973, and especially Part 3: 'Economic Development without Technological Change', pp. 203–319.

11 Mark Elvin, *op. cit.*, p. 284.

12 Mark Elvin published his book in 1973, when the Cultural Revolution was still the dominant political reality of China. He nevertheless predicted that 'to break out once and for all from the old high-level trap, it almost certainly needs to enter the international market to a far greater extent than hitherto. It is capable of doing this with an effectiveness that comes as a shock, if the decision to do so is taken', *op. cit.*, p. 319.

13 The argument for the preceding points is drawn from R. Bin Wong, *China Transformed: Historical Change and the Limits of European Experience*, Cornell University Press, Ithaca and London, 1997, Chapters 1 and 2, pp. 13–52.

14 Clifford Geertz, *Agricultural Change: The Process of Ecological Change in Indonesia* University of California Press, Berkeley, 1963.

15 *Business Week*, 1 December 1997, p. 31. A recent viewpoint by Chalmers Johnson, the noted Japan specialist, endorses the same opinion (*The Nation*, 23 February 1998).

16 BOT or 'build, operate, transfer' is a frequent contemporary arrangement for infrastructure investment.

17 Pierre-Etienne Will, 'Appareil d'état et infrastructure économique dans la Chine prémoderne' in Roland Lew (ed.), *Les bureaucraties chinoises*, Paris, L'Harmattan, 1987, pp. 11–41.

18 'Don't Worry: China Isn't Following in Japan's Footsteps', *Business Week*, 20 April 1998, p. 14.

19 Fareed Zakaria, 'The Rise of Illiberal Democracy', *Foreign Affairs*, vol. 76, no. 6, November–December 1997, pp. 22–43.

20 *Beijing Economic Daily*, 'Renminbi Exchange Rate and Financial Turmoil in Southeast Asia' by Special Commentator, 25 December 1997, pp. 1–2, FBIS-CHI-98–014.

21 Antoine Kernen and Jean-Louis Rocca, 'La réforme des entreprises publiques en Chine et sa gestion sociale: le cas de Shenyang et du Liaoning', Paris, FNSP, *Les Etudes du CERI*, no. 37, January 1998, pp. 5–6.

22 See Chapter 6, 'Challenging Asian politics'.

23 Charles P. Kindleberger, *The World in Depression, 1929–1939*, Berkeley, University of California Press, 1973, p. 21.

24 For a general account of the period, see Christopher Wood, *The Bubble Economy: The Japanese Economic Collapse*, Tokyo, Charles E. Tuttle, 1993.

25 For a pessimistic viewpoint, which has proven accurate so far, see in French Jean-Marie Bouissou, François Gipouloux and Eric Seizelet, *Japon: le déclin?*, Bruxelles, Editions Complexe, 1995.

26 Bruce Cumings, 1997, *Korea's Place in the Sun: A Modern History*, W.W. Norton, New York and London p. 336.

27 *Asian Wall Street Journal*, 18 December 1997.

28 *Far Eastern Economic Review*, 15 November 1990, p. 78.

29 According to a Morgan Stanley report cited by the *Asian Wall Street Journal*, 12 May 1998, p. 14.

30 Bank of Japan, *Comparative Economic and Financial Statistics*, Tokyo, 1997.

31 Daniel I. Okimoto, *Between MITI and the Market: Japanese Industrial Policy for High Technologies*, Stanford, Stanford University Press, 1989.

32 R. Wolf, 'Blame Government for the Asian Meltdown', *Asian Wall Street Journal*, 5 February 1998.

33 Kenichi Ohmae, *The End of the Nation State: The Rise of Regional Economies*, HarperCollins, London, 1995, p. 165.

34 Kenichi Ohmae, *ibid*.

35 Ronald I. McKinnon and Kenichi Ohno, *Dollar and Yen: Resolving the Conflict between the United States and Japan*, Cambridge, MA and London, The MIT Press, 1997.

36 I am indebted to Pierre Jacquet for recalling this declaration.

37 They were the United States, Japan, China, Australia, Singapore and Hong Kong. The group was immediately dubbed the 'G6'.

38 Personal communication.

39 C. Fred Bergsten, 'The Asian Monetary Crisis: Proposed Remedies', Statement to the Committee on Banking and Financial Services, US House of Representatives, 13 November 1997.

40 Chalmers Johnson, 'Cold War Economics Melt Asia', *The Nation*, 23 February 1998.
41 Kenichi Ohmae, *op. cit.*, p. 158.
42 Charles P. Kindleberger, *op. cit.*, pp. 291–2.
43 See Chapter 3, 'Asia, meet the rescue party'.
44 Joseph Stiglitz, Address to the Chicago Council on Foreign Relations, Chicago, 27 February 1998 (www.worldbank.org).
45 The argument, sometimes called the 'Lawson doctrine' after former UK Chancellor Nigel Lawson, is recalled in the IMF's December 1997 *World Economic Outlook*, p. 3.
46 By a fateful loophole, Korean law did not require firms to declare the liabilities of their subsidiaries when these were not guaranteed by the parent company.
47 At last news, Morgan Stanley was taken to task in Hong Kong's courts for the role they played in backing the introduction of Everbright Co., a red chip with major political connections in Beijing.
48 Bank for International Settlements, *The Maturity, Sectoral and Nationality Distribution of International Bank Lending, First Half 1997*, Basle, January 1998, Table 1, p. 6.
49 *Business Week*, special issue on 'The new business cycle', 31 March 1997. The best expert on the so-called New Economy is the neo-schumpeterian Chris Freeman, who has been predicting the current 'long wave' of prosperity based on electronics ever since 1978. See Chris Freeman *et al.*, *The Dynamics of Industrial Innovation*, Cambridge, MA: The MIT Press, 1997.
50 Messerschmitt Bulkow Blohm.
51 Cited by *Utusan Express* (Malaysia), 8 April 1998.
52 *Asiaweek*, 27 March 1998.
53 United Malay National Organization.
54 See Chapter 3, 'Asia, meet the rescue party'.
55 The central bank's executives have been sacked after an inquiry.
56 Remarks by Chairman Alan Greenspan, Thirty-fourth Annual Conference on Bank Structure and Competition of the Federal Reserve Bank of Chicago, 7 May 1998.

3 Asia, meet the rescue party

1 Joseph P. Quinlan, 'Europe, Not Asia, is Corporate America's Key Market', *The Wall Street Journal*, 12 January 1998.
2 *Asiaweek*, 27 March 1998.
3 Alan Greenspan's testimony to the US House of Representatives, 24 February 1998, from the Federal Reserve Board website.
4 *International Herald Tribune*, 24–25 January 1998.
5 *International Herald Tribune*, 6 April 1998, p. 8.
6 *Asian Wall Street Journal*, 4 February 1998.
7 *Washington Times*, 23 April 1998.
8 The French, German and Swedish ministers were in attendance.
9 Jürgen Ruland, *The Asia–Europe meeting (ASEM): Towards a New Euro-Asian Relationship?*, Universität Rostock, Rostocker Informationen zu Politik und Verwaltung Heft 5, 1996, p. 16.
10 *International Herald Tribune*, 14 January 1998.

11 *Groot-Bisgaarden De Staandard*, 13 January 1998, p. 21 (FBIS-WEU-98–013).
12 *Studies on the Economic Synergy between Asia and Europe*, background document to the ASEM Chiba (Japan) meeting, September 1997.
13 *Asian Wall Street Journal*, 1 April 1998, p. 1. The *Wall Street Journal* concluded it was probable, for example, that 1 billion dollars from Chinese reserves had been invested in Fanny Mae, the popular company that specializes in inexpensive house mortgages.
14 Bank for International Settlements, *The Maturity, Sectoral and Nationality Distribution of International Bank Lending, First Half 1997*, Basle, January 1998.
15 *Business Week*, 16 February 1998.
16 *Le Monde*, 4 April 1998.
17 Private communication, Paris.
18 *De Volksrant* (Amsterdam), 17 February 1998, p. 10 (FBIS-WEU-98–048).
19 The US holds 18 per cent of drawing rights and contributions, against 30 per cent for the combined European Union countries. But the United States' stake in the Asia-Pacific is of course larger.
20 Gerry van Klinken in *Indonesia Magazine*, 25 January 1998.
21 At www.dsbb.imf.org.
22 Testimony of Ms Karin Lissakers, US delegate to the IMF, at the House Banking and Financial Services Committee, 21 April 1998.
23 Leon Hadar, 'Will the IMF End like UN?', *Singapore Business Times*, 22 January 1998.
24 Among the list of 20-odd 'Frequently asked questions' on the IMF's web site, there figures 'How does the IMF help the poor?'.
25 Martin Khor, 'A Poor Grade for the IMF', *Far Eastern Economic Review*, 15 January 1998, p. 29.
26 Jean-Michel Severino, World Bank vice-president for the Asia-Pacific, *Les Echos*, 16 April 1998, p. 4.
27 Steven Radelet and Jeffrey Sachs, *The East Asian Financial Crisis: Diagnosis, Remedies, Prospects*, Cambridge, MA, Harvard Institute For Internatioanl Development, 20 April 1998, 44 pp., p. 9.
28 A further agreement with Indonesia in April 1998 was to raise this amount by another 7 billion dollars. At that date, however, not a single cent from the IMF's own commitment had started flowing to Jakarta.
29 Jeffrey Sachs expressed this point of view as early as September, 1997. For a reasoned critique, see Steven Radelet and Jeffrey Sachs, *op. cit.*
30 Martin Feldstein, 'Refocusing the IMF', *Foreign Affairs*, vol. 7, no. 2 March–April 1998, pp. 20–33. Martin Feldstein is chairman of the National Bureau of Economic Research.
31 See Table 3.1, International community financial assistance to Thailand, Korea and Indonesia, p. 76.
32 The Organization for Economic Cooperation and Development.
33 *IMF Bail Outs: Truth and Fiction*, January 1998, IMF website.
34 *South China Morning Post*, 29 December 1997.
35 Olle Törnquist, 'The Crisis in Asia Calls for Political Solutions', *Svenska Dagbladet*, 18 January 1998. Fascinatingly, this progressive political scientist published his disenchanted conclusion on the same day that Douglas Paal, a moderate Republican with business experience, reached the same idea from a very different premiss.
36 *New York Times*, January 14, 1998.

37 *International Herald Tribune*, 4 November 1997.
38 Address by Alassane E. Ouattara, deputy managing director of the IMF, Fez, 4 May 1998.
39 See Chapter 8, 'Conclusion: two scenarios for tomorrow'.
40 Alan Greenspan, Testimony before the Committee on Banking and Financial Services, US House of Representatives, 30 January 1998.
41 *Les Echos* (Paris), Friday 17 April 1998, p. 6.
42 *Seoul Hangyore* (weekly news magazine), 12 February 1998, pp. 34–35 (FBIS-EAS-98–043).
43 *Asian Wall Street Journal*, 2 February 1998, p. 3.
44 *Asian Wall Street Journal*, 2 February 1998.
45 Christianto Wibisono, executive director of the Indonesian Business and Data Centre in Jakarta, writing for the *Straits Times*, 20 August 1993, p. 35.
46 *The Economist*, 17 April 1993, p. 13.
47 *Agence France-Presse* news service, Jakarta, 20 February 1998.
48 Paul Kelly, 'The Suharto Family Fights Back', *The Australian*, 13 February 1998.
49 Olle Törnquist, 'The Wild Beast and the Sleeping Beauty', talk at Indonesia Hearing, Ministry of Foreign Affairs, Stockholm, Sweden, 16 March 1998.
50 During a trip to Japan, he advocated instead a range of fluctuation for the rupiah, based on a 'currency basket' involving the dollar, the yen and the euro.
51 Kurt Schuler, 'Establish Currency Boards Now', *Asian Wall Street Journal*, 12 January 1998.
52 Nouriel Roubini's website has what must be one of the world's most interesting, and in any case the lengthiest, discussion of the currency board issue at www.stern.nyu.edu/nroubini/asia:CurrencyBoardsRoubini.html.
53 Kurt Schuler, *Should Developing Countries Have Central Banks?*, London, Institute of Economic Affairs, 1996.
54 Invited to the Hong Kong East Asia Economic Summit in October 1997, Hanke delivered a starkly realistic message about monetary exchange rates and the prospect for a deflation in Asia.
55 'Rupiah Rasputin', *Fortune*, 13 April 1998.
56 *Washington Post*, 23 February 1998, p. A01.
57 *Independent*, 15 March 1998.
58 *Sankei Shimbun*, Tokyo, 22 March 1998 (FBIS-EAS-98–083).
59 Melbourne Radio Australia, 6 April 1998 (FBIS-EAS-98–096).
60 Jakarta Media Indonesia, 13 April 1998 (FBIS-EAS-98–103), reporting a meeting between Foreign affairs Ministers Ali Alatas and Tang Jiaxuan in Jakarta. China has often been said to commit a billion dollars in supplementary funds to the IMF rescue programme itself, which have never materialized.
61 *South China Morning Post*, 10 April 1998.
62 Agence France-Presse dispatch, Hong Kong, 9 April 1998.
63 See Chapter 6, 'Challenging Asian politics'.
64 Reuters News Agency, 2 June 1998.
65 Tan Sai Siong, 'S'pore's Unique Relationship with Malaysia Taken for Granted', *Singapore Straits Times*, 21 February 1998.
66 A. Nazri Abdullah, *Singapore Straits Times*, 26 February 1998.

67 Rusdi Mustapha, 'Time Now for Reunification', *Sun* (Kuala Lumpur), 18 February 1998.
68 Robert Rubin, speech at Harvard Business School, 3 June 1998, *Le Monde*, 5 June 1998.
69 See Manuel F. Montes, 'Global Lessons of the Economic Crisis in Asia', *Asia-Pacific Issues*, East–West Center, March 1998, for a soft-spoken and Singapore-based analysis that receives prominent publicity from the East–West Center.
70 'The IMF in Action', *Asian Wall Street Journal*, 19 May 1998, p. 8.
71 Some observers actually contemplate a political role for the IMF 'to bring about far-reaching political change' (Gerald Segal, 'From Indonesia, a Warning to the Authoritarians', *International Herald Tribune*, 5 June 1998, p. 5). To say the least, the goal was not part of the original charter.
72 Rudi Dornbusch, 'A Bailout Won't Do the Trick in Korea', *Business Week*, 8 December 1997, p. 10.
73 These words are attributed to Tommy Koh, Singapore's ambassador at large and executive director of the Asia-Europe Foundation, by Peter Montagnon, *Financial Times*, 9 March 1998.

4 Asian values, minus the debate: the facts behind the myth

1 François Godement, *The New Asian Renaissance: From Colonialism to the Post-Cold War*, 1997, London and New York, Routledge, pp. 276–8.
2 Kishore Mahbubani, 'The United States: Go East, Young Man', *Washington Quarterly*, vol. 17, no. 2, pp. 5–23, Spring 1994.
3 Robert D. Hormats, 'Madison's Example for the "Tigers"', *Asian Wall Street Journal*, 3–4 April 1998.
4 Mahathir reportedly blamed Jews during an electoral rally in Terenganu, the Northeast Islamist province of peninsular Malaysia. His spokesmen later denied his words, and more recently Dr Mahathir has mended fences with the World Jewish Congress.
5 *Asiaweek*, 13 April 1994, p. 55.
6 *Bangkok Post*, 1 December 1997, reprinted in FBIS-EAS-97–335.
7 As critics quickly dubbed his plan for an East Asian Economic Caucus (EAEC).
8 *South China Morning Post*, 12 March 1998.
9 Quoted by Reuters News Agency, Kuala Lumpur, 21 February 1998.
10 A Malaysian observer notes, however, that Anwar's 'chameleon-like qualities . . . of running with the American hares and hunting with the Islamic hounds remain a source of horrified worry among Malays' (M.G.G. Pillai, 'The Prime Minister moves house to Jaya Putra', 5 May 1998 (pillai @mgg.pc.my).
11 United Malays' National Organization, Malaysia's dominant political force since its creation in 1946.
12 *South China Morning Post*, 12 March 1998.
13 In another speech to the Parliament on March 1st (*Jakarta Media Indonesia*, 3 March 1998).
14 *Korea Times* 3 March 1998.
15 Indigenous Indonesians.

16 Aburizal Bakrie's call was made at a parliamentary session on 9 February 1998 (Agence France-Presse news wire, Jakarta, 10 February, 1998).

17 Kazuo Nukazawa, senior manager of Keidanren, 'The East Asian Drama of 1997–1998 and the Question of Models', Berlin, 20 January 1998, mimeo paper.

18 *Asian Wall Street Journal*, 20 January 1998.

19 P.M. Goh Chok Tong's address at the World Economic Forum, Hong Kong, 15 October 1997.

20 *Singapore Business Times*, 21 February 1998.

21 Quoted by *Singapore Business Times*, 25 February 1998.

22 *Time magazine*, 16 March 1998.

23 *Far Eastern Economic Review*, 12 March 1998, p. 12.

24 Ehito Kimura, 'The New Unequal Treaties', *Bangkok Post*, 22 January 1998.

25 *Bangkok Post*, 1 December 1997, reprinted in FBIS-EAS-97-335.

26 Martin Khor, Director of the Third World Network based in Penang, writing for the *Far Eastern Economic Review*, 15 January 1998.

27 Anwar Ibrahim, *The Asian Renaissance*, Times Books International, Singapore and Kuala Lumpur, 1996, p. 19.

28 Anwar Ibrahim, *ibid*, p. 129

29 Henry Kissinger, 'The Asian Collapse: One Fix Does Not Fit All Economies', *Washington Post*, 9 February 1998.

30 The connection between Western minority rights discourse and the 're-empowerment of the colonial other' has been noted by J.J. Clarke, *Oriental Enlightenment – The Encounter between Asian and Western Thought*, London and New York, Routledge, 1997, p. 216.

31 Benedict Anderson, *Imagined Communities: Reflections on the Origin and Spread of Nationalism*, London, Verso Books, 1991.

32 See Noordin Sopiee's speech at the Twenty-Ninth Meeting of the Pacific Basin Economic Council, Washington, 25 May 1996.

33 These principles were mutual respect for each other's integrity and sovereignty; mutual non-aggression; non-interference in one another's affairs; equality and mutual benefit; and peaceful co-existence.

34 The 'flying geese' model of regional development was created before the Pacific War by the economist Katane Akamatsu. In the 1960s, Minister of Foreign Affairs Saburo Okita would popularize it and forge the basis for comprehensive security policies with the region.

35 Asia-Pacific Economic Cooperation, founded in 1989.

36 See Richard Higgott, 'Free Trade and Asian Regionalism', in David Camroux and Jean-Luc Domenach (eds), *Imagining Asia*, London, Routledge, 1998.

37 Simon S.C. Tay, 'ASEAN, the ARF and Preventive Diplomacy: Principles and Possibilities in International Law', *ASEAN-Isis Monitor*, 1996, p. 2.

38 Cited by Mayfair Mei-hui Yang, *Gifts, Favors and Banquets: The Art of Social Relationships in China*, Ithaca and London, Cornell University Press, 1994, p. 31.

39 Branislaw Malinowski, *Argonauts of the Western Pacific*, New York, E.P. Dutton, 1961.

40 The term belongs to Joseph Nye, *Bound to Lead: The Changing Nature of American Power*, New York, Basic Books, 1991.

41 Speech at the Japanese Cultural Centre in Paris, 19 February 1998.

42 These figures and the last comment are taken from a set of research reports conducted under the aegis of the Population Studies Centre at the University of Michigan. The four-country study was finalized between February and October 1992 (Research Reports nos 92–13, 92–14, 92–16 and 92–22).

43 Lin Jiang, 'Changing Kinship Structure and its Implications for Old-Age Support in Urban and Rural China', *Population Studies*, no. 49, 1995, p. 130.

44 Lin Jiang, *ibid.*, p. 145.

45 Peter Xenos and Socorro A. Gultiano, *Trends in Female and Male Age at Marriage and Celibacy in Asia*, Hawaii, The Hawaii University Press, 1992.

46 United Nations, 1995.

47 Richard Leete and Iqbal Alam, 'The Consequences of Fertility Transition in Asia' in Richard Leete and Iqbal Alam, *The Revolution in Asian Fertility: Dimensions, Causes, and Implications*, Oxford, Clarendon Press, 1993, p. 269.

48 Richard Leete and Iqbal Alam, 'Fertility Transition of Similar Cultural Groups in Different Countries', *op. cit.*, p. 252.

49 Peter C. Smith 'Asian Marriage Patterns in Transition', *Journal of Family History*, vol. 5, no. 1, 1980, pp. 58–96.

50 Ansley J. Coale and Ronald Freedman, 'Similarities in Fertility Transition in China and Three Other East Asian Populations', in Richard Leete and Iqbal Alam, *op. cit.*, pp. 214–15.

51 We owe these remarks to James Z. Lee. See James Z. Lee, Wang Feng with Cameron Campbell, *One Quarter of Humanity: Malthusian Mythology and Chinese Reality, 1700–2000*, Cambridge, MA, Harvard University Press 1999.

52 This conclusion, and the above-mentioned data, are the result of a survey in the city of Baoding (Hebei) in 1994. See Martin King Whyte, 'The Fate of Filial Obligations in Urban China', *China Journal*, no. 38, July 1997, pp. 1–31.

5 The challenge to Asian identity

1 See James Scott, *The Moral Economy of the Peasants: Rebellion and Subsistence in Southeast Asia*, New Haven, Yale University Press, 1976.

2 Private communication.

3 Between 1958 and 1962, it is estimated that 30 million Chinese died as a result of the Great Leap Forward (Roderick MacFarquhar, *The Origins of the Cultural Revolution*, vol. 3, Oxford and New York, Oxford University Press and Columbia University Press, 1997, p. 4 and note p. 481).

4 Michael R.J. Vatikiotis, *Political Change in Southeast Asia: Trimming the Banyan Tree*, London and New York, Routledge, 1996, p. 81.

5 David I. Hitchcock, *Asian Values and the United States: How Much Conflict?*, Washington, DC, Centre for Strategic and International Studies, 1994, p. ix.

6 David I. Hitchcock, 'Cultural Side of the Asian Crisis', *Straits Times*, 15 April 1998.

7 I borrow this cue from the great historian and occasional humourist Eric J. Hobsbawm, who once explained at a centennial celebration of Karl Marx's death that the future of Marxist studies in European universities was guaranteed by the existence of the tenure system.

8 Or 'The clerics' betrayal'.

9   *Zou houmen*, the standard Chinese phrase for circumventing regulations thanks to personal relations.

10   Coincidentally, the liberalization and new regulation of the French stock exchange happened hardly two years earlier. To this day, the new watchdog committee set up to prevent insider dealing seems to find it difficult to recommend judicial proceedings in almost all cases it has investigated. The prevalence of custom over law is perhaps not uniquely Oriental.

11   The law banning payments to *sokaiya* (extortionist) underworld gangs was passed in 1982. Al Alletzhauser documented in 1990 the insider deals of Japanese finance (*The House of Nomura*, London, Bloomsbury, 1990). Both practices are still the quintessential scandals tying together corporate, government and underworld circles.

12   Eisuke Sakakibara, *Beyond Capitalism: The Japanese Model of Market Economies*, Lanham, University Press of America and the Economic Strategy Institute, 1993.

13   Personal communication. The event took place in Gaoyou district, Shandong, 1948.

14   Mayfair Mei-hui Yang, *op. cit.*, p. 172.

15   Cited by Mayfair Mei-hui Yang, *op. cit.*, p. 295.

16   Eric J. Hobsbawm, *Primitive Rebels, Studies in Archaic Forms of Social Movements in the Nineteenth and Twentieth Centuries*, Manchester University Press, new amended edition, 1971, p. 36.

17   Eric J. Hobsbawm, *op. cit.*, pp. ix–x.

18   Yunxiang Yan, 'The Culture of *Guanxi* in a North China Village', *China Journal*, January 1996, p. 6.

19   Cited by Mayfair Hei-hui Yang, *op. cit.*, p. 221.

20   Inversely, I have described how Li Peng was denounced in an allegoric film about the Qing anti-reformist movement as a court eunuch who would not even render a favour to his own relatives (F. Godement, *The New Asian Renaissance*, London and New York, Routledge, 1997, p. 234.)

21   Interviewed by *Business Week*, 4 May 1998, p. 30.

22   Land or other resources granted to a royal or aristocratic family member.

23   Pasuk Phongpaichit and Sungsidh Piriyarangsan, *Corruption and Democracy in Thailand*, The Political Economy Centre, Faculty of Economics, Chulalongkorn University, Bangkok, 1994, pp. 52–3.

24   Phongpaichit and Piriyarangsan, *ibid*, p. 20.

25   Site of New York's Municipal Council.

26   Red envelopes, which contain traditional money gifts.

27   *Far Eastern Economic Review*, 23 March 1995, p. 56.

28   *Far Eastern Economic Review*, 27 October 1994, p. 30.

29   Larry Diamond, Marc F. Plattner, Yun-han Chu, and Hung-mao Tien (eds), *Consolidating the Third Wave Democracies*, Baltimore and London, The Johns Hopkins University Press, 1997.

30   Hu Shi, 'Criticism of the Declaration for Cultural Construction on a Chinese Basis' (1935), in William Teodore DeBary (ed.), *Sources of Chinese Tradition*, vol. 2, New York, 1960, UNESCO Collection of Representative Works – Chinese series, p. 195.

31   Japanese social scientist M. Nakamura, cited by Michael R.J. Vatikiotis, *op. cit.*, p. 30.

32   Samuel P. Huntington, 'The Clash of Civilizations?', *Foreign Affairs*, Fall 1993, vol. 72, no 4, pp. 22–49.

33 Mark Juergensmeyer, *The New Cold War: Religious Nationalism Confronts the Secular State*, University of California Press, 1993, p. 4. East Asia, including Malaysia, Indonesia and the Philippines figure only in a passing remark within this work. This is telling on the low level of religious confrontation in Southeast Asia, at least compared with the rest of the Islamic world.

34 For a good statement of the arguments against Asian regional integration, see Jean-Luc Domenach, *L'Asie en danger*, 1998, Paris, Fayard, pp. 157–239.

6 Challenging Asian politics

1 Michel Crozier, *The Stalled Society*, New York, Viking, 1973.

2 See Chapter 3, 'Asia, meet the rescue party'.

3 According to Central Provident Fund statistics cited by the *Far Eastern Economic Review*, 18 June 1998, p. 63.

4 'Thai Banks Rebuilding with Foreign Capital', *Nikkei Weekly*, Internet Edition, 14 May 1998.

5 *Nikkei Weekly*, 16 February 1998, p. 1.

6 Official opinion in neighbouring Singapore firmly defended the action, however, explaining that Petronas had not overpaid Mahathir Mirzan's firm, and that the move was coherent with its own strategy to transport oil (Eddie Toh, 'Malaysia Inc Could Learn a Few Lessons from the Konsortium', *Singapore Business Times*, 4 May 1998).

7 A phrase he borrows from Joseph Schumpeter.

8 Agence France-Presse dispatch, Kuala Lumpur, 3 June 1998.

9 One of the first political prisoners to be released after Suharto's fall was Colonel Abdul Latief, in jail since 1966. He confirmed that the reason for his lifelong emprisonment was his awareness of General Suharto's fore-knowledge of a putsch against Sukarno. Suharto let the plot unfold, in order to position himself as the saviour of the day.

10 In the same fashion, no Vice-President has ever lasted more than one term.

11 The Army's Strategic Reserve Command (or Green Berets) in Jakarta. Suharto himself held the same post during the decisive 1965 events. To complicate things further, Prabowo is also the son of 'Berkeley mafia' Professor Soemitro Djojohadikusumo.

12 See Chapter 3, 'Asia, meet the rescue party'.

13 He does share the anti-Chinese prejudice with Lt. General Prabowo.

14 Salim Said, 'Who's Afraid of Habibie', *Far Eastern Economic Review*, 12 March 1998. 31. Habibie has support from former army commander Feisal Tanjung, an ex-aide to Suharto who has become Minister for Home and Interior Affairs in May 1998.

15 Mrs Siti Hardimanti Rukamanya (known as 'Tutut') is thought to be worth between 400 million and 2 billion dollars.

16 Indonesia's Human Rights Commission, reactivated after Suharto's fall, put the toll at 1,118 dead (*South China Morning Post*, 3 June 1998).

17 In 1989 China, effective Politburo control over the People's Congress Standing Committee prevented such an event from happening in an even less democratic assembly. However authoritarian Suharto's regime may have been, there is an evident difference of nature with communist states, even after these embrace market reforms.

18 The Indonesian Association of Islamic Intellectuals.

19 Seth Mydans, 'Indonesia's New Leader, Self-Styled Reformer, Hopes to Stay Awhile', *New York Times*, 3 June 1998.

20 Founded in 1965 by a Catholic Chinese who would support Suharto's New Order.

21 Founded in 1971 as a local news magazine for the middle class.

22 David T. Hill, *The Press in New Order Indonesia*, Nedlands, University of Western Australia Press, 1994, p. 45.

23 Cited by David T. Hill, *op. cit.*, p. 89.

24 Greg Fealy, 'Indonesian Politics, 1995–1996: The Makings of a Crisis', in Gavin W. Jones and Terence H. Hull, *Indonesia Assessment*, Singapore, ISEAS, 1997, pp. 25–6.

25 Or N.U., League For the Revival of Religious Scholars, founded in 1926.

26 Adam Schwarz, *A Nation in Waiting: Indonesia in the 1990s*, Boulder, Westview Press, 1994, p. 163, describes an occasion in 1992 when then Lieutenant Colonel Prabowo tried to intimidate Wahid after he had held a mass rally demonstrating the strength of NU.

27 Followers of Muhammad, founded in 1912.

28 After the so-called religious students who have taken over Afghanistan and established an Islamic regime.

29 The Pentagon replaced the official exchange and training by an informal programme unapproved by US Congress.

30 Geoffrey Robinson, *The Dark Side of Paradise: Political Violence in Bali*, Ithaca, Cornell University Press, 1995, p. 313.

31 Lisbon Radio, 13 May 1998 (FBIS-EAS-98–133).

32 *Diario de Noticias*, Lisbon, 11 May 1998.

33 Devout Muslim.

34 R. William Liddle, 'Can All Good Things Go Together? Democracy, Growth and Unity in Post-Suharto Indonesia', in R. W. Liddle, *Leadership and Culture in Indonesian Politics*, St Leonards, Allen and Unwin, 1996, p. 255.

35 Fiscal Investment and Loan Programme.

36 In May 1998, Hong Kong's chief executive Tung Chee-hwa announced the economy was entering a recession.

37 Reuters News Agency, 2 June 1998.

38 Again, there are incredibly close analogies to be found with the smaller-scale French economy. France's institutional Caisse des Dépôts et Consignations serves as a second investment budget, and no amount of political debate has allowed for its privatization. In Japan, the government has vowed to take under its own responsibility the huge deficit (213 billion dollars) of Japan Rail by October 1998. In France, under pressures from unions, the Free Railway debt has largely been transferred to the public budget. Of all European countries, France is, for political reasons, the heaviest spender on local roads and infrastructures.

39 'Japan's Real Crisis', *Business Week*, 18 May 1998, pp. 38–43.

40 Unsympathetic observers have noted that the ratio of its current account deficit to GNP matches Thailand's.

41 *Chuo Koron*, Japan's highbrow magazine, published a lengthy and scathing indictment of the ministry of finance by bureaucratic Japan's long time nemesis, Karel Van Wolferen (March 1998, pp. 64–78, FBIS-EAS-98–112).

42 *Asian Wall Street Journal*, 4 May 1998, p. 3.

43 See for example 'Discussion on MOF's Corruption Cases', *Ekonomisuto*, 24 March 1998, pp. 22–5 (FBIS-EAS-98–082).
44 Michael Green and Richard Samuels, 'Recalculating Autonomy: Japan's Choices in the New World Order', *The National Bureau of Asian Research*, vol. 5, no 4, May 1994, p. 6.
45 Throughout the period from 2 July 1997, key economic indicators for the entire region have constantly been revised downwards, turning the science of economic forecasting into a joke. Once more, it is apparent that the only valid predictive tool at times of crisis is political economy, not quantitative models.

7 A Faustian deal for Asia?

1 Merril Lynch comment, 'GDP downgrades: exports have proved disappointing', 5 June 1998.
2 *Asian Wall Street Journal*, 14 May 1998, p. 6.
3 Zhang Youwen, World Economic Institute of the Shanghai Institute of Social Sciences, China News Agency, 3 June 1998 (FBIS-CHI-98–154).
4 Song Qiang *et al.*, *Zhongguo keyi shuo bu*, Hong Kong: Ming Bao Publishers, 1996.
5 'Indon Trade Insurance Deal in Two Parts: Goh', *Star*, Malaysia, 21 April 1998.
6 Manuel F. Montes, 'Global Lessons of the Economic Crisis in Asia', *Asia-Pacific Issues*, East–West Center, March 1998, p. 4.
7 The Development Bank of Singapore.
8 *Asian Wall Street Journal*, 19 May 1998, p. 1.
9 François Godement and Gerald Segal, *International Herald Tribune*, 13 January 1998.
10 *International Herald Tribune*, 6 February 1998.
11 *New Statesman*, 17 April 1998.
12 *South China Morning Post*, 16 April 1998.
13 *Bangkok Phuchatkan*, 30 January 1998, p. 6 (FBIS-EAS-98–033).
14 *Singapore Business Times*, 4 March 1998.
15 Cesar Bautista interviewed in *Le Monde*, 13 January 1998.
16 5 March 1998.
17 Personal communication at the ADB's Board of Governors meeting in Geneva, April 1998.
18 *South China Morning Post*, 30 April 1998.
19 The Asia Society, *Asia at a Crossroads: The Path Ahead, Report of the Asia Society Eminent Persons Group on the Economic Crisis*, New York, May 1998 (www.asiasociety.org).
20 Address to the Chicago Council on Foreign Relations, 27 February 1998.
21 *Business Week*, 15 June 1998, p. 24.
22 Short for repossession, or the claiming of remaining assets by a creditor to cover a fraction of debts owed by a firm or an individual.
23 'Japanese Tepid on Korean deals', *Nikkei Weekly*, 1 June 1998, p. 1.
24 *Business Week*, 26 January 1998.
25 Gerald Segal, 'Speak Plainly to the Paper Tiger', *New Statesman*, 17 April 1998.
26 Patrick J. Buchanan, *The Great Betrayal: How American Sovereignty and Social Justice Are Being Sacrificed to the Gods of the Global Economy*, New York, Little, Brown and Company, 1998.

27 Emmanuel Todd, *L'illusion économique: essai sur la stagnation des sociétés développées*, Paris, Gallimard, 1998.
28 E.g., former communist left and neo-fascist right. Todd himself does not accept the term and claims 'an intelligent protectionism' instead.
29 Kenichi Ohmae, *The End of the Nation State: The Rise of Regional Economies*, London, HarperCollins, 1995, p. 148.
30 Speech to the International Conference on the Future of Asia, Tokyo, 5 June 1998, as cited by Agence France-Presse.
31 The Asia Society, *op. cit.*, p. 18.
32 American International Group.
33 *Asian Wall Street Journal*, 12 May 1998, p. 4.

8 Conclusion: two scenarios for tomorrow

1 Charles P. Kindlegerger, *op. cit.*, p. 24.
2 Former French premier Edgar Faure is reputed to have once said 'When a problem is too complicated to solve, appoint a committee'.
3 'Seller Beware', *The Economist*, 6 June 1998, p. 95.
4 The Asia Society, *op. cit.*, p. 9.

References

Alagappa, Muthiah (ed.) (1995) *Political Legitimacy in Southeast Asia: The Quest for Moral Authority*, Stanford: Stanford University Press.

Alletzhauser, Al (1990) *The House of Nomura*, London: Bloomsbury.

Anderson, Benedict (1991) *Imagined Communities: Reflections on the Origin and Spread of Nationalism*, London: Verso Books.

Asia Society, The (1998) *Asia at a Crossroads: The Path Ahead*, Report of the Asia Society Eminent Persons Group on the Economic Crisis, New York.

Asian Development Bank (1998) *Annual Report, 1997*, Manila.

Bank for International Settlements (1997) *The Maturity, Sectoral and Nationality Distribution of International Bank Lending, Second Half 1996*, Basle.

Bank for International Settlements (1998) *The Maturity, Sectoral and Nationality Distribution of International Bank Lending, First Half 1997*, Basle.

Bank for International Settlements (1998) *The Maturity, Sectoral and Nationality Distribution of International Bank Lending, Second Half 1997*, Basle.

Bank of Japan (1997) *Comparative Economic and Financial Statistics*, Tokyo.

Bergsten, C. Fred (1997) 'The Asian Monetary Crisis: Proposed Remedies', Statement to the Committee on Banking and Financial Services, US House of Representatives, 13 November.

Bouissou, Jean-Marie, Gipouloux, François and Seizelet, Eric (1995) *Japon: le déclin?*, Brussels: Editions Complexe.

Brown, David (1994) *The State and Ethnic Politics in South-East Asia*, London and New York: Routledge.

Buchanan, Patrick J. (1998) *The Great Betrayal: How American Sovereignty and Social Justice are Being Sacrificed to the Gods of the Global Economy*, New York, Little, Brown and Company.

Camroux, David and Domenach, Jean-Luc (eds) (1997) *L'Asie retrouvée*, Paris: Editions du Seuil. Published in English (1998) *Imagining Asia*, London: Routledge.

Clarke, J.J. (1997) *Oriental Enlightenment – The Encounter Between Asian and Western Thought*, London and New York: Routledge.

Crozier, Michel (1973) *The Stalled Society*, New York: Viking.

Cumings, Bruce (1997) *Korea's Place in the Sun: A Modern History*, New York and London: W.W. Norton.

DeBary, William Theodore. (ed.) (1960) *Sources of Chinese Tradition*, vol. 2, New York: UNESCO Collection of Representative Works – Chinese Series.

Diamond, Larry, Plattner, Marc F., Chu, Yun-han and Tien, Hung-mao (eds) (1997) *Consolidating the Third Wave Democracies*, Baltimore and London: The Johns Hopkins University Press.

Domenach, Jean-Luc (1998) *L'Asie en danger*, Paris: Fayard.

Elvin, Mark (1973) *The Pattern of the Chinese Past*, London: Eyre Methuen.

Emmott, Bill (1989) *The Sun Also Sets: The Limits to Japan's Economic Power*, Touchstone Books.

Feldstein, Martin (1998) 'Refocusing the IMF', *Foreign Affairs*, March–April, vol. 77, no. 2: 20–33.

Fernald, John, Edison, Hali and Loungani Prakash, (1998) *Was China the First Domino? Assessing Links between China and the Rest of Emerging Asia*, Federal Reserve System, International Finance Discussion Paper, no. 604.

Fischer, Stanley (1998) *The Asian Crisis: A View from the IMF*, International Monetary Fund.

Freeman, Chris *et al.* (1997) *The Dynamics of Industrial Innovation*, Cambridge, MA: The MIT Press.

Geertz, Clifford (1963) *Agricultural Change: The Process of Ecological Change in Indonesia*, Berkeley: University of California Press.

Godement, François (1993) *La renaissance de l'Asie*, Paris: Odile Jacob. Published in English (1997) *The New Asian Renaissance*, London and New York: Routledge.

Goh, Chok Tong (1997) Address at the World Economic Forum, Hong Kong, 15 October.

Gomez, Edmund Terence and Jomo K.S. (1997) *Malaysia's Political Economy: Politics, Patronage and Profits*, Cambridge: Cambridge University Press.

Green, Michael and Samuels, Richard (1994) 'Recalculating Autonomy: Japan's Choices in the New World Order', *The National Bureau of Asian Research*, vol. 5, no. 4.

Greenspan, Alan (1998) Testimony before the Committee on Banking and Financial Services, US House of Representatives, 30 January 1998.

Greenspan, Alan (1998) Testimony to the US House of Representatives, 24 February 1998.

Hill, David T. (1994) *The Press in New Order Indonesia*, Nedlands: University of Western Australia Press.

Hitchcock, David I. (1994) *Asian Values and the United States: How Much Conflict?*, Washington, DC: Centre for Strategic and International Studies.

Hobsbawm, Eric J. (1971) *Primitive Rebels, Studies in Archaic Forms of Social Movements in the Nineteenth and Twentieth Centuries*, Manchester: Manchester University Press, new amended edition.

Hooke, A.W. (1981) *The International Monetary Fund, its Evaluation, Organization, and Activities*, Washington DC: IMF.

Hsieh, Chang-tai (1998) *What Explains the Industrial Revolution in East Asia? Evidence from Factor Markets*, Berkeley: University of California Press.

Hu, Zuliu and Khan, Mohsin S. (1997) *Why is China Growing so Fast?*, Washington DC: IMF Working Paper.

Huntington, Samuel P. (1993) 'The Clash of Civilizations?', *Foreign Affairs*, Fall, vol. 72, no. 4: 22–49.

Ibrahim, Anwar (1996) *The Asian Renaissance*, Singapore and Kuala Lumpur: Times Books International.

International Monetary Fund (1997) *World Economic Outlook*, December.

International Monetary Fund (1998) *The IMF's Response to the Asian Crisis*, April.

Jiang, Lin (1995) 'Changing Kinship Structure and its Implications for Old-age Support in Urban and Rural China', *Population Studies*, no. 49: 127–45.

Jones, Gavin W. and Hull, Terence H. (1997) *Indonesia Assessment*, Singapore: Institute of South East Asian Studies.

Juergensmeyer, Mark (1993) *The New Cold War: Religious Nationalism Confronts the Secular State*, Berkeley and Los Angeles: University of California Press.

Kernen, Antoine and Rocca, Jean-Louis (1998) 'La réforme des entreprises publiques en Chine et sa gestion sociale: le cas de Shenyang et du Liaoning', *Les Etudes du CERI*, no. 37, Paris: FNSP.

Kindleberger, Charles P. (1973) *The World in Depression, 1929–1939*, Berkeley: University of California Press.

Krugman, Paul (1994) 'The Myth of Asia's Miracle', *Foreign Affairs*, November–December, vol. 73, no. 6: 62–78.

Krugman, Paul (1998) 'Will Asia Bounce Back?', Speech for Crédit Suisse First Boston Conference, Hong Kong, March.

Lee, James Z., Wang, Feng and Campbell, Cameron (eds) (forthcoming) *One Quarter of Humanity: Malthusian Mythology and Chinese Reality 1700–2000*, Cambridge, MA: Harvard University Press.

Leete, Richard and Alam, Iqbal (1993) *The Revolution in Asian Fertility: Dimensions, Causes, and Implications*, Oxford: Clarendon Press.

Liddle, R. William (1996) *Leadership and Culture in Indonesian Politics*, St Leonards: Allen and Unwin.

Lissakers, Karin (1998) Testimony at the House Banking and Financial Services Committee, April 21.

MacFarquhar, Roderick (1997) *The Origins of the Cultural Revolution*, vol. 3, Oxford and New York: Oxford University Press and Columbia University Press.

McKinnon, Ronald I. and Pill, How (1996) 'Credible Liberalization and International Capital Flows', in Takatoshi Ito and Anne Krueger (eds) *Financial Deregulation and Integration in East Asia*, Chicago: University of Chicago Press.

McKinnon, Ronald I. and Ohno, Kenichi (1997) *Dollar and Yen: Resolving Economic Conflict between the United States and Japan*, Cambridge, MA and London: The MIT Press.

Mahbubani, Kishore (1994) 'The United States: Go East, Young Man', *The Washington Quarterly*, Spring, vol. 17, no. 2: 5–23.

Malinowski, Branislaw (1961) *Argonauts of the Western Pacific*, New York: E.P. Dutton.

Montes, Manuel F. (1998) 'Global Lessons of the Economic Crisis in Asia', *Asia-Pacific Issues*, March, no. 35.

Nukazawa, Kazuo (1998) 'The East Asian Drama of 1997–1998 and the Question of Models', Berlin, 20 January mimeo paper.

Nye, Joseph (1991) *Bound to Lead: The Changing Nature of American Power*, New York: Basic Books.

Ohmae, Kenichi (1995) *The End of the Nation State: The Rise of Regional Economies*, London: HarperCollins.

Okimoto, Daniel I. (1989) *Between MITI and the Market: Japanese Industrial Policy for High Technologies*, Stanford: Stanford University Press.

Ouattara, Alassane D. (1998) *The Asian Crisis: Origins and Lessons*, International Monetary Fund, Oxford University Press.

Park, Yung Chul (1998) *The Financial Crisis in Korea: From Miracle to Meltdown?*, March 1, preliminary draft.

Phongpaichit, Pasuk and Piriyarangsan, Sungsidh (1994) *Corruption and Democracy in Thailand*, Bangkok: The Political Economy Centre, Chulalongkorn University.

Qiang, Song *et al.* (1996) *Zhongguo keyi shuo bu*, Hong Kong: Ming Bao Publishers.

Radelet, Steven and Sachs, Jeffrey (1998) *The East Asian Financial Crisis: Diagnosis, Remedies, Prospects*, Cambridge, MA: Harvard Institute for International Development.

Research Reports (1992) The Population Studies Centre, University of Michigan, nos 92–13, 92–14, 92–16 and 92–22.

Robinson, Geoffrey (1995) *The Dark Side of Paradise: Political Violence in Bali*, Ithaca: Cornell University Press.

Ruland, Jürgen (1996) *The Asia–Europe Meeting (ASEM): Towards a New Euro-Asian Relationship?*, Universität Rostock: Rostocker Informationen zu Politik und Verwaltung Heft 5.

Sakakibara, Eisuke (1993) *Beyond Capitalism: The Japanese Model of Market Economies*, Lanham: University Press of America and the Economic Strategy Institute.

Sautter, Christian (1996) *La France au miroir du Japon, croissance ou déclin*, Paris: Editions Odile Jacob.

Schuler, Kurt (1996) *Should Developing Countries Have Central Banks?*, London: Institute of Economic Affairs.

Schwarz, Adam (1994) *A Nation in Waiting: Indonesia in the 1990s*, Boulder: Westview Press.

Scott, James (1976) *The Moral Economy of the Peasants: Rebellion and Subsistence in Southeast Asia*, New Haven: Yale University Press.

Sharma, Shalendra D. (1998) 'Asia's Economic Crisis and the IMF', *Survival*, Summer, vol. 40, no. 2: 27–8.

Smith, Peter C. (1980) 'Asian Marriage Patterns in Transition', *Journal of Family History*, vol. 5, no. 1: 58–96.

Sopiee Noordin (1996) Speech at the 29th meeting of the Pacific Basin Economic Council, Washington, May 25.

Stiglitz, Joseph (1998) Address to the Chicago Council on Foreign Relations, Chicago, February 27.

Studies on the Economic Synergy between Asia and Europe (1997) Background document to the ASEM Chiba (Japan) meeting, September.

Tay, Simon S.C. (1996) 'ASEAN, the ARF and Preventive Diplomacy: Principles and Possibilities in International Law', *ASEAN-Isis Monitor*.

Todd, Emmanuel (1998) *L'illusion économique: essai sur la stagnation des sociétés développées*, Paris: Gallimard.

Törnquist, Olle (1998) The Wild Beast and the Sleeping Beauty, Talk at Indonesia Hearing, Ministry of Foreign Affairs, Stockholm, Sweden, March 16.

United Nations Report (1995).

Van Wolferen, Karel (1998) *Chuo Koron*, March: 64–78, in FBIS-EAS-98–112.

Vatikiotis, Michael R.J. (1996) *Political Change in Southeast Asia: Trimming the Banyan Tree*, London and New York: Routledge.

Wade Robert (1990) *Governing the Market: Economic Theory and the Role of Government in East Asian Industrialization*, Princeton: Princeton University Press.

Whyte, Martin King (1997) 'The Fate of Filial Obligations in Urban China', *The China Journal*, no. 38: 1–31.

Will, Pierre-Etienne (1987) 'Appareil d'état et infrastructure économique dans la Chine prémoderne' in Lew, Roland (ed.) *Les bureaucraties chinoises*, Paris: L'Harmattan: 11–41.

Wong, R. Bin (1997) *China Transformed: Historical Change and the Limits of European Experience*, Ithaca and London: Cornell University Press.

Wood, Christopher (1993) *The Bubble Economy: The Japanese Economic Collapse*, Tokyo: Charles E. Tuttle.

World Bank (1993) *The East Asian Economic Miracle – Economic Growth and Public Policy*, Oxford: Oxford University Press.

Xenos, Peter and Gultiano, Socorro A. (1992) *Trends in Female and Male Age at Marriage and Celibacy in Asia*, Hawaii, The Hawaii University Press.

Yan, Yunxiang (1996) 'The Culture of *Guanxi* in a North China Village', *China Journal*, January: 1–25.

Yang, Mayfair Mei-hui (1994) *Gifts, Favours and Banquets: The Art of Social Relationships in China*, Ithaca and London: Cornell University Press.

Young, Alwyn (1995) 'The Tyranny of Numbers: Confronting the Statistical Realities of East Asian Growth Experience', *The Quarterly Journal of Economics*, August: 641–80.

Zakaria, Fareed (1997) 'The Rise of Illiberal Democracy', *Foreign Affairs*, November–December, vol. 76, no. 6: 22–43.

Index